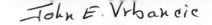
SYBASE SQL SERVER

on the World Wide Web

JOIN US ON THE INTERNET VIA WWW, GOPHER, FTP OR EMAIL:

WWW: http://www.thomson.com
GOPHER: gopher.thomson.com
FTP: ftp.thomson.com
EMAIL: findit@kiosk.thomson.com

WebExtra™

WebExtra gives added value by providing updated and additional information about topics discussed in this book. Items included in the WebExtra for *Sybase SQL Server on the World Wide Web* are:

- Code examples

- Resource list of URLs

The WebExtra features outlined above are available free of charge (except for the charges associated with accessing the Internet and the World Wide Web). Just go to the Web site for International Thomson Computer Press. The URL is:

http://www.thomson.com/itcp.html

A service of I(T)P™

SYBASE SQL SERVER

on the World Wide Web

ED ASHLEY and **BETH EPPERSON**

with **Kerri De Rosier**

INTERNATIONAL THOMSON COMPUTER PRESS

I(T)P™ An International Thomson Publishing Company

London • Bonn • Boston • Johannesburg • Madrid • Melbourne • Mexico City • New York • Paris
Singapore • Tokyo • Toronto • Albany, NY • Belmont, CA • Cincinnati, OH • Detroit, MI

Library of Congress Cataloging-in-Publication Data
Ashley, Ed.
    Sybase SQL Server on the World Wide Web / Ed Ashley, Beth
Epperson.
        p.   cm.
    Includes index.
    ISBN: 1-85032-815-3 (alk. paper)
    1. Client/server computing. 2. SQL Server. 3. Sybase. 4. World
Wide Web (Information retrieval system)   I. Epperson, Beth, 1955– .
    II. Title.
QA76.9.C55A84   1996
005.75'8--dc20
                                96–19186
                                CIP

Publisher/Vice President: Jim DeWolf, ITCP/Boston
Project Director: Chris Grisonich, ITCP/Boston
Marketing Manager: Kathleen Raftery, ITCP/Boston
Project Manager: Trudy Neuhaus
Editor: Kerri E. De Rosier
Production: Jo-Ann Campbell • mle design • 562 Milford Point Rd. • Milford, CT 06460

Dedication

I would like to thank my family and my dear friend, Paula Doss. Without her encouragement, patience and advice, I know I would never have even started writing this book.

Beth Epperson
San Diego, CA

It is with great pride that I thank my best friend for keeping me going—my wife Diana.

Ed Ashley
La Jolla, CA

To Beth, for getting me started in the world of technical editing; to my husband, Dave, who was endlessly supportive during this first "real" post-Sarah job; and to Sarah, my guiding light.

Kerri E. De Rosier
San Diego, CA

Contents

6   USING JAVA FOR CLIENT-SIDE PROGRAMMING

Preface

This book describes creating interactive database applications using the World Wide Web. Interactive database applications have exploded in popularity because the Web offers simple, easy-to-use, and platform-independent access to databases while greatly reducing the cost and complexity of custom development typically associated with such applications.

Specifically, this book explains how to interface with Sybase SQL Server using the Web as the front-end interface. There are several approaches available for creating the interface between the Web and the database: in this book, we introduce you to four of the possible approaches, and share our experiences in putting all of the pieces together.

We strongly suggest that you review Chapter 1, "Introduction." It contains several decision trees that guide you through the considerations you need to make before embarking on creating your own database-enabled Web application—such as choosing between client- and server-side processing, choosing between static and dynamic forms, choosing the appropriate programming language for creating the application, and how to approach the task.

Chapter 2, "Creating Forms" introduces you to all of the form elements and provides detailed explanations of how to code each element type and use the attributes associated with each element. The chapter shows you everything you need to know about creating effective and highly-functional World Wide Web forms.

Chapter 3, "Using ISQL to Connect to Sybase SQL Server" describes how to write Transact-SQL scripts in order to query the Sybase database, and how to insert information into the database. The chapter explains the various SQL commands needed to write basic scripts and provides tips to help you begin writing your own scripts.

Chapter 4, "Creating CGI Scripts Using Perl" provides Perl scripts that you can use in your own environment with minimal modifications, and detailed explanations of the different components in the Perl environment.

Chapter 5, "Creating CGI Scripts Using Tcl" introduces you to the Tcl language, and discusses how to pass information into scripts and validate it. The chapter shows you how to write a script to test and replace unwanted data. Each code example is explained in detail so you can quickly apply what you have read to your own needs.

Chapter 6, "Using Java for Client-side Programming" compares client-side and server-side processing to help you understand why Java is so important in reducing the load on the server. The chapter also explains the Java language, and includes examples that you can easily apply to your own HTML documents.

Chapter 7, "Using Web.sql to Streamline Data Flow" provides an overview of web.sql and how it works, and illustrates web.sql constructs using an example Web site.

Chapter 8, "Security Issues for the Web" discusses encryption methods and issues involved with establishing a secure environment for your information.

Assumptions

We need to make some assumptions about you, the reader. You should have:

- General knowledge of programming logic

- General experience navigating through various operating system file structures, such as UNIX or NT

- General knowledge of SQL, although not necessarily Sybase Transact-SQL

- Some knowledge of tables as they apply to relational database structures

- Some experience with the World Wide Web

- Basic knowledge of HTML.

We also assume that you have access to the following:

- A Web server for your specific platform that includes CGI support

- A scripting language such as Tcl or Perl for your specific platform; web.sql for your specific platform; or Java

- Sybase SQL Server for your specific platform

- Access to an editor for creating CGI scripts.

Getting the Code Sample

You can find complete code for each application in this book at the International Thomson Computer Press Web Site, WebExtra. You can find it at the following location:

http://www.thomson.com/itcp.html

Acknowledgments

Although there are only three names on the cover, there are a number of people who contributed significant work for this book. We would like to acknowledge the following people for the chapters or parts they wrote:

Kemer Thomson at Sun Microsystems, thanks for the chapter and being the guiding light on Java.

Frank Whittemore of UCSD's Administrative Computing and Telecommunications department not only keeps the administrative systems running at UCSD, but also gave us the Security chapter.

Thanks to Lyle Kafader at UCSD's School of Engineering and Computer Science. Without Lyle's deep knowledge of the Tcl language, we would have not been able to include a Tcl chapter in this book.

Gabe Lawrence at the Scripps Institute of Oceanography supplied endless energy and patience for his work on the Perl and Java chapters.

A special thanks to Alean Kirnack at Software Partners, who created the web.sql chapter with very little notice. Thanks for jumping through hoops.

Thanks to Shane Greif for providing the illustrations and diagrams.

There are many other people who made this book magically appear. Sandy Emerson at Sybase kept us all moving forward while carrying the task of running Sybase Press. Unending thanks to you, Sandy.

Also, to Jim DeWolf at International Thomson Computer Press, who stuck with us throughout. We wholeheartedly appreciate your support and your belief in what we proposed.

Thanks to Richard Rawles for a thorough review and excellent editorial advice.

Thanks also to Matthew McClure for his technical review of the book.

We now realize that the names on the cover of a book are not necessarily the ones who do most of the work. We would never in a million years want to be a Project Manager—what a job—to have to deal with folks who think they can write. With that knowledge now firmly planted, we would like to deeply thank Trudy Neuhaus for her gentleness in the editing process. Without her advice and patience, we would have never completed this project.

And finally, we want to commend you, the reader for wanting to learn as much as you can about the wonderful world of the Web. We all hope that this book will help in some small way to make you successful in connecting your Web server to Sybase SQL Server. Best wishes!

1

Introduction

In the past few years, the World Wide Web (WWW) has made static, unstructured information like that in printed texts accessible to millions of Internet users virtually instantaneously. With the Web, information is accessible 24 hours a day, and platform issues are no longer a concern. But the real promise of the Web lies in its ability to deliver information from different media *interactively* and *dynamically*, and to collect information from users.

Businesses have been quick to capitalize on this promise. In fact, many organizations are finding the Web so useful in running their business that they are making a Web browser the default front end to their corporate data assets, both on the Internet for global access by employees, customers, and partners, and as a private Intranet service for internal use. The reasons for this stampede onto the Web include ease of development, ease of use, cost considerations, and universal access.

Using the Internet instead of a proprietary wide-area network removes protocol and interface barriers, which allows global access to a company's resources and reduces costs. Moreover, Web pages are platform-independent, which means that a single Web page can be immediately available on any operating system that supports a Web browser, such as Windows, Macintosh System 7, and UNIX.

By employing basic data protection schemes such as passwords, firewalls, permissions, and encryption, you can share your corporate data assets with your customers to whatever depth or breadth is appropriate while continuing to run your business on your Intranet. The potential for customer feedback—empowering your customers to help you interactively define the best and most effective product and market strategies—is one of the most compelling arguments for running your enterprise on the World Wide Web.

Despite the potential, most Web sites today are made up of fairly static pages that present information but don't offer much opportunity for the user to interact with the information. As the Web has become more popular, there has been more demand for interactive Web applications—even applications that can accommodate on-line commerce. Following are true-life scenarios illustrating the demand:

- A government agency wants to link a Web site to a mainframe database, allowing users to look up parcel and other information of public record from their homes or from an information kiosk

- An international hotel chain wants to allow guests to place hotel reservations from their homes

- A catalog retail company wants to allow home shoppers to order items directly across the Web.

As the demand for interactive Web applications continues, Web developers are searching for tools and methods for creating applications that can access sophisticated Client/Server database systems such as Sybase SQL Server to provide customized information on demand.

The purpose of this chapter is to discuss preliminary considerations and implementation methods for linking your Web pages with Sybase SQL Server, then to point you to the appropriate chapters in this book that discuss your chosen implementation method.

Preliminary Considerations

One of the first things you need to decide is what kind of application you want to build. Should it have query or transactional capabilities? Will it provide Internet access or be used solely within your Intranet? Will the processing occur on the client or server?

After you have an idea about what you want your application to do, where you want it to reside, and how you want to process the information gathered by the application, you can then determine how you want to design your forms, how to design or modify the database, and the method you use to connect your Web application to Sybase SQL Server. In this book, we discuss the following methods for creating the Web-to-database link:

- Use Web forms for data queries or data collection, pass the data to an ISQL script using Tcl or Perl, and send it to Sybase SQL Server

- Use Web forms for data queries or data collection, pass the data to an Open Client/Open Server script using SybTcl or SybPerl, and send it to Sybase SQL Server

- Use web.sql to translate web.sql data into Open Client calls

- Use Java to perform transactional calculations and client-side processing by passing data through Open Client calls or CGI scripts.

Query vs. Transactional

In the database world there are basically two types of applications: those that get information from the database, and those that write information to the database. In making your decision between a query versus transactional application, you need to ask yourself the following questions:

- Do you want the interaction with the application to be static (with users choosing from predefined selections) or dynamic (with users filling in text fields)?

- If you plan to collect data, what specific data do you want to collect? Is it textual data (customer names, addresses, and so on) or order information (product IDs, quantity, and cost), and how it is stored, retrieved, and archived?

- Is the user expecting to perform searches or generate reports?

The answers to the questions above directly affect the design of your form(s), and the tools you choose to create the link between your Web page and database. See "Implementing the Application" for more information.

Intranet vs. Internet

Before you create your application, you need to decide whether the application will reside on an Intranet, where it is accessible by only the users in your organization, or whether you want to provide Internet access. If you decide to go with an Intranet, some of the questions you need to answer include:

- Can all employees access the database, or should you limit their access?

- Is a login required to access the forms used to interact with the database?

- If the database is to be accessed by the Internet, can you allow everyone access or do you need to reduce the access to a selected group of users?

Many companies design their systems so that Intranet users have one level of access, and Internet users have another level of access. If you're providing Internet access, you may be worried about the level to which your essential company data can be protected from inappropriate access or even damage. Several mechanisms exist for protecting Web-server data. The most common is the use of firewalls—separate computers that sit between the machine on which your Web server runs and its connection to the Internet. These firewalls validate the addresses of the clients making the HTTP (HyperText Transfer Protocol) requests to the Web server.

After you understand the level of access you want to provide, you need to review existing technology and choose the appropriate security system (for example, encryption, authentication, and so on). Chapter 8, "Security Issues for the Web" covers security issues in detail.

Server-side vs. Client-side Processing

Next, you need to think about how you want to distribute the workload between the client or server to improve productivity and prevent repeated server-side connections (in other words, preventing the eternal "Host contacted...." message). For example, suppose you have a Web page containing a purchase order form. With server-side processing, users enter line items into the purchase order form, then submit the form to be processed on the server. A CGI script created with Tcl or Perl collects the values users enter. The CGI script must then take up server processing time to calculate the results, generate an HTML page, and return the HTML page to the client. With client-side processing, processing the total dollar value of line items can occur in the client browser, with no need to ship the form off to the server for processing.

Server-side Processing

Server-side processing is clearly the best method for managing data integrity and scheduling transactions for large, centralized collections of data such as customer order histories. Server-side processing also provides centralized data lookups. You can provide a Web form allowing users to enter partial search information, query your Sybase SQL Server database, then return the results as a Web page. Suppose you want to place a directory of your valued partners on the Web to enable anyone in the world to look up your partners' contact information. You could provide a Web form allowing users to enter partial search information, and then query your Sybase SQL Server database. You would then return the results as a Web page. You can also create drill-down Web pages that provide recursive links that query the Sybase SQL Server and return the results as links that further query the database, returning more detail as links.

Using CGI and ISQL

Assume that a user wants to submit a Web form that queries Sybase SQL Server through an associated CGI program. When the user loads the Web form page into her browser and clicks the Submit button, the data collected on the form is sent by the browser to the Web server along with the data the user typed into the form. The Web server receives the form, invokes the named CGI program (written in Perl, Tcl, or C++), and passes the CGI environment variables to the CGI script. The CGI script then manipulates the variables and invokes Sybase ISQL (Sybase's Interactive SQL program) with a SQL query. ISQL connects to Sybase SQL Server and processes the query. The results come back to the CGI script, which manipulates the results and formulates a new Web page that includes the results of the query. The Web page is then returned to the Web server, which in turn sends it to the client. The user sees the new Web page in her browser. Figure 1-1 shows each step of the process.

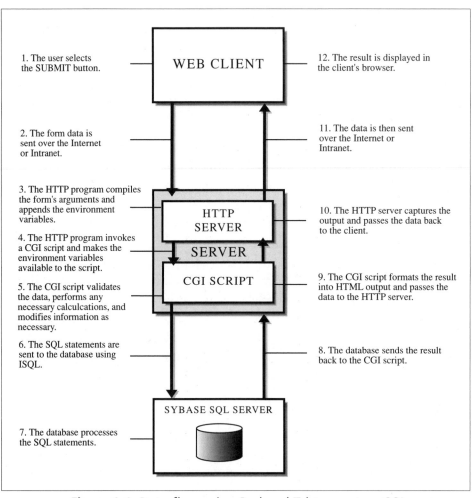

Figure 1-1. *Data flow using Perl and Tcl to create a CGI script that passes data to ISQL*

Using CGI and Open Client/Open Server

Your decision to use Open Client versus ISQL should be based on the type of interaction you require with the database and peripheral applications. Open Client calls are normally used in applications requiring a large amount of server time (such as a query requesting quarterly sales), or the requirement to call other server applications such as bcp (batch copy). Using Open Client calls also ensures that you can collect system errors and status messages. Figure 1-2 shows the data flow.

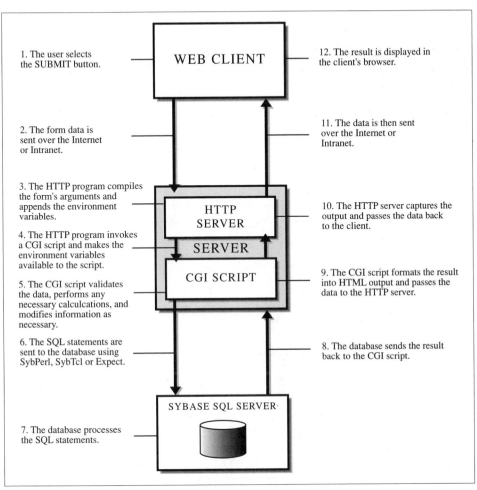

1. The user selects the SUBMIT button.

2. The form data is sent over the Internet or Intranet.

3. The HTTP program compiles the form's arguments and appends the environment variables.

4. The HTTP program invokes a CGI script and makes the environment variables available to the script.

5. The CGI script validates the data, performs any necessary calculcations, and modifies information as necessary.

6. The SQL statements are sent to the database using SybPerl, SybTcl or Expect.

7. The database processes the SQL statements.

12. The result is displayed in the client's browser.

11. The data is then sent over the Internet or Intranet.

10. The HTTP server captures the output and passes the data back to the client.

9. The CGI script formats the result into HTML output and passes the data to the HTTP server.

8. The database sends the result back to the CGI script.

WEB CLIENT

HTTP SERVER

SERVER

CGI SCRIPT

SYBASE SQL SERVER

***Figure 1-2.** Data flow using SybPerl, SybTcl, or expect to create a CGI script that passes data to Open Client/Open Server*

Using Web.sql

With the introduction of web.sql and the use of centralized data collection, you can perform many processing activities on the Web server using a single script. Using web.sql to process the information is faster than: sending variables to a CGI script; having the CGI script process the data and forward it to a SQL script that in turn interacts with the database; returning a result to the CGI script, which then returns a new Web page to the client. The latter process uses numerous scripts: using web.sql, you can embed SQL commands directly within

HTML pages and make database calls from Web pages without having to develop additional scripts that call Open Client code.

Web.sql works by placing a wrapper around an HTTP server that preprocesses web.sql queries, formats the output in HTML, and sends the resulting HTML code to the user's browser. Web.sql can bypass the CGI interface completely, allowing database connections to stay open between pages, which greatly reduces the overhead of interacting with a database. However, using web.sql with CGI scripts gives you the power to quickly Web-enable useful business applications such as order entry, order tracking, status reports, and market research. When web.sql is installed, the HTTP server is recompiled with library code that can recognize and interpret web.sql code. The Netscape API (NSAPI)—which is itself a sort of "Open Server" application—is used to maintain connections. Figure 1-3 shows the data flow between web.sql and Sybase SQL Server.

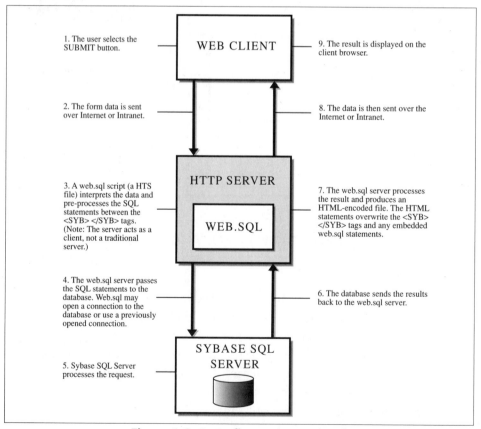

Figure 1-3. Data flow using web.sql

Client-side Processing with Java

With the advent of Sun's Java language, it is possible to add behavior and similar functionality to Web pages on the *client* side. Java can extend the power of your Web-enabled database applications by allowing you to load database results into program components such as a spreadsheet or word processing program, or enrich reports with audio comments or animation.

Java is intended to augment, not replace server-side processing. If your Web site receives a lot of traffic, users may receive the dreaded "Host contacted: Waiting for reply" message. If you can reduce the amount of secondary traffic, meaning the interactions with users who are using processor space to calculate order totals, and so on, then you can help free up processor space for new connections to the server. When a user selects a link that invokes a Java-encoded page, the Java-encoded page is then transmitted to the client, which can perform actions such as calculating a cost/quantity field. This *thin client* strategy permits Web-enabled client-server applications to be deployed to client machines that have a minimum of resources such as a fast CPU and an excellent network connection.

Java also provides some needed security for applications: because information is calculated on the fly, static pages are no longer resident on the server and that in turn produces less traffic across the Internet, which gives potential hackers less of an opportunity to "sniff" out your information.

Java is currently the only language for developing *applets* (small applications interpreted at run-time) for client-side processing. Netscape and other Web browsers are rapidly adding support for Java applets, and Sun Microsystems has developed (in Java) its own Java-specific Web browser called HotJava. Powersoft recently announced Optima++, which enables development of Java applets.

Figure 1-4 shows the data flow between Java and Sybase SQL Server.

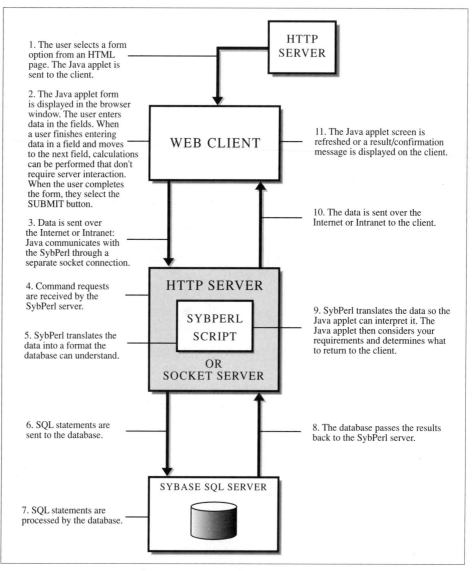

Figure 1-4. Data flow using Java

Hardware Issues

You must determine the level of activity that the environment will generate and assess whether the proposed architecture can support it. If the customer anticipates a heavy level of activity, then you most likely need to separate the Web, database, and application servers. If the anticipated activity level is small, then you might determine that two of the services can reside on the same hardware. Understanding the level of activity, knowing whether users will download information from the HTTP server verses an FTP server, and whether the application will require more server processing versus more client processing will also help you determine the size of the servers required.

Implementing the Application

Now that you've made some preliminary decisions, you're ready for some considerations related to implementing the application, which is what the rest of this book is about. You need to consider how to:

- Design the forms
- Handle the database
- Create the link between the Web site and the database.

Designing the Forms

Ultimately, the purpose of a Web application is for a user to interact with data. You should give careful consideration to making sure that the procedures and options for the interaction are intuitive and unambiguous. This involves understanding the purpose of the application, how the end-user will interact with the form, and the available user interface elements for the form.

For example, if you're building an application for business transactions, your form should represent the business transaction process. Web sites that sell products over the Web let you choose what you want first, give you a total for the purchase, and then collect personal and financial information. This type of process is known as the "shopping cart" method.

You also need to know the names of the tables and columns in the database that will eventually receive the information, and the size constraints for each column. (If your database isn't yet created, you can define names in your form, then add the corresponding tables and columns to the database later.) When you code a form, you need to supply a NAME attribute, which normally corresponds to a database column name, and in some instances, a MAXLENGTH value for the specific text-entry field.

Your security needs (discussed in "Internet vs. Intranet" in the previous section) will determine whether you need to use the POST or GET method for form submission. Chapter 2, "Creating Forms" discusses these methods in detail.

Whether your form data is dynamic or static directly affects the elements you use to create your form. For example, in a static form, you will most likely use pull-down menus, radio buttons, and checkboxes as user interface elements; use a series of drill-down menus; or mix the two together. For example, you may want to query the user through a set of drill-down menus to better understand what they want to do, such as create a new entry to be inserted into the database or update an existing account. If they choose to update, you may want to have an additional set of drill-down menus allowing them to choose the type of update (for example, changing a single field or deleting an entire record). After they choose the update criteria, you could supply them with a form to fill-in and submit.

Choosing dynamic forms drives two decisions: using text entry fields in the form, and the bigger decision, whether the form will be processed on the client or server side, as we discussed earlier. Processing on the client side involves coding in Java, while server-side processing requires the use of standard HTML FORM elements. Figure 1-5 shows the decision tree related to forms.

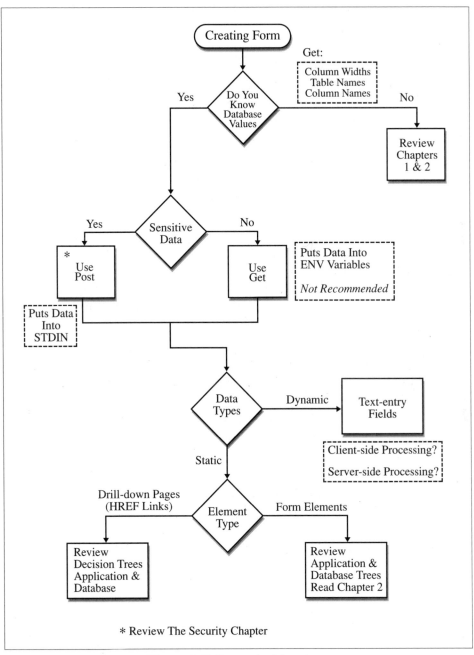

Figure 1-5. Form decision tree

Database Considerations

Database concerns can be handled at almost any point during the development process. If you're using an existing database, you need to consider whether or not the application will require slight modifications to the database, or whether it would be worth your while to create an entirely new database. Obviously, the easiest type of application to create is one that doesn't require you to modify any of the database tables, and one in which you have an existing Web site with interactions already taking place. In that situation, you may be able to borrow existing scripts and modify them to accomplish your goal.

If you need to design a new database or make significant changes to an existing database, we suggest that you use the data modeling technique. Although the process seems painful and drawn out, putting significant effort into properly modeling up front eliminates many headaches down the road. Many designers think they know what they want until they get involved in the data modeling process.

During the data modeling process, you need to regularly communicate with your customer to ensure that your models gather the information the client is requesting. You also need to watch for the tendency to put as much information as possible into a few tables. Most database designers will tell you to normalize your tables at least to level three: by doing so, you can avoid overly-redundant data. Normalizing tables also forces you to design the tables in such a way that each table contains only one type of information, such as customer data, the purchase order header, and purchase order detail information. The idea behind extensive data modeling is ensuring that you group the information into logical structures while eliminating as much redundancy as possible.

After you design the database, you then must evaluate the most appropriate method or methods for interfacing with it. You must also keep in mind the potential for growth and change. Traditionally, most clients initially want to gather data from outside and then at a later date allow users to access the database.

Figure 1-6 shows the decision tree for database issues.

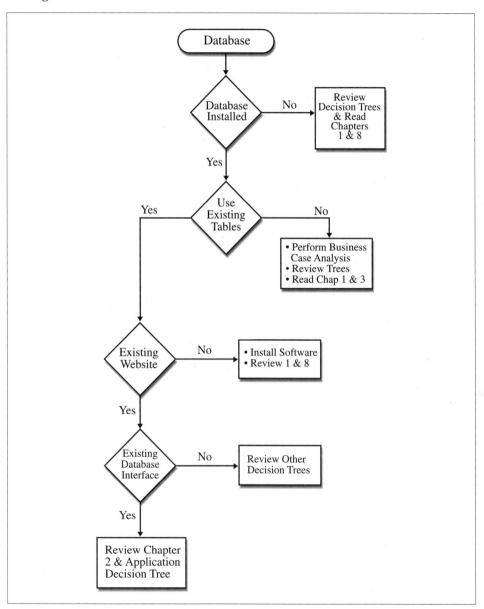

Figure 1-6. Database decision tree

Creating the Link between the Web page and the Database

The final step, of course, is implementing (and testing!) the application that links the Web page with the database. Deferring implementation until this stage almost ensures that it will proceed more quickly and with fewer bugs than if you attempt to implement the application before considering design issues.

Figure 1-7 shows a decision tree for determining the application type. If you .determined that the application is a query, you must decide whether the form or user interface will be *dynamic* or *static*. That is, whether you allow the user to enter query information (dynamic), or choose from a list of values that you provide using checkboxes, radio buttons, or pull-down menus (static).

If you decided that the application will be a static query, then you will most likely use Perl or Tcl to interface with the database via ISQL. If you want to provide a dynamic query, then you need to look at the decisions for creating a transactional application, such as deciding between: using Java to perform client-side processing, and using Java DataBase Connectivity (JDBC), Sun Microsystem's new Java API, for server-side processing; interfacing with a CGI script; or using web.sql or a CGI script for server-side processing. If you choose CGI, you can use Open Client or ISQL to interface with the database. If you choose web.sql, you can use Open Client to interface with the database.

Choosing between Java, web.sql, CGI scripts, or a combination of the three also depends upon how often the applications change. If web.sql serves all of your database connectivity needs, then you should consider using it for all of your development. If not, you may want to consider CGI development. If you already have an existing base of either Tcl or Perl, then you might want to begin with those tools. The bottom line is that you need to consider your timeline when determining whether to learn new technology or to carry on with what you already know.

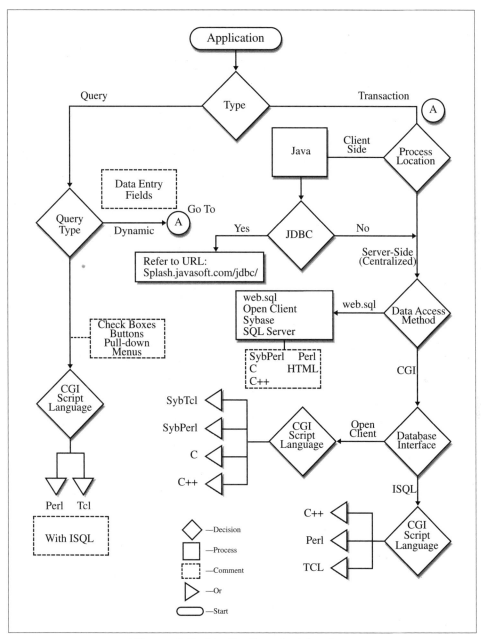

Figure 1-7. Application decision tree

The rest of this book contains detailed information about each of the programming tools. Use the following matrix to set your direction:

If you plan to:	**Go to:**
Use Web forms for data queries or data collection, pass the data to an ISQL script using Tcl or Perl, and send it to Sybase SQL Server	Chapter 2, "Creating Forms" Chapter 3, "Using ISQL to Connect to Sybase SQL Server" Chapter 4, "Creating CGI Scripts Using Perl" or Chapter 5, "Creating CGI Scripts Using Tcl"
Use Web forms for data queries or data collection, pass the data to an Open Client/Open Server script using SybTcl or SybPerl, and send it to Sybase SQL Server	Chapter 2, "Creating Forms". Chapter 3, "Using ISQL to Connect to Sybase SQL Server" Chapter 4, "Creating CGI Scripts Using Perl" or Chapter 5, "Creating CGI Scripts Using Tcl"
Use Java to perform transactional calculations and client-side processing by passing data through Open Client calls or CGI scripts	Chapter 6, "Using Java for Client-side Programming"
Use web.sql to translate web.sql data into Open Client calls	Chapter 2, "Creating Forms" Chapter 3, "Using ISQL to Connect to Sybase SQL Server" Chapter 4, "Creating CGI Scripts Using Perl" or Chapter 5, "Creating CGI Scripts Using Tcl" Chapter 7, "Using Web.sql to Streamline Data Flow"

For all methods, read Chapter 8, "Security Issues for the Web."

ABC Widget Company Example

Throughout this book, we're going to show you different workflows for managing information by providing sample forms, CGI scripts, and ISQL scripts for a fictitious company known as ABC Widget Company. ABC Widget Company is entering the realm of World Wide Web customer order processing.

The Scenario

The management team at ABC Widget Company has realized that their current ordering process is time-consuming and inefficient. Order clerks take orders by phone, write down the order information, then enter the information into a database. The management concluded that allowing customers to enter order information themselves electronically using an HTML form and CGI scripts would not only save time but eliminate keying errors. Additionally, customers could easily check mailing addresses, phone numbers, and other data, and update the information immediately.

The management also sees the benefit of using the World Wide Web within their own environment, or Intranet. They realize that allowing the sales and marketing teams to access ordering information easily and quickly will help increase internal productivity.

In addition to an order form, the ordering department wants a confirmation screen that displays the total cost of the order, and allows the customer to cancel or confirm the order. When the customer confirms the order, the department wants to display an additional screen to thank the customer for their order, redisplay the total cost of the order, and provide a purchase order number so the customer can check the status of their order if needed.

The marketing and sales groups want to quickly get sales information based on quarterly sales as well as drill-down to monthly sales within the quarter. They also want to be able to perform trend analysis to see if they're receiving few orders that are large in total value, or multiple orders that are lower in total value. They also want to know which customers order the most widgets.

Throughout this book, we place you in the role of the programmer, webmaster, or database administrator meeting the information requirements for various departments at ABC Widget Company. The book is organized so you can walk through the process step by step, or single out a particular activity that you want to learn about.

The Database

The sample database consists of four tables: client, items, order_header, and order_dtl.

Client Table

The client table is used for a customer management database. Although the table does not contain all of the necessary information required for a complete management database, it should give you an idea of how the interaction will work between the personal client information and the related purchase table.

The client table is linked to the order_header table through the client primary key called client_id, and consists of the following columns:

```
client_id       numeric (4,0)      identify      primary key
last_name       varchar (20)       not null
first_name      varchar (15)       not null
phone_number    char (13)
address         varchar (60)
city            varchar (30)
state           char (2)
zip             char (10)
```

Order_header Table

The purchase order information is divided into two tables. The reason for the division is that any purchase order can have more than one item charged against the purchase order number. Therefore, there is a one-to-many relationship between the header information of the purchase order and the items being ordered.

The order_header table and the order_dtl table are linked by the order_id column. The order_header table is basically used for linking the client table and order_dtl tables. The columns are:

```
order_id        numeric (4,0)      identity      primary key
client_id       numeric (4,0)      not null      references
order_date      datetime
```

Order_dtl Table

The order_dtl table is used to record each item ordered based on the order_id, which is the purchase order number. The columns within the order_dtl table are:

```
order_id        numeric (4,0)       not null        references
item_id         numeric (4,0)       not null        references
quantity        int
cost            numeric (10,2)
```

Items Table

The items table contains specific information about the different product offerings at ABC Widget Company. The items table is linked to the order_dtl table through the item_id column. The columns within the items table are:

```
item_id         numeric (4,0)       identity        primary key
description     varchar (60)
price           numeric (10,2)
```

Figure 1-8 illustrates the tables and their relationships.

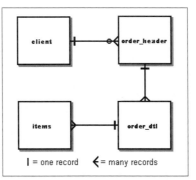

Figure 1-8. *ABC Widget Company database relationship model*

Moving Ahead

Now that you've made some decisions and decided which tools you want to use to create your application, you're ready to continue. You may need to come back to the decision trees when you're ready to begin implementing your application. Keep in mind that there's no "best" way to create a database-enabled Web application: use this book as a guideline for an approach that suits your needs.

2

Creating Forms

Forms are the key to making your database accessible from Web pages—from inside your corporate firewall or outside your corporate domain. For example, you can use forms to provide customers a way to order products and download software from the Web, and you can use forms to allow company employees access to personal benefits information. Using one user interface to access the database means one learning curve for you and your customers, saving time and money and increasing productivity. Adding forms to your Web pages means deciding on what information you want to allow the user to access, and whether or not to create an additional set of database tables to provide that information.

The ability of Web page developers to incorporate the `<FORM>` element in the HTML Document Type Definition (DTD) has resulted in the proliferation of forms on the World Wide Web. Browsing Web pages on the Internet is a great way to see how other people and companies are using forms. You'll find forms for creating simple queries, such as finding phone numbers, to more complex drill-down pages that first show summary information, then allow the user to obtain more detailed information by selecting from options returned from the original query. You can think of drill-down pages as multilayered tables of contents.

In this chapter, we're assuming that you already understand your data model and are ready to begin designing the user interface (see Chapter 1, "Introduction" for details). We'll provide some considerations for creating a form, then show you the basic constructs of a form. After you have a solid grasp of form constructs, we'll provide two sample applications to help you grasp the concepts of form creation. The J.B. Coffee Company application introduces you to the form elements, and the ABC Widget Company application re-enforces element concepts. We'll do this in the following sections:

- Considerations for Creating Forms

- Getting Started with Forms Development

- The <FORM> Element

- The <INPUT> Element

- The <SELECT> Element

- The <TEXTAREA> Element

- Form Examples

- Tips and Tricks.

Considerations for Creating Forms

Forms play two primary roles: they are used to get information from a database, and they are used to insert data into a database. The information needs of your audience—from the customer entering information to the person gathering the information—determine the complexity that is needed to be built into your form. By complexity, we mean whether or not you need to build a drill-down form to allow users to see different levels of information, and the level to which the user interacts with checkboxes, radio buttons, and picklists versus text fields into which they enter search criteria or other information. When you supply the user with a text field, for example, you must verify the accuracy and relevance of the value entered using robust CGI scripting. Using checkboxes, radio buttons and picklists saves processing work and structures the choices on behalf of the user.

Here's how it works: When a user submits a form to the database, the information is passed to the server where the CGI script resides. The CGI script then filters the information and converts it into a format that the SQL script can interpret. The SQL script then passes the variable information through Remote Procedure Calls to the Sybase database. The database returns the values requested in the form to the CGI script, which in turn formats the information into an HTML document, then sends the document back to the user.

When creating forms, you need to consider how the CGI script will filter the user-supplied information. For example, when you use text fields, filtering ensures that the information entered is in the correct format (for example, that the user entered an integer in the integer field), and ensures that special characters inserted by the system are converted back to the appropriate text values (for example, that spaces are replaced with the plus sign). After the CGI script has the information in the correct state, it can pass the information over to the SQL script for processing. The following sections describe the form components and the filtering process in more detail.

Getting Started with Forms Development

Forms are comprised of *elements* and *element attributes*. Before we describe each element and attribute, you need to understand how the Web page containing the form entries interacts with the database. In this chapter, we're assuming that the database already exists.

The first thing to do is record the necessary information about the database. Why is this important? You must know the column names for linking the form content to the CGI script and database table, and the column widths when assigning text field length values so the user can't enter more information than the column can hold. You also must know the table names for writing the CGI script. This section discusses the column names for linking the form content to the CGI script and database table. The section, "The <FORM> Element" discusses linking the form content to the CGI script and database table, and the section, "The <INPUT> Element" discusses assigning text field width values. Chapter 4, "Creating CGI Scripts Using Perl" and Chapter 5, "Creating CGI Scripts Using Tcl" discuss writing CGI scripts. Chapter 3, "Using ISQL to Connect to Sybase SQL Server" discusses writing the SQL receiving end that interacts with the database.

The form attributes that link the form with the database are NAME and VALUE. We suggest that you use the NAME attribute as your link to the database column and that you use the VALUE attribute as the data you want to be inserted or used as the search value. Consistently using the NAME and VALUE attributes ensures that you pass the correct information and that the column name is passed with the value. For example, when you use a pair of radio buttons to identify the gender of the user, the column name in the database would most likely be "gender" and the available column values would be "male" or "female." If a woman is filling out the form, then the NAME and VALUE attribute values passed to the CGI script are: gender=female. This pair of values is called a *name/value pair.* By using the table column names for the NAME attribute, you can avoid using a test-and-verify clause within your CGI script to ensure that the database column and the value being passed are linked.

You also have the option to use a value within the column as the NAME attribute value, or to use a unique value within the NAME attribute that will be used within the CGI script as a test-and-evaluate value. We'll get to those options later. First, let's look at how and why you would directly link a NAME attribute value to a specific column in the database.

Let's say that you want to collect the first and last names of your customers. The database contains a customer table containing last_name and first_name columns. When you code the text field element for the last and first names, you would use the values last_name and first_name within the NAME attribute, which correspond to the column names in the database. When a customer enters his or her name in the text field, the value they enter is entered into the column specified within the NAME attribute.

The database table columns look like this:

```
last_name       first_name
```

The NAME attribute is coded like this:

```
NAME="last_name"
```

The value passed to the CGI script is:

```
last_name=EPPERSON
```

There may be situations when it is necessary to link two or three components together and pass the information to the CGI script in a way that makes the relationship between the different components apparent. In this situation, you would not link the NAME attribute to a particular column in the database.

For example, say you want to create a form in which your customers can choose a particular coffee bean from several different choices such as Breakfast Blend, French Roast, or Kona. You also need to know whether or not customers want the coffee ground, and how much they want to buy. There are three unique values that need to be passed to the database: the type of bean (Breakfast Blend, French Roast, or Kona); ground or whole; and the quantity.

How can you code the form so the customer can make several coffee bean choices, still pass the three required bits of information for each bean type, and easily link all three entries? The easiest way to link the information is to create two text fields for each coffee bean type. One text field is used to pass the quantity information for ground coffee, and the other text field is used to pass the quantity information for whole bean. In this case, the NAME attribute values do not have a direct link to a column in the database: instead, you establish the link to all three pieces of information by entering a unique value in the NAME attribute, such as fr_grnd (for French Roast ground). You would code the NAME attributes as follows: NAME="fr_grnd" and NAME="fr_whole". Using this method, the value passed would be the quantity, and an example of a name/value pair is fr_whole=2.

Another way to use the NAME attribute value to your advantage is to specify a particular object within the NAME attribute. For example, if you need to create a form to collect quantity information for a particular product, entering the "product" column name within the NAME attribute isn't helpful, especially if you have more than one product. However, if you enter the product name or the product ID number in the NAME attribute, then you can link the specific product to a specific quantity. The information passed to the CGI script is the product and quantity. If the user orders several items, you can easily associate each product with a specific quantity.

The database may look like this:

```
product        quantity
95-1234
95-1847
```

The coded NAME attribute would look like this:

```
NAME="95-1234"
```

The value passed to the CGI script would look like this:

```
95-1234=5
```

The database, then, would be updated as follows:

```
product        quantity
95-1234        5
```

You could then determine that the user wants five 95-1234s.

Now that you are familiar with how the form interacts with the database, we'll get into the elements and attributes that make up the form.

The <FORM> Element

The <FORM> element signals the beginning of a form to the HTML browser application. Essentially, the <FORM> element (<FORM>... </FORM>) is a container for other sub-elements. The <FORM> element can contain any number or combination of the <INPUT>, <SELECT>, and <TEXTAREA> sub-elements. After we describe the <FORM> element, we'll describe each of these sub-elements in subsequent sections.

Figure 2-1 shows the <FORM> element with its associated attributes. We describe each attribute in this section.

Figure 2-1. *<FORM> element attribute window showing an example of the ACTION, ENCTYPE, and METHOD attributes*

The <FORM> element and its associated attributes are also shown in the following DTD listing. The ACTION and METHOD attributes are required. Note that the following element and attribute declarations include the content model %body.content and an associated attribute declaration. The percent sign (%) identifies %body.content as a *parameter entity*.

```
<!ENTITY % body.content "(DIV | %heading | %text | %block | HR |
ADDRESS)*">
<!ELEMENT FORM - - %body.content -(FORM) +(INPUT|SELECT|TEXTAREA)>
<!ATTLIST FORM
action %URI              #REQUIRED
method                  (%HTTP-Method) GET
enctype                 %Content-Type;
script %URI             #IMPLIED>
```

The ACTION Attribute

The ACTION attribute is the link between the form and the CGI script. The location address within the ACTION attribute (also known as the URL) points to the server, a specific directory, and the script name within the specific CGI-BIN directory.

Normally, the location address is the CGI script location and name. For example,

```
ACTION="netra1/http/cgi-bin/cgiscript"
```

ACTION="http://www.abcwidget.com/cgi_bin/example"

is a location address or URL. Figure 2-2 shows an example of the ACTION attribute.

Figure 2-2. *The ACTION attribute*

The METHOD Attribute

The METHOD attribute tells the browser software how to send the form information to the database. The information may be sent along with the URL, or sent as a separate file. When the user fills in the form and selects the Submit button, the browser software checks the ACTION attribute value to see where the information is going, and then checks the METHOD attribute to see how it is supposed to get there.

GET and POST, the two options associated with METHOD, tell the browser software how to send the form information. If you don't specify the METHOD attribute, GET is the default. Use the GET option when you want to send information to the CGI script as an attachment to the URL. Using the GET option appends the content of the form to the URL and passes it as one stream of data to the HTTP server. The data passed is sent to the server environment variable QUERY_STRING or PATH_INFO. If you create a Web form with some input text fields and name them field_one, field_two, and field_three, and the user enters the corresponding values "Alpha," "Beta," and "Delta," the QUERY_STRING looks like this:

```
?field_one=Alpha&files_two=Beta&field_three=Delta
```

Note that the data string begins with a question mark, and each data value is associated with the name of the Web form widget it represents. Do not use this method if you want to pass masked or sensitive data, as all of the information being passed is displayed in the Location line at the top of your browser window, as shown in Figure 2-3.

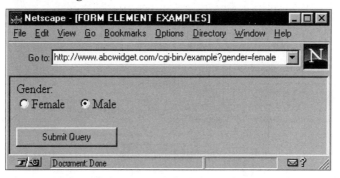

Figure 2-3. *The contents of the Location line at the top of the browser when the METHOD attribute is set to the GET option*

Use the POST option when you want to send the information as a separate file from the URL. Separating the URL from the data allows you to pass masked or sensitive data because it is not displayed on the screen, and allows you to send longer strings. The information sent via POST is received by the server through STDIN. Like the GET method, the POST method passes its arguments encoded and in the format arg1=val1&arg2=val2&...

Usually, POST is the preferred method because GET has a few limitations. For example, GET passes data values through the command line of the operating system on which the Web server program is running, but most operating systems have limitations in the number of characters that can be passed via the command line, and have different command line length limitations. As a result, if you have a large data string being passed from a Web form, you may reach the operating system's limitation and lose data. Figure 2-4 shows the same form values sent using the POST option.

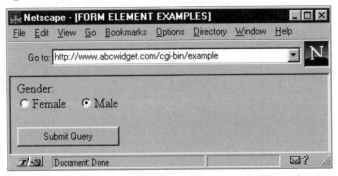

Figure 2-4. *The contents of the Location text field at the top of the browser when the METHOD attribute is set to the POST option*

Note: Do not confuse using the POST method with secure data transmission: it by no means should be considered as a secure method of transferring information. See Chapter 8, "Security Issues for the Web" for more information.

Special Characters

When a user submits a form, it is sent as a 7-bit ASCII file. There are specific characters that do not transfer into the 7-bit ASCII code set, and are viewed by the system as special characters. For example, commas and slashes are viewed as special characters and are converted to special ASCII code values preceded by a % sign to indicate that they have been converted. Spaces are converted to a plus sign (+). You also need to remember that the HTML submission process is based on the ASCII standard, and the browser software applications have been coded to separate attributes with the ampersand (&).

You should know the characters that get transferred as special ASCII values, and their ASCII equivalents. Within the CGI script, you need to convert the ASCII information back to an appropriate value before storing the information into the database. For example, if someone places a space in a text field, it is interpreted by

(cont.)

the system as a + sign. In the CGI script, write an expression substitution to convert the + sign back to a space. You also need to use the ampersand (&) as a separation tool within the CGI script. The & is your begin or end point for finding a name and value pair. For example, here are a few conversions that you may encounter (for a complete list of all conversions, see Appendix D, "ASCII Conversion Chart").

Special Character	ASCII Equivalent
comma	%2C
space	+
return	%0D%0A
back slash(\)	%5C
forward slash (/)	%2F
colon	%3A
double quote (")	%22
single quote (')	%27

The ENCTYPE Attribute

The ENCTYPE attribute (ENCoding TYPE) is used to specify the MIME type (Multipurpose Internet Mail Extensions). MIME is the standard used for sending information through the Internet e-mail environment. The encoding type default for World Wide Web documents is part of that standard. The default value for the ENCTYPE attribute is:

```
application/x-www-form-urlencoded
```

For more information about the MIME standard, please refer to Borenstein, N., and N. Freed, *MIME (Multipurpose Internet Mail Extensions): Mechanisms for Specifying and Describing the Format of Internet Message Bodies*, RFC 1521, Bellcore, Innosoft, September, 1993.

The SCRIPT Attribute

The SCRIPT attribute is a newly-defined attribute that was introduced with the HTML 3.0 specification, but is being adopted into the HTML 2.0 extended specification. The functionality permits you to call a form generator script that resides on the server from within your HTML document. When a user selects a link to access a form, the browser interprets the SCRIPT attribute, accesses the

CGI script, and displays the form coded within the script. This enables real-time creation of forms, or automatic form generation. For more information about this attribute, consult the HTML 3.0 DTD.

Formatting the Form

The <FORM> element can contain almost any other markup elements in the HTML DTD such as <HEAD>, <BODY>, <BOLD>, and <TABLE>. You can use the <BOLD> and <TABLE> elements to make the form easier to follow. For example, if your form requires the user to enter their last name, first name, and address, you can use the <TABLE> element to make the entries flush left, and vertically align the text entry boxes. We show you how to use the <TABLE> element to format form entries in the "Form Examples" section at the end of this chapter.

The <INPUT> Element

The <INPUT> element is the foundation of forms creation. The TYPE attribute of the <INPUT> element allows you to create checkboxes, radio buttons, text fields, masked password boxes, and Submit and Reset buttons. Because the TYPE attribute drives the use of the other attributes within the <INPUT> element, we'll discuss the TYPE attribute first. The other attributes of the <INPUT> element are listed in alphabetical order in the "Other <INPUT> Element Attributes" section. (Each attribute definition includes the TYPE attribute with which it can be used.) Figure 2-5 shows an example of the <INPUT> element attributes.

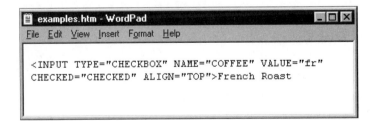

Figure 2-5. *An example showing the <INPUT> element attributes:*
TYPE, NAME, VALUE, ALIGN, and CHECKED

The TYPE Attribute

The TYPE attribute is used to determine the type of field displayed on the Web page. There are ten TYPE options available: CHECKBOX, FILE, HIDDEN, PASSWORD, RADIO, RANGE, RESET, SCRIBBLE, SUBMIT, and TEXT. This section describes the TYPE attribute options in detail so you can gain an understanding of when and where to use each one.

CHECKBOX Option

Use checkboxes when you want to offer several choices to the user. How you handle the boxes checked by the user depends upon the amount of information being processed. You may want to pass the values to one column in the database, or pass the values to several columns in the database. In this section, we'll discuss when one method is better than the other, and show you some other options related to checkboxes.

The CHECKBOX option uses the NAME and/or VALUE attributes to pass information to the CGI script. If you use the NAME attribute by itself, the associated value passed with it is on, meaning that the user selected the checkbox, or blank, meaning that the user didn't select the checkbox. Use only the NAME attribute when you want to gather several values from a group of checkboxes and insert them into a column or columns.

Using the NAME Attribute Alone

If you're collecting multiple data-values for multiple columns, using just the NAME attribute is the way to go. When using checkboxes for multiple column entries, you only need to insert one row of information.

Let's use an example to illustrate. You have a table in the database that you are using to collect order information for coffee. The table has three columns: one for collecting Breakfast Blend information (bb); one for French Roast information (fr); and one for Kona information (ko). You code three checkboxes on your form as follows:

```
<INPUT TYPE="CHECKBOX" NAME="yes">Breakfast Blend
<INPUT TYPE="CHECKBOX" NAME="yes">French Roast
<INPUT TYPE="CHECKBOX" NAME="yes">Kona
```

Remember that data passed to the database comes over as a complete row, so when the user selects "Submit" on your form, one row of information is inserted into the database table. If the user chooses two of the three checkboxes and submits the form, the following information is passed to the database:

```
yes=on&yes=on
```

Which of the three coffees did the user choose? You can't tell because the same value ("yes") is used for the NAME attribute. If you use unique values for the NAME attribute instead, as shown below, you can determine the type of coffee chosen by the user.

```
<INPUT TYPE="CHECKBOX" NAME="bb">Breakfast Blend
<INPUT TYPE="CHECKBOX" NAME="fr">French Roast
<INPUT TYPE="CHECKBOX" NAME="ko">Kona
```

If the user chooses two of the three checkboxes and submits the form, the following information is passed to the database, and their choices are clear:

```
fr=on&bb=on
```

Note: There are some cases when you want the NAME attribute to be the same: one example is when you are coding radio buttons. See the "RADIO Option" section for more information.

Using the NAME and VALUE Attributes Together

If you need to capture multiple rows of information that will go into one column, you need to use the NAME and VALUE attributes together.

For example, the checkbox <INPUT TYPE="CHECKBOX" NAME="fr"> passes the name/value pair fr=on to the CGI script, which then places an on indicator value into the "fr" column in the table. When you want to pass a specific value to the database instead of the on indicator, use the NAME and VALUE attributes. For example, the checkbox <INPUT TYPE="CHECKBOX" NAME="coffee" VALUE="fr"> passes the name/value pair coffee=fr to the CGI script.

When you use the NAME and VALUE attributes together, the data-value of each checkbox NAME attribute can be the same or unique. In all cases, the data-value of the VALUE attribute must be unique. In general, use only the NAME attribute when you have a column into which you want to enter on or off values, or when you have multiple columns requiring only an on or off value. The on or off value can then be tested and evaluated within the CGI script: at that time, you can then determine what should be inserted into the database column.

You can specify a default checkbox selection using the CHECKED attribute within the <INPUT> element. The code looks like this:

```
<INPUT TYPE="CHECKBOX" NAME="coffee" VALUE="fr" CHECKED="CHECKED">
```

If you wanted to allow the user to choose one or more options and also provide a default choice, you would code the selection like this:

```
<FORM ACTION="http://www.jbcoffee.com/cgi_bin/example">
<INPUT TYPE="CHECKBOX" NAME="bb" ALIGN="TOP">Breakfast Blend
<BR>
<INPUT TYPE="CHECKBOX" NAME="fr" CHECKED="CHECKED" ALIGN="TOP">French
Roast
<BR>
<INPUT TYPE="CHECKBOX" NAME="ko" ALIGN="TOP">Kona
<BR>
<INPUT TYPE="SUBMIT" VALUE="Submit" ALIGN="TOP">
</FORM>
```

Notice that the NAME attribute is used by itself. When the user selects a box, the indicator for the checkbox is on. When a user doesn't select a box, the indicator is off. Only the on values are passed to the CGI script. The CGI script links the data to the appropriate column, so if the user selects two boxes, the row gets two additional column entries. Figure 2-6 shows how checkboxes look on a Web page, and the associated HTML code.

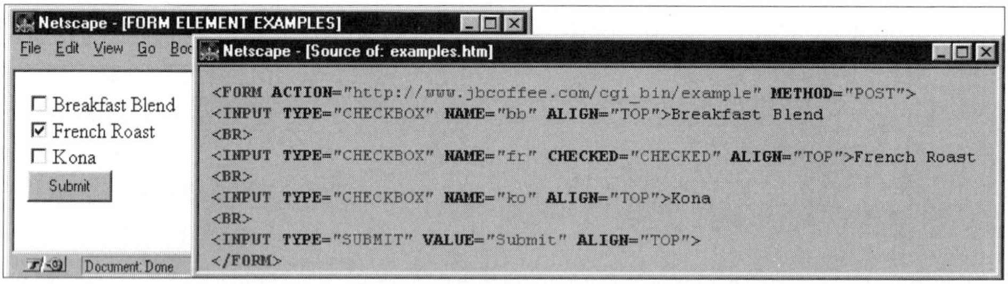

Figure 2-6. Checkbox option using the NAME attribute only, where the NAME attribute is unique across all related checkboxes

If the user selects all three coffee selections, the string passed to the CGI script includes three unique NAME attribute values, as shown below:

```
'http://www.jbcoffee.com/example?bb=on&fr=on&ko=on'
```

Remember, if you want to allow for unique values to be passed that designate the value as on or off, you need to assign unique NAME attributes to each checkbox.

You may want to have the same NAME data-value for all of the related checkboxes. In the example below, the NAME data-value is coffee. In this situation, the VALUE attribute data-value must be unique. You would code the <INPUT> elements like this:

```
<FORM ACTION="http://www.jbcoffee.com/cgi_bin/example">
<INPUT TYPE="CHECKBOX" NAME="coffee" VALUE="bb" ALIGN="TOP">Breakfast
Blend
<BR>
<INPUT TYPE="CHECKBOX" NAME="coffee" VALUE="fr" CHECKED="CHECKED"
ALIGN="TOP">French Roast
<BR>
<INPUT TYPE="CHECKBOX" NAME="coffee" VALUE="ko" ALIGN="TOP">Kona
<BR>
<INPUT TYPE="SUBMIT" VALUE="Submit" ALIGN="TOP">
</FORM>
```

The checkbox or checkboxes the user chooses determines the data-values passed to the CGI script. Using the name/value pairs means that the CGI script searches for a specific name/value pair instead of an on indicator. As in the previous example, if the user chooses two or more values, the CGI script adds two or more row entries to the appropriate column. Figure 2-7 shows how the checkboxes look on the page and in the associated HTML code. Notice that the checkboxes on the browser page do not look any different from those in the previous example. What is different is the way the NAME and VALUE attributes are coded, which in turn affects what information is passed to the CGI script.

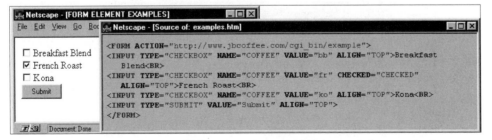

Figure 2-7. *Checkbox example using name/value pairs, in which the NAME attribute is common across the related checkboxes, but the VALUE attributes are unique to each checkbox*

If the user selects all three options, the following string is passed to the CGI script:

```
'http://www.jbcoffee.com/example?coffee=bb&coffee=fr&coffee=ko'
```

FILE Option

The FILE option is used to append attachments to forms. FILE is a new <INPUT> element option that has been adopted into the HTML 2.0 extended specification. When you use it, the browser displays a text field box with a BROWSE button, allowing the user to browse for the file they want to attach prior to submitting the form.

The following code shows the <INPUT> element with the FILE option:

```
<FORM ACTION="http://www.jbcoffee.com/cgi_bin/example">
Attach File<BR>
<INPUT TYPE="FILE" NAME="text" TYPE="file" ACCEPT="text/*">
<BR>
<BR>
<INPUT TYPE="SUBMIT" VALUE="Submit" ALIGN="TOP">
</FORM>
```

Figure 2-8 shows how the FILE option looks on a Web page.

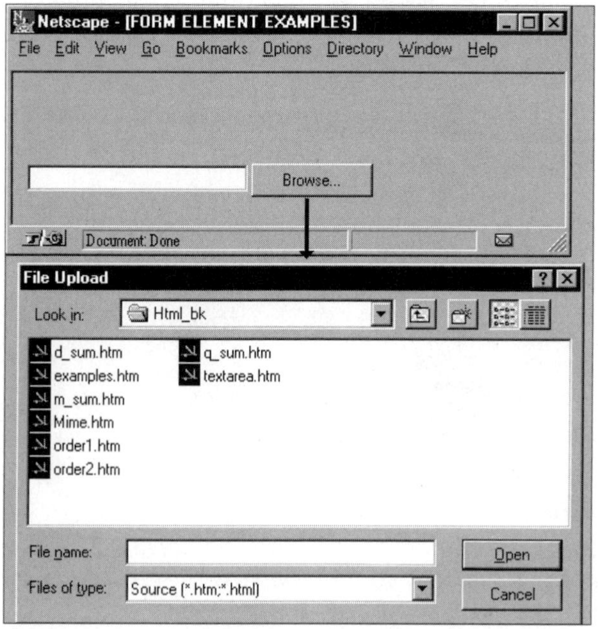

Figure 2-8. *File option example showing the FILE option text field and the related browse dialog box displayed when the Browse button is selected*

HIDDEN Option

Hidden boxes are useful for passing information that you want to be hidden from the user. For example, if you have several remote offices and each office submits data independently, you can use the HIDDEN option to indicate the remote site from which the information originated. (The presumption is that each remote site has its own HTTP server, and that the form resides on each server.) It may not make sense for the user to code in the branch number or location number: in fact, they may not even know the number. Using a hidden field, you can enter the location information for them. Remember, however, that users can see hidden boxes when they view the source of the form.

Following is an example of how to code the <INPUT> element to track the remote sites sending the data:

```
<FORM ACTION="http://www.mountainvalley.com/cgi_bin/example">
<INPUT TYPE="HIDDEN" NAME="source" VALUE="girdler" ALIGN="TOP">
<BR>
<INPUT TYPE="SUBMIT" VALUE="Submit" ALIGN="TOP">
</FORM>
```

The value string sent to the CGI script would be:

```
'http://www.mountainvalley.com/cgi_bin/example?source=girdler'
```

The string indicates that the form came from your remote office in Girdler.

PASSWORD Option

The PASSWORD option masks each character typed into a field. You can see the number of characters entered, but not the characters themselves. However, when the form is submitted, the characters are readable and visible in the text stream.

> **Note:** Masking the characters does not mean that the data is secure. You must use an encryption method to ensure the security of the data. See Chapter 8, "Security Issues for the Web" for more information.

Additionally, if you use the GET option instead of POST for the METHOD attribute, the masked data is displayed in the Location text field at the top of the browser window when the form is submitted. (See "The METHOD Attribute" in this chapter for more information about GET and POST.) With a secure Web server, password masking, and the use of the POST option, you can ensure complete confidentiality.

Following is an example of how you would code the <INPUT> element to include the PASSWORD option. Figure 2-9 shows how the coded PASSWORD option looks on a form.

```
<FORM ACTION="http://www.jbcoffee.com/cgi_bin/example">
Enter your password:
<INPUT TYPE="PASSWORD" NAME="password" SIZE="15" MAXLENGTH="12"
ALIGN="TOP">
<BR>
<INPUT TYPE="SUBMIT" VALUE="Submit" ALIGN="TOP">
</FORM>
```

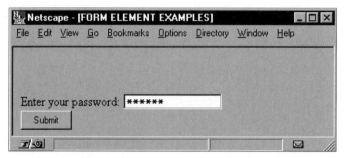

Figure 2-9. Example showing how the password is masked from the viewer within the password text field

If the user enters the password "456289" in the password block and you're using the GET option for the METHOD attribute, the string visible within the Location text field at the top of the browser window is:

```
'http://www.jbcoffee.com/cgi_bin/example?password=456289'
```

RADIO Option

Unlike the CHECKBOX option, radio buttons require the user to select a single option. For radio buttons to work correctly, the NAME attribute of each related radio button must have the same data-value, and the VALUE attribute must have a unique data-value.

Using the same example as that for the checkbox option, the NAME attribute data-value is "coffee," which corresponds to a column in the database. Like the checkbox example, the default selection is French Roast, but setting a default is optional. The value passed is "fr," "ko," or "bb." The <INPUT> elements are coded like this:

```
<FORM ACTION="http://www.jbcoffee.com/cgi_bin/example">
<INPUT TYPE="RADIO" NAME="coffee" VALUE="bb" ALIGN="TOP">Breakfast Blend
<INPUT TYPE="RADIO" NAME="coffee" VALUE="fr" ALIGN="TOP" CHECKED="CHECKED"
>French Roast<BR>
<INPUT TYPE="RADIO" NAME="coffee" VALUE="ko" ALIGN="TOP">Kona<BR>
<BR>
<INPUT TYPE="SUBMIT" VALUE="Submit" ALIGN="TOP">
</FORM>
```

Figure 2-10 shows how the above-coded RADIO option looks on a form. The radio button for French Roast is the default option.

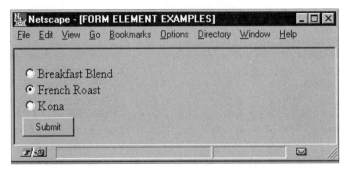

Figure 2-10. *Radio button example*

If the user selects the option "French Roast," the following string is passed to the CGI script:

```
'http://www.jbcoffee.com/cgi_bin/example?coffee=fr'
```

RANGE Option

RANGE is another newly-proposed option that is not yet fully supported by any of the more popular browsers like Netscape, Mosaic, and Microsoft Internet Explorer. The purpose of the option is to allow the end user to choose a value within a specified range. The range checking is actually performed on the client side, but this is not yet supported by the browsers.

An example of using the RANGE option is if you wanted to allow your users to rate your products or service department on a scale of 1 to 10. You would code minimum and maximum values using the MIN and MAX attributes and provide a text box into which the user would enter a value. The browser would ensure that the value is within the specified range: however, to be on the safe side, your CGI script should test the user's response against the MIN and MAX values to ensure they rated within the appropriate range.

Following is an example of how to code the <INPUT> element to include the RANGE option.

```
<FORM ACTION="http://www.jbcoffee.com/cgi_bin/example">
<INPUT TYPE="RANGE" NAME="value_range" MIN="1" MAX="10" ALIGN="TOP">
Select appropriate value from 1-10
<BR>
<INPUT TYPE="SUBMIT" VALUE="Submit" ALIGN="TOP">
</FORM>
```

Figure 2-11 shows how the RANGE option is currently represented on a form.

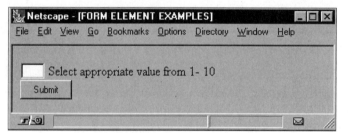

Figure 2-11. The RANGE option

If the user gives your service department a rating of 5, the following string is passed to the CGI script:

```
'http://www.abcwidget.com/cgi_bin/example?value_range=5'
```

RESET Option

The RESET option is used to reset the values within a form back to the original or default state, giving the user filling in the form the option to start over. Following is an example of coding the <INPUT> element to include the RESET option. Note that the default text "Reset" is changed to "Clear Entry" using the VALUE attribute.

```
<FORM ACTION="http://www.jbcoffee.com/cgi_bin/example">
<INPUT TYPE="RESET" VALUE="Clear Entry" ALIGN="TOP">

</FORM>
```

Figure 2-12 shows how the above-coded RESET option looks on a form.

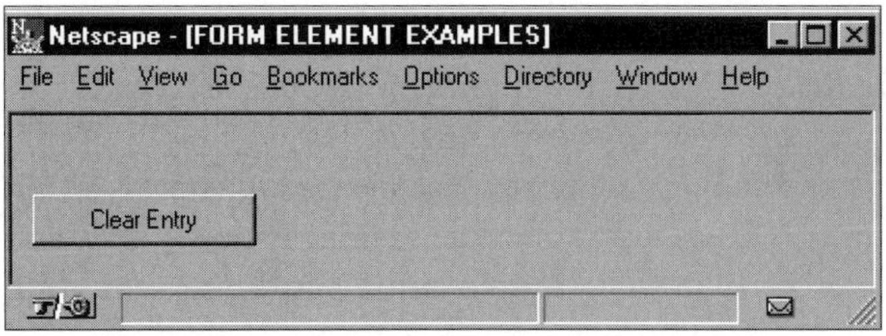

Figure 2-12. *Resulting Clear Entry button*

We highly recommend that you place the Reset button and associated instructions toward the end of a form.

SCRIBBLE Option

SCRIBBLE is a newly-proposed TYPE option within the HTML 3.0 specification that has been carried over into the HTML 2.0 spec. The purpose of the option is to allow the end user to *scribble* on an image referenced in the SRC attribute—without affecting the original image.

If you have ever used Microsoft PowerPoint, the scribble feature is similar to selecting the pen icon and drawing on a slide during a presentation. Your scribbles are not saved as part of the file. If you were interfacing with an engineering or drafting group and were asked to review an image, you could use the scribble feature to overlay comments or show specific change requests without affecting the original image. If your browser does not support this option, you can provide a text field in which users can enter comments instead.

The <INPUT> element with the scribble option looks like this:

```
<FORM ACTION="http://www.jbcoffee.com/cgi_bin/example">
<INPUT TYPE="SCRIBBLE" NAME="scribble_pad" SIZE="15"
SRC="file:///c|/html_bk/btn_home.gif" ALIGN="TOP"> Scribble Pad
<BR>
<INPUT TYPE="SUBMIT" VALUE="Submit" ALIGN="TOP">
</FORM>
```

If the user enters "Overwrite" in the Scribble Pad box, the following string is passed to the CGI script:

```
'http://www.jbcoffee.com/cgi_bin/example?scribble_pad=Overwrite'
```

Notice that the SRC value isn't passed with the rest of the information. This is a good indication that the browser does not support this function.

SUBMIT Option

The SUBMIT option is used to create a Submit button that signals the browser software that the user has submitted the form. When the user selects the Submit button, the browser software checks the ACTION attribute in the <FORM> element to execute the URL, and then checks the METHOD attribute within the <FORM> element to see how the information is supposed to get there. We suggest that you place the Submit button and instructions concerning the submission process at the end of the form. You can rename the default text displayed on the Submit button by entering a new name in the VALUE attribute, as shown below:

```
<FORM ACTION="http://www.jbcoffee.com/cgi_bin/example">
<INPUT TYPE="SUBMIT" VALUE="Submit Order" ALIGN="TOP">
</FORM>
```

Figure 2-13 shows how the above-coded SUBMIT option looks on the form. Note that the name of the Submit button has been changed to "Submit Order."

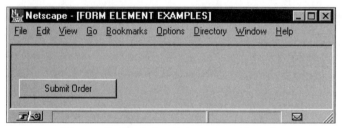

Figure 2-13. Submit button example

TEXT Option

The TEXT option is used for single-line entries such as names, address lines, and phone numbers. The data-value you enter for the NAME attribute normally corresponds to a specific column name in the database. One of the better features of this option is the ability to limit the number of characters the user can enter, which is beneficial if you have limited column widths.

Use the SIZE and MAXLENGTH attributes to specify the display width of the text field and the number of characters the user can enter. The SIZE attribute is used to define the physical width of the text field on the browser. Set the SIZE attribute value to one or two points greater than the MAXLENGTH value to allow for white space around the text entered by the user. Ensure that the MAXLENGTH attribute doesn't exceed the length of the column in the database, or you'll lose data.

The <INPUT> element with the TEXT option looks like this:

```
<FORM ACTION="http://www.jbcoffee.com/cgi_bin/example">
Text field: <INPUT TYPE="TEXT" NAME="comment" SIZE="30" MAXLENGTH="28"
ALIGN="TOP">
<BR>
<INPUT TYPE="SUBMIT" VALUE="Submit" ALIGN="TOP">
</FORM>
```

Figure 2-14 shows how the above-coded TEXT option looks on a form.

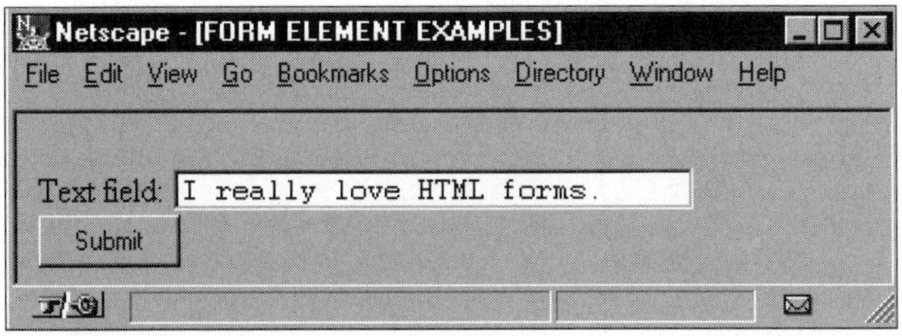

Figure 2-14. *Text option example showing a fixed text field width*

If the user enters the comment "I really love HTML forms," the following string is passed to the CGI script:

```
'http://www.jbcoffee.com/cgi_bin/example?comment=I+really+love+HTML+forms.'
```

Other <INPUT> Element Attributes

Following is a DTD listing of the remaining <INPUT> element attributes. This section defines in alphabetical order each attribute and indicates the TYPE attribute options that can be used with the attribute.

```
<!ENTITY % attrs
        'id        ID       #IMPLIED
         lang      CDATA    "en.us"
         class     NAMES    #IMPLIED'>
<!ENTITY % InputType "(TEXT | PASSWORD | CHECKBOX | RADIO | SUBMIT
                     | RESET | RANGE | FILE | SCRIBBLE | HIDDEN)">
<!ENTITY % REAL "CDATA">
<!ENTITY % URI "CDATA">
```

```
        "Uniform Resource Identifiers" by Tim Berners-Lee
   http://info.cern.ch/hypertext/WWW/Addressing/URL/URI_Overview.html
<!ENTITY % url.link
        "md      CDATA   #IMPLIED">

<!ELEMENT INPUT - O EMPTY>
<!ATTLIST INPUT
%attrs;
type %InputType TEXT
name   NAME                       #IMPLIED
value CDATA                       #IMPLIED
disabled (disabled)               #IMPLIED
error CDATA                       #IMPLIED
checked (checked)                 #IMPLIED
size NUMBER                       #IMPLIED
maxlength NUMBER                  #IMPLIED
min %REAL                         #IMPLIED
max %REAL                         #IMPLIED
accept CDATA                      #IMPLIED
src   %URI                        #IMPLIED
%url.link;
align  (top|middle|bottom|left|right) top >
```

ACCEPT – Acceptable file type

Required: FILE

Not Allowed: CHECKBOX, HIDDEN, PASSWORD, RADIO, RANGE, RESET, SCRIBBLE, SUBMIT, or TEXT

Contains the MIME content type for the attached files. For a complete listing of allowable MIME types, refer to the MIME standard:

> Borenstein, N., and N. Freed, *MIME (Multipurpose Internet Mail Extensions): Mechanisms for Specifying and Describing the Format of Internet Message Bodies*, RFC 1521, Bellcore, Innosoft, September, 1993.

ALIGN – Alignment

Allowable: RESET, SCRIBBLE, and SUBMIT

Optional: CHECKBOX, FILE, HIDDEN, PASSWORD, RADIO, RANGE, or TEXT

Sets the background alignment using the textual baseline. The allowable values are left, right, top, middle, or bottom.

CHECKED – Check default indicator

Allowable: CHECKBOX, RADIO

Not Allowed: FILE, HIDDEN, PASSWORD, RANGE, RESET, SCRIBBLE, SUBMIT, or TEXT

The check default indicator is a flag that sets the CHECKBOX or RADIO button to the "set" or "on" position.

CLASS – Classification

Optional: All

The classification setting of an element is used to assign a specific class or sub-class. The classification value can be hierarchical. For a more complete definition of the CLASS attribute, refer to the SGML standard, *International Organization for Standardization (ISO). ISO 8879:1986. Information Processing - Text and Office Systems - Standard Generalized Markup Language (SGML).*

DISABLED – Disable write

Optional: All

Allows you to set read-only values such as information in a text box.

ERROR – Error script

Optional: All

Allows you to enter an error code or message that is displayed if the user enters an incorrect value.

ID – Identifier

Optional: All

The ID attribute is used for uniquely naming an element for the purpose of linking data within HTML documents. For a more complete definition of the ID reference link, refer to the SGML standard, *International Organization for Standardization (ISO). ISO 8879:1986. Information Processing - Text and Office Systems - Standard Generalized Markup Language (SGML).*

LANG – Language

Optional: All

The Language attribute indicates to the browser or parser the language used to display an element. The data-value for this attribute is composed of two values: the first value specifies the language, and the second value specifies the country. All of the examples in this book use the data-value "en.us," in which "en" refers to the English language, and "us" refers to the United States.

MAX – Maximum RANGE value

Required: RANGE

Not Applicable: All others

The maximum numeric value for the RANGE option.

MAXLENGTH – Maximum entry characters

Allowable: PASSWORD, SCRIBBLE, TEXT

Not Applicable: All others

Specifies the maximum number of characters the user can enter into PASSWORD and TEXT entry boxes. We recommend that you set a maximum length for entry boxes associated with short columns in the database. Otherwise, the data is truncated to fit the column width if the user enters too much information.

MIN – Minimum RANGE value

Required: RANGE

Not Applicable: All others

The minimum numeric value for the RANGE option.

NAME – Input name data-value

Highly recommended: CHECKBOX, FILE, HIDDEN, PASSWORD, RADIO, RANGE, SCRIBBLE, and TEXT

Not allowed: RESET and SUBMIT

A unique value that may or may not represent a column name within a database. The name you choose depends on what you want to do with the information after it is sent to the CGI script. See the section, "Getting Started with Forms Development" for more information about the NAME attribute.

SIZE – Specify visible size

Allowable: PASSWORD, SCRIBBLE, or TEXT

Not Allowed: All others

Allows you to specify the width of a text entry box. This sets only the physical size of the box: it does not limit the number of characters that the user can enter. Use this attribute with the MAXLENGTH attribute to ensure that the user cannot enter more characters than the column can handle.

TYPE – Element type

Required: All

This attribute is used to define the type of entry fields in a form. There are currently ten options for this attribute: CHECKBOX, FILE, HIDDEN, PASSWORD, RADIO, RANGE, RESET, SCRIBBLE, SUBMIT, or TEXT (the default). For more information about these options, see "The TYPE Attribute" section.

VALUE – Data-value

Highly Recommended: CHECKBOX, HIDDEN, RADIO

Allowable: RANGE, RESET, SUBMIT, or TEXT

Do not use with: FILE, PASSWORD, or SCRIBBLE

Use the VALUE attribute with the TEXT attribute to set a default value within a text box. When used with the CHECKBOX, HIDDEN, and RADIO options, the data-value entered is the value passed to the CGI script along with the NAME data-value. When used with the SUBMIT and RESET options, the text is displayed on the button.

The <SELECT> Element

The <SELECT> element is used to create options that appear in a scrollable list or pull-down menu. The <SELECT> element is an alternate selection method to the CHECKBOX or RADIO options that saves space on the form by condensing the list of choices. You can design the list or menu so users can select one or multiple options, but allowing multiple selections requires more space.

You use the <SELECT> element with the <OPTION> element to display the values the user sees on the picklist. The values are passed with the NAME data-value to compose the name/value pair.

A pull-down menu allowing one selection is coded as follows. Note that the French Roast option is set as the default value using the SELECTED attribute.

```
<FORM ACTION="http://www.jbcoffee.com/cgi_bin/example">
<SELECT LANG="en.us" NAME="coffee">
<OPTION>Breakfast Blend</OPTION>
<OPTION SELECTED="SELECTED">French Roast</OPTION>
<OPTION>Kona</OPTION>
</SELECT>
<BR>
<INPUT TYPE="SUBMIT" VALUE="Submit" ALIGN="TOP">
</FORM>
```

Figure 2-15 shows how the above-coded <SELECT> element looks on a form.

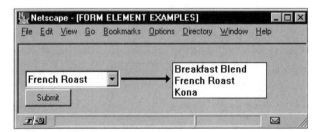

Figure 2-15. *A pull-down menu allowing selection of one option*

Selecting "French Roast" sends the following string to the CGI script:

```
'http://www.jbcoffee.com/cgi_bin/example?coffee=French+Roast'
```

Notice that the name/value pair passed to the CGI script is very similar to the name/value pair passed with the RADIO option, which also allows only one selection.

Use the MULTIPLE attribute within the <SELECT> element to allow the user to select multiple options, as shown below. Note that "French Roast" is set as the default value using the SELECTED attribute within the <OPTION> element.

```
<FORM ACTION="http://www.jbcoffee.com/cgi_bin/example">
<SELECT LANG="en.us" NAME="coffee" MULTIPLE="MULTIPLE">
<OPTION>Breakfast Blend</OPTION>
<OPTION LANG="en.us" SELECTED="SELECTED">French Roast</OPTION>
<OPTION>Kona</OPTION>
</SELECT>
<BR>
<INPUT TYPE="SUBMIT" VALUE="Submit" ALIGN="TOP">
</FORM>
```

Figure 2-16 shows how the above-coded <SELECT> element looks on a form:

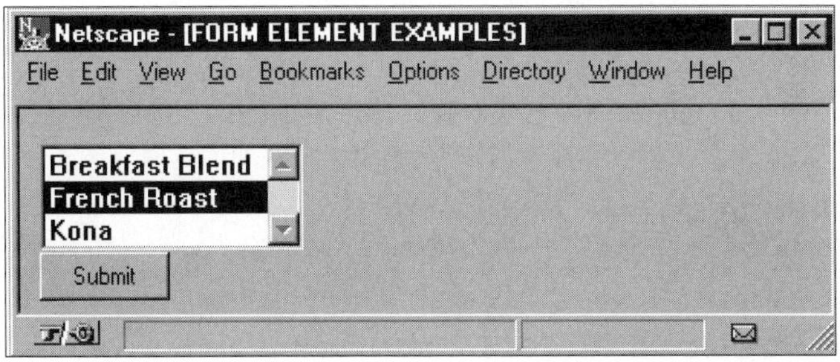

Figure 2-16. *Select example with multiple selections allowed*

Note that the format shown doesn't intuitively tell the user how to choose more than one option. We suggest that you provide instructions in a leading paragraph. For example, if the user is using Microsoft Windows and wants to select two consecutive options, they need to select the first option, then press the SHIFT key and select the second option. If, however, they want to select two options that are not consecutive, they must select the first option, then press the CTRL key and then select the second option.

Selecting "French Roast" and "Kona" passes the following string to the CGI script:

```
'http://www.jbcoffee.com/cgi_bin/example?coffee=French+Roast&coffee=Kona'
```

Notice that the name/value pairs passed are exactly the same as the name/value pairs passed when using the CHECKBOX option.

There may be times when you want the values within the picklist to be different from the code values sent to the CGI script. For example, you may want to offer the user the following choices:

```
Breakfast Blend
French Roast
Kona
```

but you may need to pass the abbreviated value for each coffee type—bb for Breakfast Blend, fr for French Roast and ko for Kona—into the database. You can do this using the VALUE attribute within the <OPTION> element, as shown below:

```
<FORM ACTION="http://www.jbcoffee.com/cgi_bin/example">
<SELECT LANG="en.us" NAME="coffee">
<OPTION VALUE="bb">Breakfast Blend</OPTION>
<OPTION VALUE="fr">French Roast</OPTION>
<OPTION VALUE="ko">Kona</OPTION>
</SELECT>
<BR>
<INPUT TYPE="SUBMIT" VALUE="Submit" ALIGN="TOP">
</FORM>
```

Other <SELECT> Element Attributes

Following is a DTD listing of <SELECT> and <OPTION> element attributes. This section defines (in alphabetical order) each attribute, and indicates the elements that can be used with the attribute.

```
<!ENTITY % attrs
        'id       ID      #IMPLIED
         lang     CDATA   "en.us"
         class    NAMES   #IMPLIED'>

<!ENTITY % SHAPE "CDATA"
<!ENTITY % URI "CDATA">
       "Uniform Resource Identifiers" by Tim Berners-Lee
  http://info.cern.ch/hypertext/WWW/Addressing/URL/URI_Overview.html
<!ENTITY % url.link
        "md      CDATA   #IMPLIED">
```

```
<!ELEMENT SELECT - - (OPTION+) -(INPUT|TEXTAREA|SELECT)>
       <!ATTLIST SELECT
       %attrs;
       name CDATA                #REQUIRED
       multiple (multiple)       #IMPLIED
       disabled (disabled)       #IMPLIED
       error CDATA               #IMPLIED
       src  %URI                 #IMPLIED
       %url.link;
       width  NUMBER             #IMPLIED
       height NUMBER             #IMPLIED
       units  (en|pixels)        pixels
       align  (top|middle|bottom|left|right) top >

<!ELEMENT OPTION - O (#PCDATA)>
       <!ATTLIST OPTION
       %attrs;
       selected (selected)       #IMPLIED
       value  CDATA              #IMPLIED
       shape %SHAPE;             #IMPLIED
       disabled (disabled)       #IMPLIED
       error CDATA               #IMPLIED >
```

ALIGN – Alignment

Optional: SELECT and OPTION

Sets the background alignment using the textual baseline. The allowable values
are left, right, top, middle, or bottom.

CLASS – Classification

Optional: SELECT and OPTION

The classification setting of an element is used to assign a specific class or subclass. The classification value can be hierarchical. For a more complete definition of the CLASS attribute, refer to the SGML standard, *International Organization for Standardization (ISO). ISO 8879:1986. Information Processing - Text and
Office Systems - Standard Generalized Markup Language (SGML).*

DISABLED – Disable write

Optional: SELECT and OPTION

Allows you to set read-only values by preventing users from editing a value such
as information in a text box.

ERROR – Error script

Optional: SELECT and OPTION

Allows you to enter an error code or message that is displayed when the user enters an incorrect value.

HEIGHT – Picklist height (if SRC is used)

Optional: SELECT

Allows you to specify a specific height for the image referenced in the SRC attribute.

ID – Identifier

Optional: SELECT and OPTION

The ID attribute is used for uniquely naming an element for the purpose of linking data within HTML documents. For a more complete definition of the ID reference link, refer to the SGML standard, *International Organization for Standardization (ISO). ISO 8879:1986. Information Processing - Text and Office Systems - Standard Generalized Markup Language (SGML).*

LANG – Language

Optional: SELECT and OPTION

The LANG attribute indicates to the browser or parser the language used to display an element. The data-value is composed of two values: the first value specifies the language, and the second value specifies the country. All of the examples in this book use the data-value "en.us," where "en" refers to the English language, and "us" refers to the United States.

MD – Message Digest

Optional: SELECT

Used to include a checksum or value that allows you to check the integrity of an image.

MULTIPLE – Multiple selections allowed

Optional: SELECT

Allows the user to select multiple options.

NAME – Select name data-value

Required: SELECT

A unique value that may or may not represent a column name within a database. The name you choose depends on what you want to do with the information after it is sent to the CGI script. See the "Getting Started with Forms Development" section for more information about the NAME attribute.

SELECTED – Select default choice

Optional: OPTION

This attribute indicates the default value for the picklist.

SHAPE – Image map shape location

Optional: OPTION

This attribute allows you to define *hotzones* within an image that reflect a particular option. Hotzones are similar to image maps. If you want to learn more about hotzones, refer to the extensive information on the WWW concerning image maps. Access any of the search engines on the Web and enter "IMAGE MAP."

SRC – Image source

Optional: SELECT

Contains the path and image name used as a backdrop. The SRC attribute used here is the same as the SRC attribute used with the <IMG> element. For more information about the <IMG> element, see the HTML DTD.

UNITS – SRC height and width unit type

Optional: SELECT

This attribute specifies the unit in which an image's width and height are measured. The default unit is pixels (72 pixels per inch).

VALUE – Data-value

Optional: OPTION

The VALUE attribute is directly linked to the NAME attribute. If you don't use this attribute, the default data-value is the value surrounded by the <OPTION> element. If you use the VALUE attribute, it takes precedence over the default value.

WIDTH – Picklist width

Optional: SELECT

Allows you to specify a specific width for the image referenced in the SRC attribute.

The <TEXTAREA> Element

The <TEXTAREA> element provides the user with a larger text entry area than is available with the <INPUT> element's TEXT option. The <TEXTAREA> element is commonly used for user comments.

The major drawback of the <TEXTAREA> element is that you can't specify an upper limit of allowable characters. The ROWS and COLS attributes allow you to set the size of the text entry box for the screen. The ROWS attribute determines the number of lines displayed at any given time. If the number of lines exceed the space available, the user can scroll the text entry box. The COLS attribute determines how many characters are displayed across the screen. If the number of characters exceeds the space available, the user can scroll the text entry box.

The <TEXTAREA> element is coded as follows. Note that the ROWS and COLUMNS attributes are used to create a text area that is four rows high and 25 characters wide.

```
<FORM ACTION="http://www.jbcoffee.com/cgi_bin/example">
<TEXTAREA LANG="en.us" NAME="comment_field" ROWS="4" COLS="25">
</TEXTAREA>
<BR>
<INPUT TYPE="SUBMIT" VALUE="Submit" ALIGN="TOP">
</FORM>
```

Figure 2-17 shows how the above-coded <TEXTAREA> element looks on a form.

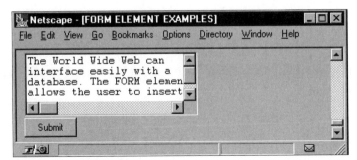

Figure 2-17. *<TEXTAREA> element example showing a display area that is four rows high and 25 characters wide*

The following example shows how a string from a text entry box looks when it's passed to the CGI script:

```
'http://www.jbcoffee.com/cgi_bin/example?comment_field=The+World+Wide+Web+c
an+interface+easily+with+a+database.+The+FORM+element+allows+the+user+to+in
sert+information+into+a+database+or+query+for+information+from+a+database.'
```

<TEXTAREA> Element Attributes

Following is a DTD listing of <TEXTAREA> element attributes. This section defines (in alphabetical order) each attribute, and indicates whether the attributes are optional or required.

```
<!ENTITY % attrs
        'id       ID      #IMPLIED
        lang      CDATA   "en.us"
        class     NAMES   #IMPLIED'>

<!ELEMENT TEXTAREA - - (#PCDATA) -(INPUT|TEXTAREA|SELECT)>
<!ATTLIST TEXTAREA
        %attrs;
        name CDATA              #REQUIRED
        rows NUMBER             #REQUIRED
        cols NUMBER             #REQUIRED
        disabled (disabled)     #IMPLIED
        error CDATA             #IMPLIED
        align  (top|middle|bottom|left|right) top
 >
```

ALIGN – Alignment

Optional

Sets the background alignment using the textual baseline. The allowable values are left, right, top, middle, or bottom.

CLASS – Classification

Optional

The classification setting of an element is used to assign a specific class or subclass. The classification value can be hierarchical. For a more complete definition of the CLASS attribute, refer to the SGML standard, *International Organization for Standardization (ISO). ISO 8879:1986.Information Processing - Text and Office Systems - Standard Generalized Markup Language (SGML).*

COLS – Textarea display width

Required

Sets the width of the text area as viewed in the browser: it does not set user entry character limits.

DISABLED – Disable write

Optional

Allows you to set read-only values by preventing users from editing a value, such as information in a text box.

ERROR – Error script

Optional

Allows you to enter an error code that is displayed if the user enters an incorrect value.

ID – Identifier

Optional

The ID attribute is used for uniquely naming an element for the purpose of linking data within HTML documents. For a more complete definition of the ID reference link, refer to the SGML standard, *International Organization for Standardization (ISO). ISO 8879:1986.Information Processing - Text and Office Systems - Standard Generalized Markup Language (SGML).*

LANG – Language

Optional: All

The LANG attribute indicates to the browser or parser the language used to display an element. The data-value is composed of two values: the first value specifies the language, and the second value specifies the country. All of the examples in this book use the data-value "en.us," in which "en" refers to the English language, and "us" refers to the United States.

NAME – Textarea name data-value

Required

A unique value that may or may not represent a column name within a database. The name you choose depends on what you want to do with the information after it is sent to the CGI script. See the section, "Getting Started with Forms Development" for more information about the NAME attribute.

ROWS – Textarea display height

Required

Sets the height of the text area within the browser: it does not set user entry limits.

Form Examples

The examples in this section show you how to code HTML forms to insert data into a database table, and to query database tables. Although we use the same elements in both types of forms, the coding and overall structure for each is different.

For each form, we will first explain the purpose of the form, show the supporting code, and then show the resulting form as seen through a browser.

The forms order1.htm (order form), order2.htm (order confirmation form), q_sum.htm (quarterly summary form), m_sum.htm (monthly sales form) and d_sum.htm (detailed monthly sales form) are described and shown in this section and can also be found on the "WebExtra" Web Site.

Inserting Data Using Forms

The ABC Widget Company sells three different types of widgets: Widget A, Widget B, and Widget C. Customers can order any combination of the three products. The first form shown to the customer allows them to indicate the number of widgets they want to order. The form shows the item number, description, and quantity for each widget. When the customer is ready to submit the order, they select the Submit button, which displays the confirmation order form.

The confirmation order form is used to collect personal data from the customer. The top of the form confirms the order information and displays the total cost of the order. The presumption is that existing customers have access to the WWW ordering process. If the customer is new, the form also collects the payment method, credit card type, credit card number, and expiration date. After the customer completes the form, they again select the Submit button. A "thank-you" page is returned to the browser displaying the PO#.

In this section, we show you how to create a form for inserting information into the database. We'll show you how to link name/value pairs to a specific column in the database, and how to trigger a CGI script that inserts data into the columns based on the name/value pairs it evaluates. After we show you the complete code, we'll break it down and go over it step-by-step in the "Form Review" section.

The Code

Following is the code for the form requesting order information. Note that the text fields are coded within a table so they can be aligned for easier viewing.

```
<HTML>

<HEAD>
<TITLE>ABC Widget Company</TITLE>
</HEAD>

<BODY BACKGROUND="../images/backgrnd.gif">
<BODYTEXT>
<H1><IMG SRC="../images/howto.gif" ALT="How to Order"><BR>ABC Widget
Company Order Form</H1>
```

```
<P>Please enter the quantity of each item you wish to order. Once you have
entered the quantity, please select the "Place Order" button.</P>

<FORM ACTION="http://www.abcwidget.com/cgi-bin/order">

<TABLE>

<TR>
<TH>Item</TH>
<TH>Description</TH>
<TH>Quantity</TH>
<TH>Price/Unit</TH>
</TR>

<TR>
<TD>WA111</TD>
<TD>Widget A, circular</TD>
<TD><INPUT TYPE="TEXT" NAME="1" SIZE="4" MAXLENGTH="3" ALIGN="TOP"></TD>
<TD>$19.99</TD>
</TR>

<TR>
<TD>WB222</TD>
<TD>Widget B, square</TD>
<TD><INPUT TYPE="TEXT" NAME="2" SIZE="4" MAXLENGTH="3" ALIGN="TOP"></TD>
<TD>$24.99</TD>
</TR>

<TR>
<TD>WC333</TD>
<TD>Widget C, triangle</TD>
<TD><INPUT TYPE="TEXT" NAME="3" SIZE="4" MAXLENGTH="3" ALIGN="TOP">
</TD>
<TD>$29.99</TD>
</TR>

</TABLE>

<BR>

<INPUT TYPE="SUBMIT" VALUE="Place Order" ALIGN="TOP">
</FORM>

<HR>
<ADDRESS>Please submit any comments to our
<A HREF="mailto:webmaster@abcwidget.com">Webmaster</A>
</ADDRESS>

<A HREF="http://www.abcwidget.com/">
<IMG SRC="btn_home.gif" ALIGN="TOP">
</A>
```

```
<P>Prices and availability may change at any time. All prices shown are
for the USA only.<BR>

<P>Return Policy: We accept returns of unopened products only. Products
must be returned within 30 days of delivery. Damaged or defective goods
must be returned within 45 days. The buyer is responsible for the cost of
return shipment. Returns will not be accepted without a return authoriza-
tion code. Please call our customer service office any time Monday-Friday
from 8am to 5pm PST.</P>

</BODYTEXT>
</BODY>
</HTML>
```

Figure 2-18 shows the order form page displayed by the browser.

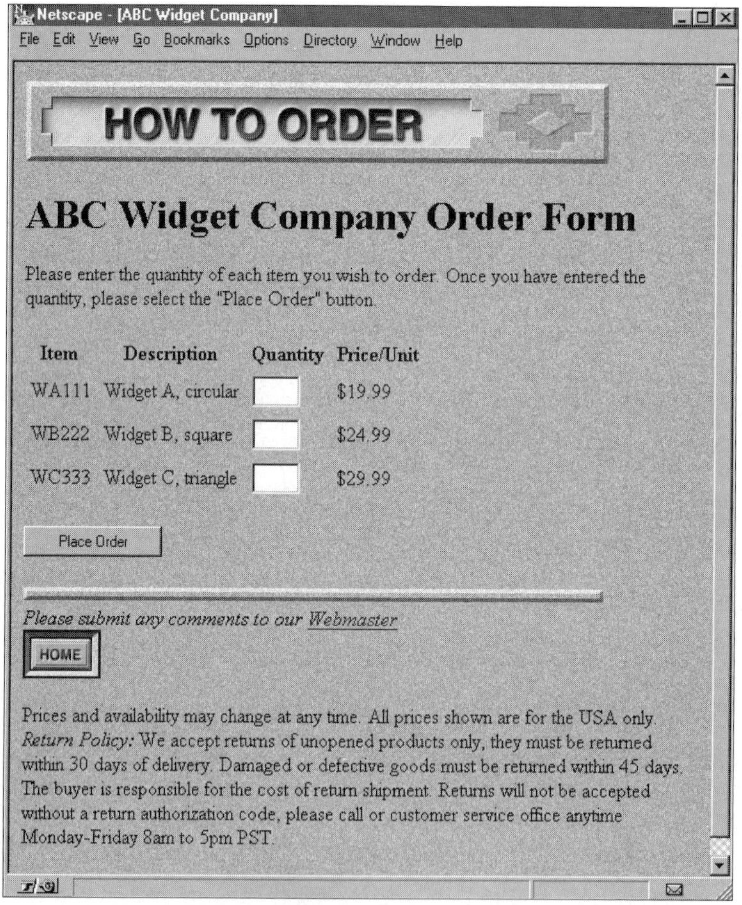

Figure 2-18. *ABC Widget Company product order form*

Form Review

This section is a step-by-step guide to creating the form shown in Figure 2-18.

When you begin creating the form, you must first enter the <FORM> element, then the required ACTION attribute. If you want the form to be submitted with the METHOD attribute equal to POST, enter the METHOD attribute. If you do not enter the METHOD attribute, the default GET option is used. The <FORM> element coded using the POST option is shown below:

```
<FORM ACTION="http://www.abcwidget.com/cgi-bin/order" METHOD="POST">
```

If you want to align the information in the form, use the <PRE> or <TABLE> elements. The advantage of using the preformat element (<PRE>) is that you can use spaces and hard returns to position the information. The disadvantage is that you need to toggle back and forth between the various browsers to see how each browser handles the positioning information.

Tables are easier to manipulate, but they can be frustrating, especially when you want to span rows and columns. However, after you become familiar with the code, you will find tables easy to use.

The code example below begins with the <TABLE> element. Within the <TABLE> element, you must insert a <TR> (Table Row) element for each row in the table. It helps to map out the table in advance so you know how many rows you'll need. Use a table row for column headings or data. To insert column heads, use the <TH> (Table column Heading) element. To insert data, use the <TD> (Table cell Data) element.

The example below shows four column headings indicated by the <TH> element: Item, Description, Quantity, and Price/Unit. Using four <TH> elements creates a table containing four columns: one <TH> element for each column.

```
<TABLE>

<TR>
<TH>Item</TH>
<TH>Description</TH>
<TH>Quantity</TH>
<TH>Price/Unit</TH>
</TR>
```

Each additional row in the table contains the table data. There are three rows: one for each widget.

Column three in each row contains an <INPUT> element that allows the user to enter a specific quantity value for each type of widget. The <INPUT> element has the TYPE attribute set to TEXT, allowing the user the flexibility to enter any value. The NAME attribute data-value is set to the database PRODUCT_ID value for the specified widget. Using the PRODUCT_ID value assists in a more efficient search on the database side.

The MAXLENGTH attribute data-value is set to 3 for this example. Even though experience shows that no customers have ordered more than 50 widgets at a time, the length of the quantity column is set to INTEGER to accommodate a large value just in case someone wants to order 999 widgets. The SIZE attribute is set to be one character larger than the MAXLENGTH attribute data-value, which allows for a little white space around the number being entered.

The following code shows the area in the form that allows the user to choose the widget and the quantity they want to buy:

```
<TR>
<TD>WA111</TD>
<TD>Widget A, circular</TD>
<TD><INPUT TYPE="TEXT" NAME="1" SIZE="4" MAXLENGTH="3" ALIGN="TOP"></TD>
<TD>$19.99</TD>
</TR>

<TR>
<TD>WB222</TD>
<TD>Widget B, square</TD>
<TD><INPUT TYPE="TEXT" NAME="2" SIZE="4" MAXLENGTH="3" ALIGN="TOP"></TD>
<TD>$24.99</TD>
</TR>

<TR>
<TD>WC333</TD>
<TD>Widget C, triangle</TD>
<TD><INPUT TYPE="TEXT" NAME="3" SIZE="4" MAXLENGTH="3" ALIGN="TOP">
</TD>
<TD>$29.99</TD>
</TR>

</TABLE>
```

After you insert the last row, make sure that you end the table using the close table element </TABLE>. This is called *normalizing*, which is the practice of using both opening and closing indicators for each element.

The only remaining action required for the form is creating a Submit button. We could have included a Reset button, but with only three entry boxes, it isn't necessary. You may want to establish a cut-off point for when to use or not use a Reset button so you are consistent from form to form.

The VALUE attribute is not required for the Submit button unless you want to change the button name from "Submit." Note in the code below that the VALUE attribute is used to name the button "Place Order."

```
<BR>

<INPUT TYPE="SUBMIT" VALUE="Place Order" ALIGN="TOP">
</FORM>
```

The initial order form is complete. Now all that remains is testing the form to ensure that the appropriate data is being passed to the CGI script. The easiest way to test the output of your form is to fill it in and submit it to your e-mail address by setting the METHOD attribute of the <FORM> element to POST, and changing the ACTION attribute to your e-mail address. You must include the keyword mailto. The <FORM> element should look like this:

```
<FORM ACTION="mailto:your e-mail address" ACTION="POST">
```

Replace the string *your e-mail address* with your e-mail address.

Following are a few simple measures that you can perform to help eliminate issues that may arise after your form is on the Web:

- Verify that all related radio buttons have the same NAME attribute data-value
- Verify that the checkboxes contain the correct name/value pair data-values
- Double-check the ACTION and METHOD attribute data-values for the <FORM> element
- Check the length fields in the database against the specified values in the MAXLENGTH attribute
- Make sure you have included a Reset button where appropriate
- Verify that you have included a Submit button
- Scan the form from several browsers to check the physical placement of the form components

- Make sure you are not using the `<TEXTAREA>` element for limited-length database fields

- Re-evaluate your decision to allow multiple- or single-selection options

- Perform several "dummy" submissions to ensure that the correct information is passed to the CGI script.

Figure 2-19 shows the confirmation order form and the thank-you page as viewed from the browser:

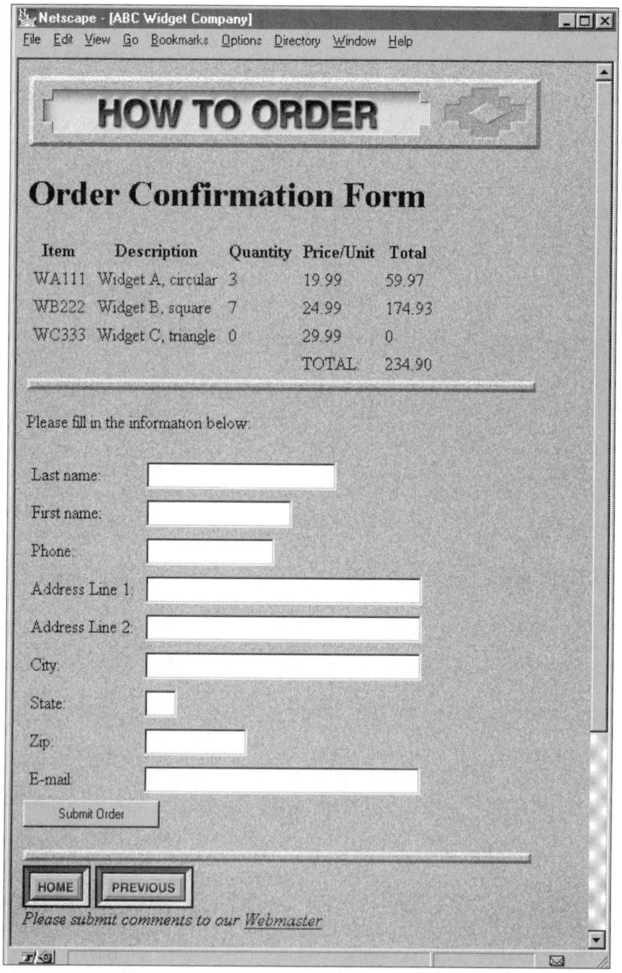

Figure 2-19. *Order confirmation form displaying the previously-chosen options in a read-only format, and personal information query data fields that are to be filled in by the user*

Query Form Example

In this section, we'll show you how to design a form that allows ABC Widget Company's sales and marketing personnel to view and analyze sales figures from the previous four quarters.

The form first prompts the user to select the quarter they want to analyze, then sends the query to the database. The query accesses the database, analyzes the total sales by month, and returns an HTML page to the browser displaying the sales totals for each month within the selected quarter.

The user can then drill-down to see a more detailed analysis for a selected month. When the monthly detailed page is returned, the user can drill-down further for more detailed information. When the user selects the Submit button, the query again accesses the database, analyzes the sales by purchase order for the month, and returns another page for review. Each purchase order (PO) is listed with the amount of the sale. The user can then select a specific PO and review related information.

In this section, we'll show you the complete code required to create a drill-down form, then break it down and go over it step-by-step in the "Form Review" section.

The Code

The quarterly summary request form is shown below:

```
<HTML>

<HEAD>
<TITLE>ABC Widget Company</TITLE>
</HEAD>

<BODY BACKGROUND="../images/mar_bck.gif">
<BODYTEXT>
<H1 ALIGN=CENTER><IMG SRC="../images/info.gif" ALT="Information"><BR>MarCom
Analysis Sheet</H1>
<H3>Quarterly summary:</H3>
<P>The quarterly summary contains sales information for the past four
quarters. Fiscal year analysis is found on the Fiscal year summary
report.</P>
<HR>
<FORM ACTION="http://www.abcwidget.com/cgi_bin/qrtr">
<P>Select the year you wish to review:</P>
<SELECT NAME="year">
<OPTION VALUE=90>1990
<OPTION VALUE=91>1991
```

```
<OPTION VALUE=92>1992
<OPTION VALUE=93>1993
<OPTION VALUE=94>1994
<OPTION VALUE=95>1995
<OPTION VALUE=96>1996
</SELECT>
<P>Select the quarter you wish to review:</P>
<FORM ACTION="http://www.abcwidget.com/cgi_bin/qrtr">

<PRE>
Quarter      Select
1st Quarter   <INPUT TYPE="RADIO" NAME="qrtr_sum" VALUE="1" ALIGN="TOP">
2nd Quarter   <INPUT TYPE="RADIO" NAME="qrtr_sum" VALUE="2" ALIGN="TOP">
3rd Quarter   <INPUT TYPE="RADIO" NAME="qrtr_sum" VALUE="3" ALIGN="TOP">
4th Quarter   <INPUT TYPE="RADIO" NAME="qrtr_sum" VALUE="4" ALIGN="TOP">
</PRE>

<INPUT TYPE="SUBMIT" VALUE="Quarterly Search" ALIGN="TOP">
</FORM>

</BODYTEXT>
</BODY>
</HTML>
```

Figure 2-20 shows the quarterly query form page as viewed by the browser.

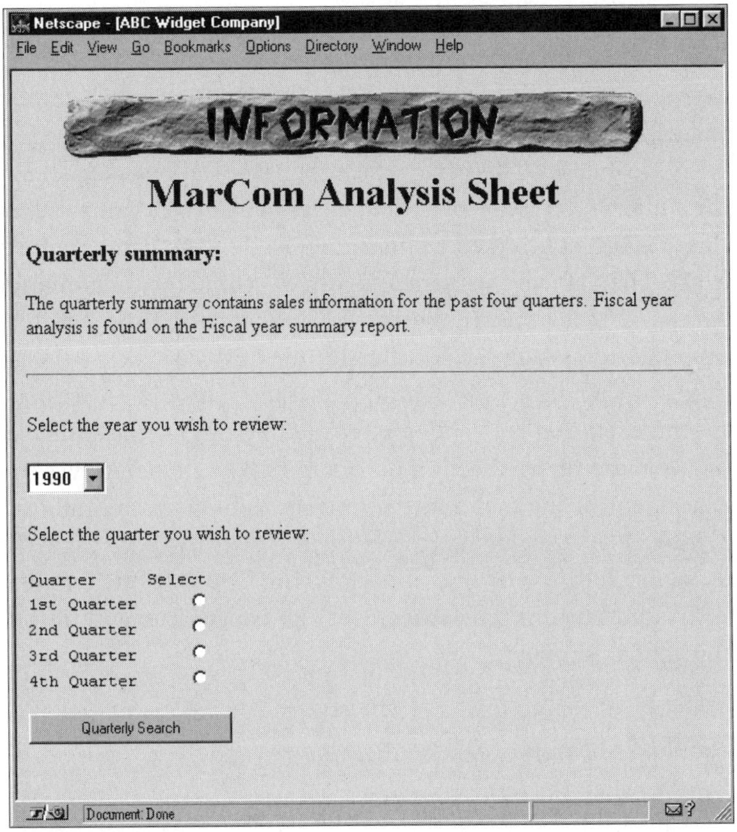

Figure 2-20. *Quarterly summary report form example showing radio button options that result in a drill-down query*

Form Review

Use this section as a step-by-step guide to help you create a drill-down query form page.

As in the data insertion form example, you must first enter the <FORM> element, then the required ACTION attribute. If you want the form to be submitted with the METHOD attribute equal to POST, enter the METHOD attribute as shown below:

```
<FORM ACTION="http://www.abcwidget.com/cgi_bin/qrtr" METHOD="POST">
```

For this example, we'll show you how to use the <PRE> element instead of a table to place the form elements, which means that you need to manually enter spaces and hard returns. In this example, "Quarter" and "Select" are separated by five spaces. These are the column headings.

The four rows are the entries for each of the four quarters. Each row contains the name of the quarter in question, three spaces (used for placement), and an <INPUT> element. This time, the user is not allowed to enter a value. Instead, they must select one of four quarters. The data-value entered in the VALUE attribute is directly linked to the value used in the database for the quarter they select. The database uses an assigned ID value for each quarter: 1 is for the first quarter; 2 is for the second quarter; 3 is for the third quarter; and 4 is for the fourth quarter. Using the ID value for the quarter makes database searches more efficient. Whatever you can do on the front-end to reduce the time required on the back-end is deeply appreciated by the user and the server!

Placing the radio button section within the <PRE> element gives you control over the placement of the text and the buttons. Notice in the following example that all four <INPUT> elements have the same NAME attribute value. Because of this, the user can choose only one option. Setting the NAME attribute to the same value is how radio buttons work together. The coded area within the form for the radio buttons is shown below:

```
<PRE>
Quarter     Select
1st Quarter    <INPUT TYPE="RADIO" NAME="qrtr_sum" VALUE="1" ALIGN="TOP">
2nd Quarter    <INPUT TYPE="RADIO" NAME="qrtr_sum" VALUE="2" ALIGN="TOP">
3rd Quarter    <INPUT TYPE="RADIO" NAME="qrtr_sum" VALUE="3" ALIGN="TOP">
4th Quarter    <INPUT TYPE="RADIO" NAME="qrtr_sum" VALUE="4" ALIGN="TOP">
</PRE>
```

The last action required for any form is the Submit function. A Reset button is not required for this form because the user can make only one choice. If the user wants to exit from here, they can select the "Back" function from the browser or select the "Home" button on the bottom of the page. The <INPUT> element used to display the Submit button is shown below:

```
<INPUT TYPE="SUBMIT" VALUE="Quarterly Search" ALIGN="TOP">
</FORM>
<HR>
<ADDRESS>Please submit any comments or issues to the <A HREF="mailto:web
master@abcwidget.com">Webmaster</A></ADDRESS>
<A HREF="index.html"><IMG SRC="home.gif" ALT="Return Home">
</A>
</BODYTEXT>
</BODY>
</HTML>
```

Figure 2-21 shows the monthly sales summary, and Figure 2-22 shows a detailed monthly summary as viewed from a browser.

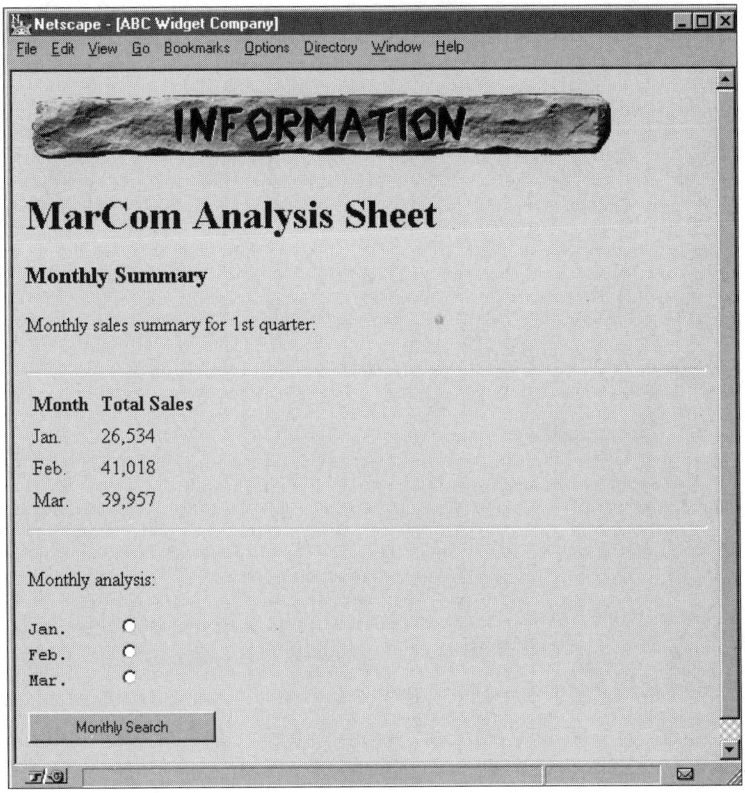

Figure 2-21. Monthly sales summary example

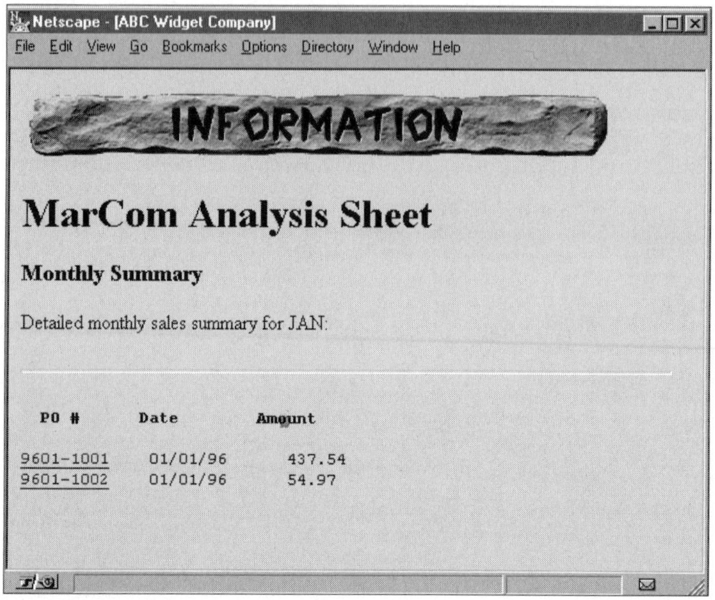

Figure 2-22. Detailed monthly sales summary for a specified month.
The PO number is a link to the database values
associated with the PO

Tips and Tricks

Keep the following pointers in mind when you're ready to create your own, fabulous form:

- Know ahead of time the name of each column that is to be accessed

- Know the width of each column

- Sketch out the specific information you want to present on the form. This will help you decide if you need to use the `<TABLE>`, `<PRE>`, or other formatting elements within the form.

- Know the physical location of the CGI scripts so you can code the `ACTION` attribute for the `<FORM>` element correctly

- If you create a lengthy form, always include a RESET option

- Know ahead of time whether you want to capture multiple or single entries to ensure that you use the correct <INPUT> type

- Before using the <TEXTAREA> element, ensure that the database column is long enough to accept long text entry blocks

- This tip is great for testing purposes: in the <FORM> element, set the METHOD attribute to POST, and the ACTION attribute to your e-mail address. For example:

```
<FORM METHOD="POST" ACTION="mailto:your e-mail">
```

When you submit the form, it will be posted to your mailbox. When you go to the directory containing attachments, you will see a file named "FORMPOST" that contains the contents of your form. Look through this file to see what is sent to the server, and to see how special characters are converted.

Summary

Forms are a wonderful tool for allowing users to access your database through a controlled environment. You hold all of the cards, and you decide how to play the hand. You can lay the entire deck on the table, or you can cautiously lay down a few cards at a time. That decision is up to you.

There are literally hundreds of great form examples on the Web. Browse around for places that allow you to buy a product or service, then look at their HTML code to see how they format their information (which you can do by selecting "View Source" from the browser window). See whether they use the POST or GET options for the METHOD attribute, and how they organize their information. Do they use radio buttons or checkboxes? Do they use text fields or text area boxes? Do they use tables or the <PRE> element to align the information? Apply the best examples to your own form.

3

Using ISQL to Connect to Sybase SQL Server

Now that you have learned about creating forms, you're ready to write the SQL receiving end that interacts with the database, and take time to consider how your database is set up. After the receiving end is done, you will need to link the form information with the SQL commands. As stated in Chapter 1, you have four options for creating the link:

- Pass the data to an ISQL script using Tcl, Perl, or C++, and send it to Sybase SQL Server

- Pass the data to an Open Client/Open Server script using SybTcl, SybPerl, C, or C++, and send it to Sybase SQL Server

- Use web.sql to translate web.sql data into Open Client calls

- Use Java to perform transactional calculations and client-side processing by passing data through Open Client calls or CGI scripts.

CT-Lib/DB-Lib are the application programming interfaces (APIs) to Open Client connectivity software. Chapter 4, "Creating CGI Scripts Using Perl," and Chapter 7, "Using Web.sql to Streamline Data Flow" contain a few of the CT-Lib/DB-Lib calls you can use to customize Open Client and Open Server, the server-side connectivity software, but the task really warrants a separate book. We'll provide a brief overview of Open Client/Open Server in the next section.

When you call ISQL from a separate CGI script, the CGI script calls the ISQL script, which initiates a process that connects to Sybase SQL Server. When Sybase SQL Server returns the results to the ISQL script process, the ISQL script process finishes and the output of the ISQL script becomes input back into the CGI script, which can then manipulate the data or return codes resulting from the ISQL program. This description works whether the ISQL program is retrieving data from a Sybase SQL Server database or updating (including inserting and deleting) data in a database.

In this chapter, we're going to tell you what you need to know to use ISQL as the CGI-to-SQL Server link. This chapter contains the following sections:

- Overview of Open Client/Open Server
- SQL Commands
- Using Transact-SQL to Manipulate Data in the Sybase SQL Server Database
- Maintaining Transact-SQL Code
- Fixing the Width for Result Sets
- Working with Multiple Hosts
- Filtering
- Tips and Tricks.

Overview of Open Client/Open Server

Open Client/Open Server, designed by Sybase, is a set of libraries and tools that allow users to access Sybase SQL Server data as well as other servers and services on the network. With the ability to connect with other servers and services, users can interact with other data sources or system applications as if they were resident on the Sybase SQL Server.

Open Client provides an interpreter that translates client information into a Tabular Data Stream (TDS), which is a format recognized by Open Server. After Open Server receives the TDS data, it can act upon it.

Open Client is responsible for managing the communications between an Open Client tool or application and an Open Server application, and consists of several applications: Client-Library, Net-Library, DB-Library, Embedded SQL, XA-Library, and interfaces to Microsoft's ODBC.

Client-Library is designed to interface with the Open Server architecture, and is based on application programming interfaces (APIs) that are referred to as Client-Library API Routines. The Client-Library layer and the User Application layer (Embedded SQL, XA-Library) interface with the Protocol Services layer. The Protocol Services layer interprets the User Application layer so data and commands can be sent across the network.

Net-Library provides Open Client with interfaces to numerous transport protocol implementations. Because of its ability to have a standard interface for a wide range of transport protocols, Net-Library allows for a very high level of operating system independence. Imagine being able to design applications independent of any particular network protocol!

Since it was introduced in 1987, DB-Library has undergone numerous changes. Because of the extent and complexity of the changes, the basic fundamental backbone of DB-Library cannot withstand any additional major rewrites. Although DB-Library is the most widely-used API for Open Client/Open Server applications, the time has come for other, more advanced interfaces such as Client-Library to replace it. Client-Library is a full-featured, high performance, next generation interface.

Embedded SQL is used specifically with C and COBOL programming languages. The SQL precompilers provide a preprocessor for embedding SQL statements, which allows for the support of stored procedures for precompiled applications, and for the conversion of SQL statements to Client-Library calls (or stored procedures).

XA-Library allows Client-Library to interact with mainframe databases that utilize transaction monitors.

For more information about Open Client/Open Server, contact Sybase and ask about the *Sybase Technical Whitepapers*, or view the Sybase website at

www.sybase.com

Using the $ISQL Environment Variable

The environment variable $ISQL is not required for using ISQL, but we use it to hold the explicit path to the ISQL executable. It is always installed in the bin directory under the Sybase home directory. For example, if the Sybase home directory is:

```
/export/home/sybase
```

the value in the $ISQL environment variable would be:

```
/export/home/sybase/bin/isql
```

Thus, whenever we use $ISQL, we are referring to the explicit path to the ISQL executable, which will be unique to your system. If you want, you can explicitly code the path in each script, but it's easier to maintain using the environment variable.

SQL Commands

In this section, we're going to cover the basic set of SQL commands used in this book. This section is not intended to be a tutorial on SQL programming, as there are many books on the market that fully describe SQL command structures.

Before we get to the commands, we'll discuss basic table constructs, and how SQL accesses the database using those constructs. We'll provide code examples to help you grasp the concepts.

Table Basics

When you design a table, you need to think about the information you want to assign to rows and columns. You should define each column by its intended purpose or content, such as a user's last name, and then determine the appropriate data type to associate with that content. Rows are used to store multiple data-types. The intersection of a column and row is a field or cell, which is where the data resides.

SQL is designed around *set processing*, in which one or more rows are manipulated at once. For example, you can retrieve ten rows of data, modify the values of one column in 50 rows, or insert one complete row. Data retrieval is based upon matching some given criteria. For example, let's say that you want to display the following report:

Table 3-1. *Example Report*

last_name	first_name	id
Epperson	Brent	555505555
Epperson	Charlene	555505556
Epperson	Christy	555505557
Epperson	Dale	555505558
Epperson	Drew	555505559
Epperson	Glenn	555505560
Epperson	Jessica	555505561
Epperson	Shirley	555505563

If you wanted to query the database using the last name "Epperson," you would first need to reference the column name, then declare the table from which you want to extract the data. Using our example, you would choose the "user" table, then indicate the data value that you want to search on within the "last_name" column using the following SQL script statement:

```
select last_name,first_name,id
from user
where last_name = 'Epperson'
```

Within ISQL, you would need to enter the GO statement for the action to occur. Entering the GO statement here would return eight rows of information.

The "id" column in the table contains a unique value for each row and is used as the key field for the table. Keys are important for several reasons, but the main purpose of keys is ensuring that your table doesn't contain duplicate data. For example, if your database contains two Drew Eppersons, you can use keys to create a separate ID value for distinguishing between them, and thus ensure a better level of integrity within the database. For a more elaborate definition of keys, please consult one of the many database books available. We'll talk about the "id" column later in this section.

Basic Commands

SQL has four basic table-level statements that you need to be aware of:

- `select`, which indicates that the following information will be used to query the database

- `insert`, which adds a new row

- `update`, which changes or modifies the table

- `delete`, which removes an existing row or several rows.

This section defines each statement and provides examples for using each one.

How the SELECT Statement Works

The `SELECT` statement is used to specify the specific columns you want to access. The example below shows the commonly-used syntax for the `SELECT` statement:

```
select <col|*|literal>
```

You can specify any number of columns in any order, specify all the columns in the table, or replace a column name with a literal value.

```
from <table>
```

Specifies the table from which you want to get the data.

```
where <expression>
```

Specifies criteria for the data that you are attempting to receive using a column name or value. For example, the following code uses the column name, operand, and column value as criteria for returning data:

```
where <col><operand><col|value>
```

There may also be situations where you are unsure how the values were entered into the table. For example, you have no way of knowing if the data entry person typed all of the last names in uppercase, lowercase, or mixed case. By using the SQL keyword `UPPER` to force all the values to be uppercase, you can then compare a specified value in the `WHERE` clause against exact case matches from the database.

Using the example in the previous section with the UPPER keyword, the following SQL script:

```
select upper(last_name), first_name, id
from user
where last_name = 'EPPERSON'
```

returns the following rows from the table:

```
Epperson, Brent, 555505555
Epperson, Charlene, 555505556
Epperson, Christy, 555505557
Epperson, Dale, 555505558
Epperson, Drew, 555505559
Epperson, Glenn, 555505560
Epperson, Jessica, 555505561
Epperson, Shirley, 555505563
```

Use the ORDER BY statement to return the information in a specific order. Using our example, if you want to return the first name first, you would enter the following command:

```
select last_name, first_name
from user
where last_name = 'Epperson'
order by first_name
```

How the UPDATE Statement Works

The UPDATE statement does exactly what its name implies: it updates a row or field within a table. The command structure for the UPDATE statement is as follows:

```
update <table>
set <col> = value
```

The value can be alphanumeric. Character data must be within single or double quotes.

```
where <expression>
```

The expression is the row qualifier.

To change Jessica Epperson's first name to "Jessie," you would enter the following SQL statement:

```
update user
set first_name = 'Jessie'
where last_name = 'Epperson' and id = 555505561
```

Note that the `last_name` value is within quotes, and that the `id` value is not. Because character data can have spaces and other types of characters, the value must be within quotes, while numeric data, such as in the `id` value does not require quotes.

How the INSERT Statement Works

The `INSERT` statement allows you to insert a new row of data into an existing table. The `INSERT` statement should not be confused with the `UPDATE` statement: the `UPDATE` statement updates an existing row, while the `INSERT` statement inserts a new row.

The `INSERT` statement is coded as follows:

```
insert into <table> {(col)}
values ('...', '...', '...')
```

If you are inserting data into every column in the table, you don't need to list the column names. However, it is a good practice to do so and indicate that the column values have some type of entry. For example, columns where data is not present warrant a `NULL` declaration value: otherwise, you could place a blank within the column. What you enter is determined by how the column was defined when it was created.

When you create a table, each field is specified to be `NULL` or `NOT NULL`. `NOT NULL` means that the field must contain data. You should set unique columns such as ID or Key fields to `NOT NULL`, which means that each occurrence of that column must have a valid value.

To insert a new row into the example database, you would use the following code:

```
insert into user (last_name, first_name, id)
values ('Epperson', 'Margaret', 555505562)
```

How the DELETE Statement Works

The `DELETE` statement physically removes one or more rows from a table. Entering `DELETE user` deletes all the rows from the user table. Be careful when you use this command, as the rows can't be recovered unless you have a good backup of the table.

The DELETE statement is coded as follows:

```
delete from <table>
where <expression>
```

Make sure to enter the statement very carefully, as people have been known to delete an entire table by forgetting to enter the FROM clause. The WHERE clause identifies rows for the deletion.

If you wanted to delete the row containing Christy Epperson from our example database, you would enter the following DELETE statement:

```
delete from user
where last_name = 'Epperson'
and id = 555505557
```

Joining Tables Using the WHERE Clause

Joining tables is one result of using the WHERE clause. Use the WHERE clause when you have information that spans across several tables. For example, you may have two or three tables defining product information that need to be checked against a database request for specific product information.

When you join tables, each table must contain a common field or a *primary key* and *foreign key*. The data within the key fields must match your particular query in order to work correctly. Using the WHERE clause, you can establish a relationship between tables by linking the table and column names with a period (.) character. The following code shows an example of this:

```
select *
from table1, table2, table3
where table1.id=table2.id
and
table1.id=table3.id
and
table2.id=table3.id
```

This may seem like an overly-coded comparison structure, but it is better to be overly cautious rather than not cautious enough.

To expand upon the join concept, let's use an example of joining a Customer table, Order table and Customer Support table (Support). The Customer table contains the records of all of the customers who have the product and a valid registration number; the Order table contains records of all customers who have purchased the product; and the Support table contains records of all customers who have requested technical support. Not all customers send in their registration information, nor do all customers utilize customer support services.

Tables 3-2, 3-3, and 3-4 show the tables for our example.

Table 3-2. *Customer Table*

cust_id	last_name	first_name	registration_no
3256	Appleton	Lester	95-122389
1896	Smith	Bruce	95-101742
7452	Jones	Chris	95-101367
1685	Thomson	Claire	95-072122
4191	Grafton	Don	95-080993
3694	Kline	Fred	95-110101
4146	Webster	Greg	95-112345
1187	Masterson	Steve	95-121675

Table 3-3. *Order Table*

cust_id	order_id	service_rep_id	order_date
3256	DSE-100230	110	12/23/95
1896	STD-237756	110	10/17/95
3324	DSE-100043	107	07/12/95
1894	DSE-100011	112	09/09/95
2659	STE-302145	112	09/24/95
3694	STD-243356	112	11/01/95
4146	STD-244232	107	11/23/95
1187	STD-244934	110	12/16/95

Table 3-4. *Support Table*

cust_id	log_number	log_date	level
3256	005231	1/5/96	2
1896	005232	1/5/96	2
3324	005233	1/5/96	2
7452	005234	1/5/96	3
1685	0052354	1/5/96	2

The join criteria you use determines which records are returned. For example, if you wanted to write a script that retrieves customers who have ordered and registered your product and requested technical support, you might begin with the following script that retrieves customer IDs for customers with entries in the Order and Customer tables:

```
select cust_id
from order, support, customer
where customer.cust_id = support.cust_id
```

The resulting string contains the following entries:

```
3256
1896
7452
1685
```

This particular join statement doesn't return the results you are looking for because it misses the technical support information. Next, you try joining the order and support tables with the idea that you will reach all customers that reside in the customer table. This is a common mistake made by many programmers. The presumption is that because the customer table has the primary keys and the other two tables are support tables, any value in the support table must also exist in the primary table. As you can see, that isn't always the case. Take a look at the following script:

```
select cust_id
from order, support, customer
where order.cust_id = support.cust_id
```

The resulting table contains the following entries:

```
3256
1896
3324
```

This result is not accurate, either. To accurately write a join that retrieves customers who have ordered and registered your product and requested technical support, you need to combine the two previously-written joins within the same script, and add a third join that links all three tables together, as shown in the following script:

```
select cust_id
from order, support, customer
where order.cust_id = support.cust_id
and customer.cust_id = support.cust_id
and customer.cust_id = order.cust_id
```

The result set from this query returns all customers who have entries within each of the three tables:

```
3256
1896
```

Not including the third join criteria could in some cases return a larger number of records than is accurate because it verifies that all three tables contain the requested entries.

Using Transact-SQL to Manipulate Data in the Sybase SQL Server Database

This section shows you how to use Transact-SQL code to manipulate data in the Sybase SQL Server database. In this chapter, we assume that you're using ISQL in batch mode for security reasons. For more information about using ISQL in batch mode, see Chapter 8, "Security Issues for the Web."

You can supply the Transact-SQL code after the password (pwd) command and before the quit statement. The following example invokes the Transact-SQL stored procedure sp_help, which shows all of the tables. Note that the sp_help command is terminated with a go statement.

```
#!/bin/csh
$ISQL -U WWW_User << EOF
`cat /export/home/WWW_User/.WWW_Userid_Pwd`

sp_help
go
quit
EOF
```

Next, you need to specify the database to query using the use statement. There is a default database for each user ID, but it is dangerous to assume that the default will remain static. It is much safer to code a use statement as follows:

```
#!/bin/csh
$ISQL -U WWW_User << EOF
`cat /export/home/WWW_User/.WWW_Userid_Pwd`

use customer
go

sp_help
go
quit
EOF
```

In this example, we are setting the database to "customer" before we invoke `sp_help`. It is wise to make a habit of placing the `use <database>` statement at the beginning of each batch ISQL query.

Technically, the results of this script go to `stdout`. However, recall the UNIX behavior that returns the `stdout` of a called program as `stdin` to the calling program. If a CGI script calls our `sp_help` csh script, the results of the `sp_help` command are returned as input to the CGI script. In the CGI script, you can manipulate those results as needed.

You could supply raw SQL if necessary, as shown below:

```
#!/bin/csh
$ISQL -U WWW_User << EOF
`cat /export/home/WWW_User/.WWW_Userid_Pwd`

use customer
select * from authors
go
quit
EOF
```

You can supply anything that you would normally type at the prompt in an interactive ISQL session here.

Maintaining Transact-SQL Code

You need to consider how to maintain Transact-SQL code. For example, simply changing the name of a table could require you to update many scripts. To avoid having to update numerous scripts every time you make a simple change, you can take advantage of the ISQL command-line option `-i` to indicate the input file name, which allows you to read in Transact-SQL commands from another file, and thus create a central storage location for Transact-SQL scripts. The following code shows how to place `sp_help` commands in a file called `sp_help.sql`.

```
use customer
go

sp_help
go
```

You could then structure your csh script as follows:

```
#!/bin/csh
$ISQL -U WWW_User -i  /export/home/WWW_User/sp_help.sql << EOF
`cat /export/home/WWW_User/.WWW_Userid_Pwd`

quit
EOF
```

Fixing the Width for Result Sets

ISQL by default supplies result lines that are 80 characters wide. This can cause some problems in a CGI script if the result set is longer than 80 characters. For example, consider the following result set:

```
one two three four five six seven eight nine ten eleven twelve thirteen
fourteen fifteen sixteen seventeen eighteen nineteen twenty
```

Because the default width of ISQL for output is 80, a CGI script would see the above as two incoming lines, separated as follows:

```
one two three four five six seven eight nine ten eleven twelve thirteen
fourteen <line break>
fifteen sixteen seventeen eighteen nineteen twenty
```

Sybase provides the command-line option -w in the ISQL utility to indicate the width of output lines. Adding the following option to the ISQL statement in your csh script tells Sybase SQL Server that lines should not break unless they are greater than 4096 characters in width, thus ensuring that output lines will not break prematurely:

```
-w 4096
```

Working with Multiple Hosts

So far in this chapter, we have described situations that assume the database server is running on the same machine as the Web server. This will probably not be the case in larger application environments, mainly for performance reasons. There are two factors that affect the performance of Web connections: one is the throughput of the network, and the other factor is the server machine itself. Although we cannot guarantee the future, network performance will most likely improve over time. In fact, the nation's network infrastructure is currently being upgraded, and, as applications on the Web become more efficient (using languages such as Java), there will be reduced traffic for applications.

While we all wait for network improvements, you can do something about your Web server performance. Web sites such as Netscape get up to 30,000,000 connections or *hits* per day. This number of connections causes any machine to bog down. Imagine the performance of a Web server getting this many hits if it was also running the database server that connects to the Web server. Placing the database server and Web server on separate machines prevents these types of bottlenecks. The next two sections describe how to connect to database server machines across the network.

Specifying the Instance of Sybase SQL Server

ISQL provides the -s command-line option for specifying the server with which to make the connection. With the -s option, you can connect to a Sybase SQL Server running on the local machine (the same machine as the Web server), or connect to a remote machine half way around the world. We will discuss how this option works with ISQL when developing our Web applications.

So far, we have not shown you how to specify a server in an ISQL script. Not indicating a server creates a connection to the default server specified by the Sybase SQL Server environment variable DSQUERY. You have a couple of choices when you specify the server. You can reset the DSQUERY environment variable for each csh script you use, or you can use the -s option.

To reset the DSQUERY environment variable, consider the following csh script. Assume that you have a local database server called "local_db" that resides on the same machine as the Web server, and a remote server called "remote_db" that resides on a separate machine. You would specify servers via csh scripts as follows:

```
#!/bin/csh
#----------------------------------------------------------#
#— This script connects to a local database server—#
#— using the DSQUERY environment variable ————#
#----------------------------------------------------------#
```

```
setenv DSQUERY local_db

$ISQL -U WWW_User -X -i
/export/home/WWW_User/sp_help.sql << EOF
`cat /export/home/WWW_User/.WWW_Userid_Pwd`

quit
EOF
```

The second csh script connects to the remote database server.

```
#!/bin/csh
#-----------------------------------------------#
#— This script connects to a remote database server —#
#— using the DSQUERY environment variable ————#
#-----------------------------------------------#

setenv DSQUERY remote_db

$ISQL -U WWW_User -X -i /export/home/WWW_User/sp_help.sql << EOF
`cat /export/home/WWW_User/.WWW_Userid_Pwd`

quit
EOF
```

Now, let's take a look at implementing each of these two scripts using the
-S ISQL option. The command-line specifies the name of the server in place of
setting the DSQUERY environment variable.

```
#!/bin/csh
#-----------------------------------------------#
#— This script connects to a local database server —#
#— using the ISQL option -S ————————————#
#-----------------------------------------------#


$ISQL -U WWW_User -X -S local_db -i
/export/home/WWW_User/sp_help.sql << EOF
`cat /export/home/WWW_User/.WWW_Userid_Pwd`

quit
EOF
```

The following code makes the connection to the remote server:

```
#!/bin/csh
#————————————————————————————————————————#
#— This script connects to a remote database server —#
#— using the ISQL option "-S" ———————————————#
#————————————————————————————————————————#


$ISQL -U WWW_User -X -S remote_db -i
/export/home/WWW_User/sp_help.sql << EOF
`cat /export/home/WWW_User/.WWW_Userid_Pwd`

quit
EOF
```

Other Factors for Connecting to Multiple Servers

There is some preparatory work that you need to perform before connecting to multiple servers. First, you must make ISQL aware of the remote servers using the "interfaces" file. The interfaces file is created when Sybase SQL Server is installed, and identifies all the servers, local and remote, to which the machine can connect. ISQL uses the interfaces file to find a server when you specify its name via the -S option. To connect to a remote server, you must place an entry in the interfaces file on the local machine referencing the server on the remote machine. Contact your database administrator for information about updating the interfaces file. To be safe, you should use the -I <interfaces-file-location> option of ISQL in your scripts so the script doesn't rely on having the SYBASE environment variable set correctly.

Filtering

You need to filter a few things that appear as part of the result set. For example, you should filter out column headings, dashes that appear between the column headings and the first line of output, and the result count row that appears at the end of the output. Chapter 4, "Creating CGI Scripts Using Perl" discusses how to filter for specified strings. At this point, be aware that they exist and will need some attention in the future.

Tips and Tricks

You can reduce the amount of coding required to create CGI scripts by taking advantage of the fact that SQL allows you to hard-code literals in your SQL query.

For example, to create an unordered list of items to retrieve from a database, you would have to trap each line in your CGI program and append a `<LI>` tag before each line. The following code shows you how to do the same thing using SQL to hard-code literals into your output stream as list items back to the client (which is what the user sees as the response from the query):

```
select '<LI>', last_name
from customer
go
```

You still need to supply the `<UL>` and `</UL>` tags around the block of list items (unless you have a list with one item), but this example makes coding the list items themselves very easy. With a simple literal, you can append HTML tags around data you retrieve from your Sybase SQL Server database.

For another example, consider a Web page with employee contact information. Instead of coding the `mailto` information in the CGI script, you can code it as part of the SQL statement. For example:

```
select '<A HREF='"mailto:', $email, '">', last_name, first_name, '<\A>'
from employee
go
```

This technique stores the Webmaster contact information centrally in a database instead of hard-coding it in all of the pages. You could then create a similar query to return the Webmaster's e-mail and contact information so it could be placed dynamically at the bottom of the Web pages.

Summary

Whether you intend to make direct CT-Lib/DB-Lib calls or use ISQL continuously, you should start using ISQL. It is easy to implement and provides you with immediate feedback when you're setting up your Sybase SQL Server connections and developing Web-based Sybase SQL Server applications. There are many aspects to using ISQL. We showed you the ones that have proven most helpful to us when developing Web applications.

4

Creating CGI
Scripts Using Perl

This chapter shows you how to create a link between your Web pages and Sybase SQL Server using CGI and Perl, the Practical Extraction and Report Language. Using CGI and Perl allows you to create dynamic, interactive Web pages instead of static ones.

Perl was originally designed for UNIX system administrators whose detailed text-manipulation, file-handling, and report-writing needs have traditionally been met by several UNIX tools. Perl is very attractive because it contains the functionality of many of these programs in a single application.

Because Web development requires many of the same text-manipulation, file handling, and report-generating features that Perl was originally designed to fill, Perl is a powerful language for creating CGI scripts to provide interaction between Web pages and Sybase SQL Server. SybPerl, an extension to Perl, provides the connectivity routines to interface with the database.

One example of an interactive link between a Web page and Sybase SQL Server is when a user running a browser selects a Submit button on a Web page form. The form is then sent to the Web server program for processing and/or storage into a database. The server invokes the CGI script, passing environment variables to it, then the CGI script processes the information and calls SybPerl.

An alternative to SybPerl is ISQL. SybPerl uses Open Client calls; ISQL is a direct, interactive interface to the database. We suggest that you use ISQL until you're more proficient with SybPerl. Thereafter, you may want to use SybPerl with Open Client. For more information about ISQL, see Chapter 3, "Using ISQL to Connect to Sybase SQL Server."

Some of the most exciting enhancements in Perl5 are its object extensions that allow you to re-use code. Because most of the resources available on Perl cover Perl4 and miss many of the powerful enhancements Perl5 has to offer, we've taken special care to pull together all of the reference information you need to have a good understanding of Perl5. Using the reference information as a foundation, we'll show you how to use CGI to build an object library for handling HTML forms.

Next, we'll discuss SybPerl, which allows Perl programs to communicate with Sybase SQL Server. SybPerl implements DB-Lib and CT-Lib, and is compatible with previous versions of SybPerl. Our discussion centers on CT-Lib, as this library closely mirrors the SQL/CLI standard (Call-Level Interface), assuring that the concepts you learn here will apply not only to Sybase, but also to any other RDBMS.

Finally, we'll help you pull together what you've learned about SybPerl and creating a CGI library by showing you how to create an Internet shopping site complete with order forms and reporting tools. This application contains many techniques that you can use in your own applications.

We'll cover all of this material in the following sections:

- Perl Basics

- Using Perl to Create CGI Scripts

- Using SybPerl to Talk to Sybase

- Using CGI Scripting and SybPerl to Build an Internet Application

- Tips and Tricks

- Useful Internet Sites.

Perl Basics

This section arms you with a strong foundation in Perl5 by explaining all the basic concepts you need to write programs in Perl and the object extensions to

Perl5. If you are anxious to start using Perl for CGI scripts and communicating with Sybase, or if you are already familiar with Perl5, skip to "Using Perl to Create CGI Scripts" and refer back to this section to clarify any confusion you may have.

This section begins by explaining the different variable types found in Perl. Next, we'll show you how to combine simple Perl statements to build complex expressions, then discuss how to use subroutines to bundle code into useable blocks. Finally, we'll show you how to use Perl5's object extensions to create re-usable code.

Variables

Perl uses four main variable types to represent different kinds of data: scalars, arrays, associative arrays, and file handles. This section defines each variable type and indicates when to use each one. If you have programmed in a language that has stronger typing, you may notice that Perl uses variable types differently from C, Pascal, C++, and other languages that require your code to distinguish between numeric, character, and binary data. Instead, Perl allows you to hold all of these data types within any scalar, array or associative array. The internal storage automatically changes to match the type.

Scalars

Scalars are useful for holding single items of data such as a person's last name, birthday, age, and the hostname of the computer on which the Perl program is running. Data types for scalars are determined by their context. For example, adding two scalars together treats their values as numeric information even if they hold strings. Concatenating two scalars treats their values as strings. Both "This is a string" and 42 are literal scalars, even though one is a string and the other is an integer.

References to scalars begin with a $. The following are all legal scalars:

5150	A literal integer
10.13	A literal float
5E-10	A literal scientific notation float
0xca	A literal integer represented in Hex
0352	A literal integer represented in Octal
"This is a string"	A literal string

$day   A scalar variable

$days[5]   6th element of the array days

Arrays

Arrays are lists that contain a set of scalars. Arrays are indexed beginning at zero, and can grow dynamically. There is no need to specify the dimension explicitly as in many other languages: if you use an array with a higher index, Perl automatically extends the array to accommodate more elements.

Array references always begin with @. You can reference a specific element in an array by referencing a scalar of the array name with the element number in square brackets. Table 4-1 shows some examples of arrays.

Table 4-1. Array Examples

Array	Description
('Sunday', 'Monday', 'Tuesday', 'Wednesday', 'Thursday', 'Friday', 'Saturday')	A literal array of strings
@months	An array reference
$#months	Length of array months (note that this is a scalar)
$months[0]	Scalar reference to the first item of array months (note that this is a scalar)

Associative Arrays

Associative arrays, sometimes called hashes, are one of Perl's most powerful features because of their ability to use any scalar reference (strings in particular), not just integer scalars. This means that you can use a string to create an index to an associative array. For example, associative arrays allow you to take a value such as a month name and use it to get information about that month, such as the number of days in the month. (See the following code for an example.) You can also use associative arrays as containers for WWW form arguments. Their dynamic character, as well as their meaningful way of referencing make them especially useful for WWW programs. We'll show you how to use associative arrays as containers for WWW form arguments in the section, "Using CGI Scripting and SybPerl to Build an Internet Application."

Associative array references begin with a %. The elements in an associative array are referenced as scalars using curly braces. The following example illustrates an associative array being used to store the number of days in each month. The code first builds the array, then uses it to answer some questions about months. The lines beginning with a # symbol are comments.

```
#Assign days to elements in Assoc. array
$DaysInMonth{'January'} = 31;
$DaysInMonth{'February'} = 28;
$DaysInMonth{'March'} = 31;
$DaysInMonth{'April'} = 30;
$DaysInMonth{'May'} = 31
$DaysInMonth{'June'} = 30;
$DaysInMonth{'July'} = 31;
$DaysInMonth{'August'} = 31;
$DaysInMonth{'September'} = 30;
$DaysInMonth{'October'} = 31;
$DaysInMonth{'November'} = 30;
$DaysInMonth{'December'} = 31;

#Print some examples to the screen

print "July has ",$DaysInMonth{'July'}," Days.\n";
print "December has ",$DaysInMonth{'December'}," Days. \n";
print "May has ",$DaysInMonth{'May'}," Days. \n";
```

Executing a Multi-line Perl Program Using UNIX

To execute a multi-line Perl program using UNIX, you need to create a program file containing all the lines of code you want to execute when the file is run. Using #! notation, you can tell the shell which program to use to execute the file, as shown below:

```
#!/bin/perl
```

Replace the path to the perl executable (/bin/perl) with the one on your machine.

From this simple example, you can see how easily you can use associative arrays to search for any kind of data using an index that exists in the domain of your data instead of using a simple numeric value. Associative arrays are also very fast at accessing elements, so incorporating an associative array into your code can greatly increase performance, especially if it replaces a long sequence of conditional comparisons.

You can use associative arrays in the following ways:

- As an index into a local database

- To make code clearer

- As a container for any open set of data

- As a container for WWW form arguments.

File Handles

File handles are constructs used to reference files and streams. You use a file handle whenever you output something to the screen, read input in from the user, or talk to a Web server. Perl provides three built-in file handles used by the Web server to communicate with your program: STDIN, STDOUT, and STDERR. These file handles are analogous to file handles found in almost all UNIX tools.

STDIN is the default input to your program. If you don't explicitly open a file, you read from STDIN. Web servers use STDIN to pass form information to the CGI script.

STDOUT is the default output of your program, and when used with CGI is the location where the server expects to find the HTML information to return to the client. If you don't supply output functions with a file handle, the output is placed in STDOUT.

STDERR is the default destination to which your program sends error messages when it encounters a problem.

You can create additional file handles as needed. It is good Perl style to use all uppercase letters in file handle names, as they don't use leading punctuation to set off their data type.

A file handle enclosed in angle brackets (<>) is called an *input symbol*, which is one method for reading data into your Perl program. Evaluated in a scalar context, an input symbol returns the next line. Evaluated in an array context, the input symbol pulls the whole file into the array (assuming you have enough memory).

Note: Using an array context when you mean to use a scalar context with the input symbol is a common mistake that can cause memory problems if the file pulled in by the input symbol is too large.

The null input symbol <> is used to emulate the input functionality of awk and sed. It references STDIN, and pulls in information from files specified on the command line.

Packages

Packages group expressions, routines, and variables into a single unit, allowing you to protect Perl expressions, subroutines, and variables from interfering with code you are reusing. Within a package, all elements such as variables and subroutines must have unique names. Between packages, it is OK to have elements with the same name, which allows you to use libraries without worrying that their subroutines, variables, and other named objects will interfere with yours.

You can reference elements in other packages by fully-qualifying a named reference. $SomePackage::AScalar references a scalar variable located in $SomePackage. If no package is explicitly specified as the default package, main is assumed, which means that every Perl program you write is protected from included libraries.

Naming Variables in Perl

Variable names can be any string of alphanumeric characters, and should start with a letter. Each data type has its own name space, so you can use the same name for a scalar, an array, an associative array, a file handle, a subroutine, and a format without worrying about conflicts. However, you need to make sure that you don't name your variables with any of the reserved words, which are the built-in commands in Perl and all lowercase. Perl is an ever-expanding language, and the reserved word list grows with each new release. You can avoid possible conflicts by using capitalization to distinguish your names.

Using capitalization is a style issue, and many Perl programmers ignore this convention because Perl also uses punctuation to make the distinction. Distinguishing names is especially important with labels and handles that don't have $, @ or % prepended to them. Scalars, arrays, and associative arrays always start with $, @, or %, so the reserved words are not reserved for these data types.

Special Variables

Following is a subset of the Perl special variables that we have found to be particularly useful, and appear in almost every Perl program.

@ARGV

@ARGV is the array containing the command-line arguments. Perl, unlike many UNIX tools, does not pass the name used to invoke the program in @ARGV. This name has its own special variable, which is $0.

@ISA

An array that holds the parent classes for a Perl object.

%ENV

An associative array that holds entries for all the environment variables set by the shell.

$_

$_ holds the default value in the current block. If you don't explicitly specify a source, $_ is used.

Expressions

So far, we've shown you how to use Perl variables. In this section, we're going to show you how to use *expressions* to create a working application. You can create *simple expressions*, which are unconditionally executed and accomplish a single goal, and can be anything from a simple assignment to a function call. The following simple expression opens a file handle:

```
open(THEFILE,"/tmp/Perl.tmp");
```

You can also create *complex expressions*, which are groupings of simple expressions. Complex expressions allow you to conditionally execute a simple expression, treat multiple expressions as a single, simple expression, and group Perl code to control program flow. In this section, we will cover various types of complex expressions Perl offers.

Conditional Execution

Perl allows you to conditionally execute expressions based on the truth value of a test expression. Any expression can be followed by a single modifier. In Perl, truth is any expression that evaluates to a non-empty value. For instance, 0 and " " are considered false, while 1, -1 and "\n" are considered true. Note that a string actually has a boolean value, and that the only false string is an empty string. The possible constructs follow:

```
EXPR1 if EXPR2;
EXPR1 unless EXPR2;
EXPR1 while EXPR2;
EXPR1 until EXPR2;
```

In the case of if, the first expression is only evaluated if the second evaluates to true. In unless, the first expression is only evaluated when the second evaluates to false. In the while and until case, the first expression is continuously evaluated until the expression becomes false or true, respectively.

For example, you could use the following statement to terminate your program when it encounters an error while opening a file:

```
die "File didn't open properly!\n" unless open(THEFILE,"/tmp/Perl.tmp");
```

The code evaluates open, and, if it is unsuccessful, returns false and calls the die function. Die is a built-in Perl function that signals an error and ends execution. Notice how this differs from the open call at the beginning of this section.

Joining Expressions

You can join expressions using the logical conjunction (&&) and disjunction (||) operators. Using these operators to join code offers you an elegant and powerful way to conditionally execute code but may also sacrifice readability.

```
EXPR1 || EXPR2;
EXPR1 && EXPR2;
```

The disjunction operator evaluates expressions until it finds one that evaluates to true. The conjunction operator works exactly the opposite, evaluating until it hits a false. Another way to think of these operators is that they continue to evaluate expressions until they hit a truth value that dictates the truth of the entire statement. In a conjunction, any false value makes the entire truth value false. In a disjunction, any true value makes the entire truth value true.

The Perl motto is that there is more than one way to do everything. For example, you could use the following logical conjunctions to terminate your program when it encounters an error while opening a file:

```
open(PASSWORD,"/etc/passwd") || die "Couldn't open file!\n";
```

This is similar to the previous example, but the open expression is evaluated first. If it returns a true value, evaluation can stop because the expression is true. The call to `die` only occurs if `open` fails and returns false.

The Conditional Expression

There may be situations where you want to choose between two values based on some logical expression. For example, you may want to determine which number is larger, 5 or 10. You can easily do this using simple statements, logical conjunctions, or even flow-control statements, but all of these methods have more overhead and more complexity than seems necessary to make the determination. Conditional expressions, on the other hand, allow you to express the relationship in a single expression.

The `?:` operator, shown below, evaluates the second or third expression depending on the truth value of the first expression. If the first expression evaluates to true, the second expression is evaluated. If it evaluates to false, the third expression is evaluated.

```
EXPR ? EXPR2 : EXPR3;
```

The `?:` operator allows you to easily assign the maximum or minimum value of two variables to a third variable. You can evaluate this statement using constructs discussed earlier, but you'll find this method much more elegant. In the following example, the test `$val1>$val2` determines which value to return and assign to the variable `$max`. If `$val1>$val2` evaluates to true, `$val1` is assigned to `$max`. If it is false, `$val2` is assigned.

```
$max = $val1 > $val2 ? $val1 : $val2;
```

Blocks

Blocks allow you to group a series of Perl statements into a compound statement. The default block is the file or package that contains the code. You can also delimit blocks using curly braces. The syntax for blocks follows:

```
[LABEL:] BLOCK [continue BLOCK]
```

A block by itself is equivalent to a loop construct that evaluates only once. Because of this, it is possible to use any of the loop control statements to leave or restart the block. The loop control statements are next, last, and redo. Users can break out of a block using the last command because last does not execute the continue block. Next moves on to the next iteration and executes the continue block. Redo restarts the current iteration.

Using any of the loop control statements without arguments allows the user to break out of the current block. You can name blocks using *labels* to make the loop control statement refer to the named block, not the current one. Labels are simply legal Perl symbols, although it is good style to capitalize labels to offset and protect them from colliding with one of the reserved words.

> **Note:** All Perl reserved words are lowercase (and they are likely to stay that way), so mixing case allows you to ensure that you won't end up colliding with a reserved word.

Flow Control Statements

You can use the following flow control statements to conditionally evaluate blocks of code. The following flow control statements behave similarly to their simple statement counterparts.

```
if (EXPR) BLOCK [[elsif (EXPR) BLOCK …] else BLOCK]
unless (EXPR) BLOCK [else BLOCK]
[LABEL:] while (EXPR) BLOCK [continue BLOCK]
[LABEL:] until (EXPR) BLOCK [continue BLOCK]
do BLOCK while EXPR;
do BLOCK until EXPR;
```

C programmers may notice that Perl is lacking the switch construct. This is not an oversight: it's just that there are already several ways to construct the above flow control statement. Following is an example of how to imitate the switch construct using labels:

```
SWITCH: {
      do { print "This message is from Tom\n"; last SWITCH;} if /Tom/;
      do { print "This message is from Dick\n"; last SWITCH;} if /Dick/;
      do { print "This message is from Harry\n"; last SWITCH;} if
/Harry/;
      print "I don't know who this message is from!\n";
}
```

This block compares $_ to Tom, Dick, and Harry. If it finds a match, it prints the message and exits from the block. If it doesn't find a match, it prints a message indicating that it can't identify where the message originates.

Another type of flow-control statement is an iteration construct. There are two main types of iteration constructs. The first iteration construct closely mirrors that of C, while the second utilizes Perl's more advanced data structures, allowing you to iterate over an array and execute the block for each value. The syntax determines which type of iteration construct is being used. For this discussion, we will use the for construct in the traditional C style, and foreach in the Perl style to avoid any confusion.

In the C style for, the first expression is an initialization. It is executed only once, and is the first thing executed during the for loop. The second expression is a test. The for loop continues as long as the test expression returns true. If the test expression returns false the first time around, the block in the for loop is never executed. The last expression is executed each time, and can be used to increment the variable. The syntax for the standard for loop follows:

```
[LABEL:] for (INIT_EXPR; END_EXPR; STEP_EXPR) BLOCK
```

The array form of for, foreach, takes an optional variable and an array. The variable is set to each element of the array, and the block is executed. The variable is optional, as $_ can be used instead. In the following foreach loop syntax, note that unlike for, foreach does not need an end or step expression.

```
[LABEL:] foreach VAR (ARRAY) BLOCK
```

Perl Operators

Perl operators allow you to edit, manipulate, and change Perl data. We will briefly describe the major Perl operators here: consult the Perl documentation noted in the section "Useful Internet Sites" at the end of this chapter for a complete description of Perl operators.

Like mathematical operators, Perl operators have an order of precedence, shown below.

->	Arrow operator
++ —	Auto increment and autodecrement
~ !	Logical negation
=~ !~	Match operators
* / % x	Multiplicative operators
+ - .	Additive operators
<< >>	Relational operators
< > <= >= lt gt le ge	Equality operators
== != <=> eq ne cmp	
&&	Conjunction operator
||	Disjunction operator
= += -= *= etc.	Assignment operator

It is always a good idea to use parenthesis instead of relying on the order of precedence. This makes it easier for others to read your code and protects you from any quirks in your Perl implementation

The Arrow Operator

The -> or arrow operator is primarily used to allow access to Perl objects. You use the arrow operator by supplying an instance of a class, or a class on the left side. On the right side, you can supply the method name or property you want to access. The following code example calls the showSvrArgs method in the instance of a class $form.

```
$form->showSvrArgs();
```

Autoincrement and Autodecrement

The ++ and – operators allow you to easily increase or decrease the value of an expression. If they are used before the expression, the value is updated before the value is used; if they are used after the expression, the value is updated after it is used. The following statement steps through ten values of I, 0 through 9. During each iteration, I is increased by one using the ++ operator.

```
for (I=0; I<10; I++) {}
```

Logical Negation

Perl has two forms of negation, logical and binary. Logical negation, which uses the ! operator, turns true into false and false into true. Binary negation, which uses the ~ operator, flips the bits from 0 to 1 and 1 to 0.

Match Operators

The =~ and !~ operators match an expression to a regular expression and return a truth value depending on the success of the pattern match. The !~ operator returns the logical negation of the truth value of the =~ operator. For more information, see the sidebar, "Perl's Search-and-Replace Engine."

Multiplicative Operators

The multiplicative operators are as follows:

* * Multiplies two numbers.
* / Divides two numbers.
* % Computes the modulus of the two numbers, which is the remainder of a division.
* x Is the repetition operator that repeats the string value the number of times specified.

Additive Operators

The additive operators work as follows:

* + Returns the sum of two numbers.
* - Returns the difference of two numbers.
* . Concatenates two strings.

Relational Operators

The <, >, <=, and >= operators compare numeric values; lt, gt, le, and ge compare string values.

Equality Operators

The `==`, `!=`, and `<=>` operators check for equality with numeric values; `eq`, `ne`, and `cmp` check for string values.

Conjunction Operator

The `&&` operator returns the conjunction of the truth values for its expressions. If both sides resolve to a true value, it returns true; if either side is false, it returns false.

Disjunction Operator

The `||` operator returns the disjunction of the truth values for its expressions. It returns true if either side resolves to true but doesn't necessarily stop executing. See the discussion under "Joining Expressions" in the "Expressions" section for more information about using this feature.

Assignment Operator

The assignment operator sets the value of the item on the left to that of the expression on the right. The = operator does a straight assignment. You can also combine the assignment operator with other operators to modify the value of the item on the left. Using the extended assignment operator, you can simplify the expression `$a= $a +2;` to `$a+=2;`.

Perl Subroutines

You can combine Perl expressions to form subroutines. Subroutines are blocks of code that are grouped together and called as a single unit, allowing you to modularize your code to make it easier to read and debug.

Perl subroutines are declared using the `sub` call. A name is optional. If it is not present, Perl returns an anonymous subroutine. Below, you will find the syntax for the subroutine call:

```
sub NAME BLOCK
```

Values passed into a subroutine are passed into the array `@_`. The subroutine's `return` value is the value of the last expression or the value supplied to form `return`. For example, the following code displays its arguments.

```
#It's good style to name the arguments by assigning them to a local vari-
able. It makes it much easier to come back and figure out what's going
on.

sub printMyArgs {

my @args=@_;
        foreach (@args) {
                print $_,"\n";
        }
}


printMyArgs(6,5,3,4);
```

Perl Objects

In Perl, objects are packages with a constructor. The constructor returns a reference that has been *blessed* to the type. Blessing indicates to a reference the package to which it belongs, which means that a *blessed reference* can be used to tell the Perl interpreter where to look for a function definition. Following is an example of creating a Perl object:

```
package MyFirstPerlObject;

sub new {
bless {};
}
```

The above code returns a blessed anonymous associative array that is an object of type MyFirstPerlObject. This reference is called an instance of the object, or *instance*.

Functions that can be called by a blessed reference are called *methods*. The first parameter in a blessed method is the object that called it, which is traditionally called $self. The built-in list function shift returns the first value in the list, then removes it from the list. Remember that a function called without an argument uses $_ or @_, depending on whether it wants a scalar or array context. The first line in any method uses a shift, implicitly using @_ as its argument to assign the object to $self, as shown below:

```
sub MyFirstMethod {
        $self = shift;
print "Welcome to my first method!\n";
}
```

Properties are variables tied to an instance. Because we are using associative arrays as objects, it's easy to make instance variables elements in the associative array. Following is a constructor that declares some instance variables and a method that displays the values of these properties.

```
package PerlObjectWithProperties;

sub new {
        $self= {};
        $self->{'name'}="Elvis";
        $self->{'Last Sighting'}="Indianapolis 500, Car # 45";
        bless $self;
}
sub WhereIsHe {
        $self=shift;
        print $self=->{'name'}," was last seen at ",$self->{'Last
Sighting'},"\n";
}
```

Inheritance

So far, you've seen that object programming doesn't give you many more capabilities than procedural programming, aside from a handy way to reference data and methods in a separate package. The real power of object programming comes from the ability to re-use code without copying it. This concept of code re-use is called *inheritance*. Inheritance allows code to use code from another class, requiring you to *override* or rewrite only the portions of the class that are different. Inheritance allows you to add methods and properties that did not exist in the parent class, and extend methods by adding extra code and calling the parent classes' version. This process of adding additional code to existing code is called *extending*.

The special array @ISA is used to tell Perl which parents of the class to use. Perl allows you to have multiple inheritance, where a single class inherits from more than one parent class. In general, you will not need to use this feature.

The following code shows you how to use inheritance to extend and override a parent class. Note that the constructor uses a two-argument version of bless. This allows subclasses to use the parent's constructor, and still retain the proper class membership.

```perl
#Set up a class. Remember, classes are just packages!

package foo;

#Build a constructor. Use the two argument bless so subclasses can use it.

sub new {
        $type = shift;
        $self = {};
        bless $self $type;
}
#Create a method that will be defined only in foo.

sub FooSub {
        $self = shift;
        print "FooSub in Foo!\n";
}
#Create a method that will be overridden by bar.

sub FooBarSub {
        $self = shift;
        print "FooBarSub in Foo\n";
}
#Create a new class, bar.

package bar;
use foo;

#Tell Perl that bar is a subclass of foo.

@ISA=("foo");          .

#Create a new method.

sub BarSub {
        $self = shift;
        print "BarSub in Bar!\n";
}
#Override a method from bar.

sub FooBarSub{
        $self= shift;
        print "FooBarSub in Bar!\n";
}
#Actually use these classes.

package main;
use bar;
use foo;

#Create an instance of each object.
```

```
$fooinstance = new foo;
$barinstance = new bar;

#Call FooSub, this calls the version in Foo.

$foo->FooSub();

#Call FooBarSub. This calls the version in foo, not the one in bar.

$foo->FooBarSub();

#ERROR in the line below! Parents don't know anything about their chil-
dren. Foo has no idea about the method BarSub!

$foo->BarSub();

#This works though, as children inherit from their parents.

$bar->FooSub();

#This calls the version overridden in bar.

$bar->FooBarSub();

#This works because BarSub is a bar method.

$bar->BarSub();
```

Using Perl to Create CGI Scripts

Now that you know the basic constructs of Perl programming, you're ready to apply your knowledge to using Perl to create CGI scripts. Perl is a powerful language for creating CGI scripts because it has very strong file- and text-processing capabilities. In this section, we'll show you how to use these file- and text-processing capabilities and Perl's object-oriented capabilities to parse form results and communicate with a client machine sending a form.

We'll use a *top-down programming* problem-solving approach to processing form results, allowing you to define needs as you go and call code that you haven't written yet. Top-down programming can be compared to starting a business. You have to get slightly immersed in a business before you know all of your staffing requirements. As your needs become apparent, you can hire a new employee, or an entire division, and let the employees decide if they need additional support.

CGI Headers

CGI headers are lines that begin an HTTP request to indicate to the server the type of data to return. In this book, we are focusing on servers that return HTML, so the CGI header is:

```
Content-type: text/html
```

The line must be generated exactly as it appears above. Some versions of Lynx (a program that enables character-mode-only connections to Web servers) require case-sensitive Content-type CGI headers. For example, the following Content-type header caused several headaches until we discovered the case-sensitivity in Lynx:

```
content-type: text/html
```

Subtle change. Big problem. Always generate your headers in the same case as listed in the first example.

There are several types of headers that CGI supports. The more common ones are as follows:

```
Content-encoding
Content-length
Content-type
Expires
Location
Status
```

The scripts we develop will mainly contain the Content-type header. The header types are explained in the following sections.

Content-type

The Content-type header is sent by the client to the server telling the server what type of data or document to return. The value of the Content-type header is in type/subtype pairs. For example, the Content-type header requested by the client could be:

CGI Headers (cont.)

```
application/octet-stream
audio/basic
image/gif
message/rfc822
multipart/mixed
text/html
video/mpeg
```

For HTML documents being returned to the client, the value would most likely be text/html. The value of the header can be acquired in the CONTENT_TYPE CGI environment variable.

Content-encoding

The Content-encoding header is used to indicate a compression type for data that is passed to the CGI program as compressed. Possible values are:

```
x-gzip
x-compress
```

Expires

The Expires header indicates to the client program the date that the file should be considered as expired.

Content-length

The Content-length header is like the CGI variable in that it indicates in bytes the length of the data value being passed.

Location

The Location header contains a URL or virtual address of a new file to be retrieved. It is used to redirect a client or server to a new location.

Status

The Status CGI header indicates the error codes mentioned in Appendix C, "CGI Environment Variables and Return Codes." An incorrectly formed CGI header usually causes a return code of 500.

Parsing Form Results

When the client sends user input from the forms to the Web server, the CGI script needs to know how to handle the information in the different fields. In this section, we'll show you how to create a CGI script to parse form results sent from a client machine. We're going to break the task into three sub-tasks:

- Creating the object that contains a reference to the parse subroutine

- Creating the parse subroutine that handles the form arguments

- Creating a subroutine to unencode the values sent from the client machine.

Because we're using top-down programming, we can reference subroutines before they're created. For example, when we create the object, we reference a *parseForm* subroutine that isn't yet written. When we write the parse subroutine, we reference a yet-to-be-written *hextotext* subroutine. This ability to write code in manageable chunks makes the programming process more flexible, helps you identify requirements, and reduces errors.

Creating the Object

To create an object, you first need to declare a package for the object as shown in the following code:

```
package cgisub;
```

Unlike earlier object-oriented examples, we are going to use the constructor to do some special things. When thinking about a form result, there are two things that you need to consider: the form arguments, and the method used to extract the form arguments. Because you will most likely re-use these two functions, we'll have the object parse the form arguments and store them as an associative array reference in a property (in other words, store them in a table), and pull out the method and store it as a scalar property (in other words, pulling out one row at a time). Here, we are hiding complexity from the user by putting this initialization code in the constructor. This way, you can call the code without having to involve the user.

```
sub new {

#Get the type for the two argument bless.

    my $type = shift;

#Set up a reference to an anonymous array to serve as the object.

    my $self = {};

#Set up a the associative element args using a function called parseForm.
We haven't written this yet, but when we do we know that it will return a
reference to an associative array.

    $self->{'args'} = parseForm();

#Store the value of the environment variable REQUEST_METHOD. This variable
is set by the server, and tells us what kind of method was requested by
the client. the %ENV associative array is a special one that holds all
environment variables set by the OS.

    $self->{'method'} = $ENV{'REQUEST_METHOD'};

#Return our object. Remember that a subroutine will return the value of
the last expression, so the return form is optional here.

    bless $self, $type;
}
```

Notice that the above code contains a reference to the parseForm subroutine, which isn't yet written. Next, we'll show you how to write the parseForm subroutine.

Writing the parseForm Subroutine

We begin by defining the problem that parseForm needs to solve: to handle the form arguments passed from the Web client to the server using CGI conventions. Because parsing the form is done repeatedly, we'll divide the coding into two chunks: one for handling the form arguments; and one for parsing.

Handling Form Arguments

Before we get into how to handle form arguments, you should review the discussion on GET and POST, CGI's methods for handling form arguments in the section, "The <FORM> Element" in Chapter 2, "Creating Forms." We will make the parseForm subroutine work for both.

While we have relied on object-oriented programming to this point, we will mix object-oriented programming and traditional procedural programming to handle form results. Because parseForm is used in the constructor, it is not intended to be used outside of the current library, so we do not need to add the complexity of making it object-oriented. We will instead simply make parseForm a Perl subroutine using the following code. Note that the name/value pairs are placed in the variable $rawFormData.

```
sub parseForm {

#Declare a temporary variable to hold the results of parse.

  my %res;

#Determine which method we used, note the use of eq for strings, == for numerics.

  if ($ENV{'REQUEST_METHOD'} eq "POST" ) {

#If it's a post, read in the data from STDIN. We will store the results in
$rawFormData.

        read(STDIN,$rawFormData,$ENV{CONTENT_LENGTH});
  } else {

#It's a get, so set $rawFormData to the environment variable.

        $rawFormData=$ENV{QUERY_STRING};
  }
#Check to see if there were any arguments, if there were, parse them.

  if ($rawFormData) {

#Note that parse returns a reference to an associative array. It also lets us
choose what the separator will be between argument pairs.

        %res=%{parse($rawFormData,'&')};
  }

#Return a reference to the associative array.

  return \%res;
}
```

Note that the above code references a subroutine called *parse*. The parseForm subroutine simply determines where it should look for its arguments based on whether it was called using the GET or POST method. The parse subroutine then accepts two variables: the encoded arguments and the separator, and returns an associative array containing the values in a usable format.

Writing the Parse Subroutine

The parse subroutine is the real meat of our CGI argument processing code. Its job is to pull out all the name/value pairs and create an associative array, which is best tackled using a combination of Perl's pattern-matching and list-handling features.

Perl has a function called `split` that breaks a scalar into a list using a pattern as the delimiter. The parse subroutine can then loop over this list, breaking up each name/value pair and putting them into the associative array.

Web clients send their arguments to Web servers in an encoded format, so parse also needs to do some translation. Some browsers send characters instead of spaces, and all of them encode special characters as %##, where ## corresponds to the hexadecimal value of the ASCII code for that character. For more information about hexadecimal to ASCII conversions, see Appendix D, "ASCII Conversion Chart." Following is the parse subroutine:

```
sub parse {

#Get our two arguments, the form arg, and the split character.

   local ($wwwArgs,$splitCharacter) = @_;

#Use split to break $wwwArgs up into a list.

   foreach (split(/$splitCharacter/, $wwwArgs)) {

#Check to see that this entry matches name/value. Using the .* means it
will match zero or more non newline characters. Note that the parenthesis
allow us to refer to each side of the equal sign within the body of the
if using the $1 and $2 special variables.

      if ( /(.*)=(.*)/ ) {

#Give $1,$2 more meaningful names.

         local ($varName, $val) = ($1, $2);

#Translate any +'s to spaces in the value using the substitution operator.

         $val =~ s/\+/ /g;

#Translate any +'s to spaces in the name using the substitution operator.
```

```
        $varName =~ s/\+/ /g;
```

#First we translate any encoded special characters. Note that we are only
doing this for the value, so if you try and use special characters in
your name you will also have to decode that. Then, we assign this to the
associative array using the name as the key.

```
        $pArgs{$varName}=hexToText($val);
    } else {
```

#If it wasn't in the name/value format, signal an error.

```
        print("Error Parsing $_\n");
        }
    }
```

#Return a reference to the associative array we built.

```
    return \%pArgs;
}
```

Note that the above code references a subroutine called *hexToText*. This subroutine unencodes the special characters. Writing the hexToText subroutine in the final step.

Writing the hexToText Subroutine

The hexToText subroutine has a simple job: take a string and find instances of %## (where ## represents a digit), and replace them with the ASCII character that has that value. Our hexToText subroutine is going to be lax in its checking and assume that the server is passing valid encoded information. This means that any % character in the scalar will signal the subroutine that the two characters following it are the hexadecimal value of a character. If you are planning on having Perl pass any of this information to other programs, you should also examine the value for any possible security implications. See Chapter 8, "Security Issues for the Web" for more information.

We will use the substitution operator to handle the translation. We have to give the substitution operator two arguments so it will detect every occurrence of an encoded character. Arguments are supplied to the substitution operator after the final slash. The g (global) option indicates that all occurrences will be replaced. The e option indicates that the substitution string should be evaluated as an expression, not just blindly substituted.

Using the parenthesis in our pattern, we can reference the hexadecimal value and translate it to an ASCII character. The built-in function `pack` uses a scheme to translate a number into a character. The first argument to `pack` tells it what scheme to use to translate, and the second argument tells it what value to use. The `c` scheme translates the number into an ASCII character.

```perl
sub hexToText {

#Get the value to translate.

  local($value) = @_;

#Substitute any %.. sequence in $value with the ASCII value of the hexa-
decimal number.

  $value =~ s/%(..)/pack('c',hex($1))/eg;

#Return the translated value.

  return $value;
}
```

Perl's Search-and-Replace Engine

Perl's pattern-matching abilities make it an extremely powerful language for CGI scripting. With the addition of SybPerl, Perl's powerful search-and-replace engine can be used to manipulate data on your SQL Server. Because pattern-matching is so powerful, we will spend a little time talking about the finer points. In our hexToText subroutine, we use pattern-matching for a simple search and replace, but pattern-matching can also be used to break out information that is encoded into a single column in a database or to manipulate complex data from the server.

Perl has two pattern-matching operators. The first, the match operator, is used to detect an occurrence of a particular pattern. The match operator m// or // (the m is optional if you use / as the delimiter) searches for a match to the pattern specified between the slashes. The match operator returns true if it detects a match, and false if it fails to find one.

The second matching operator is the substitution operator, s///. The s/// operator works in a similar fashion to the // operator, but in addition to returning true or false, it substitutes the value between the second and third delimiter for the matched pattern.

Patterns (cont.)

Patterns are comprised of characters. The characters in a pattern
match against themselves or a special value. For a match to occur,
the pattern must be an exact subset of its search space. Within a
pattern, there are special characters that allow you to arbitrarily
specify complex patterns. To match one of these characters, you
need to escape them. The special characters are +?.*()[]{}|\.

+	Matches the preceding pattern at least once, and possibly many times.
?	Matches the preceding pattern zero to one times.
.	Matches anything excluding new lines.
*	Matches the preceding pattern zero to many times.
(...)	Groups a series of pattern elements into a single element. This is used with the $1..$9 and \1..\9 pattern matching special variables.
[...]	Matches anything in the set specified within the parenthesis. A ^ at the beginning matches anything not in the specified set.
{MIN,MAX}	Matches anything that matches the pattern at least MIN times, and at most MAX times.
{MIN}	matches anything that matches the pattern at least MIN times.
{MAX}	matches anything that matches the pattern MAX times.
(...|...|...|...)	Matches anything that matches one of the patterns separated by the vertical bar.
\	Is used to escape one of the special characters. To match a \, you need escape it, so you search for \\ instead.

To see pattern-matching in action, we'll show you how to
implement a program that searches for phone numbers in a text
file, and prints a result when the pattern-matching criteria is met.
To do this, you need to read a file and print any pattern that
matches seven digits, as shown below:

```
while (<>) {
    print $1 if /[0..9]{7}/g;
}
```

Special variables in patterns (cont.)

Perl gives you the following set of special variables that allow you
to refer back to matched elements within the pattern-matching
and substitution operators as well as the current block of code.

`\1..\9`	Back references variables to patterns matched with parentheses. These are used within the match. Use `$1..$9` for references outside of the match.
`$1..$9`	Contain the subpatterns enclosed in parenthesis from the last pattern match. If there are no corresponding matches, the undefined value is returned.
`$``	References the string preceding whatever was matched.
`$'`	References the string following whatever was matched.
`$&`	References the last value matched.

Useful CGI Subroutines for Sending Information Back to the Client Machine

Now that we've shown you how to parse the information sent from the client
machine, we're going to show you how to send information back to the client
machine using the showHeader, getArg, ShowFormArg, and ShowSvrArg subroutines. ShowHeader sends information back to the client indicating what to
do with your response. The getArg subroutine returns the value of an argument.
ShowFormArg and ShowSvrArg display the arguments passed from the client
and server in a table and are mainly used for debugging purposes.

Sending Back a Properly-formatted HTML Document

All responses from an HTTP server begin with a simple statement telling the
client what kind of information it should expect to receive. Because this is a
common requirement for all CGI scripts, we'll create a subroutine called
showHeader to return the proper header for a standard HTML document.
ShowHeader returns the minimal header needed for an HTML response, which
is the MIME type of the document. Note that everything printed to STDOUT is
sent to the client's browser. STDOUT is the default destination for print.

```perl
sub showHeader {

#Get my object.

   my $self = shift;

#Display the mime type for HTML.

   print "Content-type: text/html\n";

#One more return to end the header portion of an HTTP response.

   print "\n";

#Signal success.

   return 1;
}
```

Returning the Value of a Form Argument

The getArg utility subroutine returns the value of a form argument. When CGI code calls getArg and supplies it with the name of an argument, getArg returns the value that the Web client passed to the server. For example, calling getArg with HTTP_USER_AGENT as the argument returns the name of the user's Web browser.

The getArg subroutine is an *accessor function,* meaning that it is used to hide the internal representation of the form argument properties. You could easily have users dereference the associative array that holds the arguments, but this adds a needless level of complexity. Hiding the internal representation of form argument properties also allows you to change the internal representation at some point by simply updating the getArg subroutine.

```perl
sub getArg {

#Get my object.

   my $self = shift;

#Get the argument to lookup.

   local($arg) = @_;

#If Arguments exist, look for ours.

   if ($self->{'args'}) {
```

```
#Get the argument's associative array.

        %args = %{$self->{'args'}};

#Return the value from the associative array.

    return $args{$arg};
  } else {

#If no args, return the empty string.

        return "";
  }
}
```

Troubleshooting Form Input

In testing HTML forms, we've found that it is very helpful to have a routine that shows everything passed to the CGI script so you can look for possible typos in input field names and inspect the values transmitted to your script. In the following subroutine called ShowformArgs, we will put all the library subroutines we've created so far together and display the server arguments. The code for the function to display all the form arguments is included in the WebExtra Web site. ShowformArgs uses the same strategy as ShowSvrArgs, so we'll look at ShowSvrArgs first, then describe how ShowformArgs is different.

ShowSvrArgs begins by returning the HTML code to begin a table. It then uses the built-in function keys, which returns all the key names in an associative array, giving us the title of each argument passed by the server. Having the key, we can then open a new row and add a header cell to it. We put the argument name into the cell, and then open a data cell. In the data cell, we use the argument name to retrieve its value from the environment associative array, and display the value. After we've done this for all the argument names, we display a caption and close the table. ShowformArgs is similar to showSvrArgs, except that it loops over the keys in the form argument's associative array instead of the environment's associative array. Figure 4-1 shows the results of showSvrArgs:

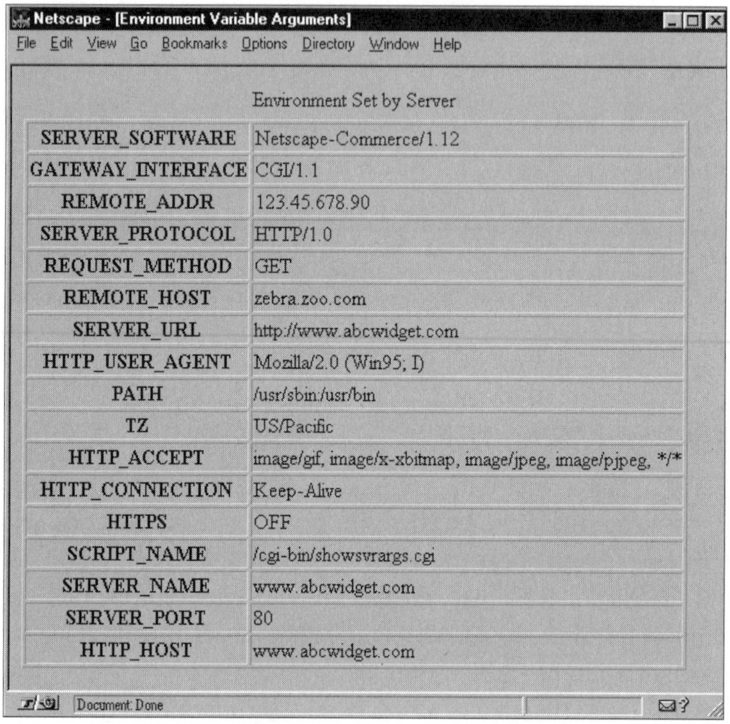

Figure 4-1. The results of showSvrArgs

```
sub showSvrArgs {
  my $self = shift;

#Open the HTML table, have it show a border.

  print "<TABLE BORDER=BORDER>\n";

#Loop over all the keys in %ENV.

  foreach (keys(%ENV)) {

#Start a new row.

      print "<TR>";

#Display a header cell, with the current key($_) as the value.

      print "<TH>",$_;

#Display the value associated with the current key as a cell.

      print "<TD>",$ENV{$_};
```

```
#End the row.

    print "</TR>\n";
  }
#Display a caption for the table.

  print "<CAPTION> Environment Set by Server</CAPTION>";

#End the table.

  print "</TABLE>\n";

#Return 1 to signal success.

  return 1;
}

#Finally, return 1 so that the module can be used.

1;
```

Using SybPerl to Talk to Sybase

SybPerl 2.0 is an add-on library to the standard Perl distribution. SybPerl implements three Sybase extension modules, `Sybase::DBlib`, `Sybase::CTlib`, and `Sybase::SybPerl`. `Sybase::DBlib` is a subset of the Sybase DB-Library API. DB-Library is being phased out in favor of the CT-Library API. The CT-Library offers precise, powerful, and useful tools for communicating with databases. CT-Library is Sybase's API for System 10, and is the library that we will use in this section. `Sybase::SybPerl` is a backward-compatibility module for scripts written in SybPerl 1.0.

In this section, we will show you how to use SybPerl to issue a `select` statement to the server, and display the row results as a table in an HTML document. The algorithm we develop here will be the basis for the example application in the next section, "Using CGI Scripting and SybPerl to Build an Internet Application."

Setting Up the Callback Routines

The first thing we need to do is use the `Sybase::CTlib` package to access the CT-Lib calls.

```
use Sybase::CTlib;
```

After importing the CT-Lib calls, we'll use APIs to set up one server callback and one client callback to display any Open Client messages. You can customize the callback routines we will create to appear as HTML comments, to log to a file, or whatever else you may desire. Note that the client takes a reference to the subroutine while the server just takes the subroutine's name.

```
ct_callback(CS_CLIENTMSG_CB, \&msg_cb);
ct_callback(CS_SERVERMSG_CB, "srv_cb");
```

For more information about the CT-Lib API, see Appendix E, "The CT-Lib API."

Connecting to the Database and Issuing a Select Statement

Now, we will prepare to connect to the database. We need to set up some user ID's and server information to be used in the connect call.

```
$user = 'epresley';
$pass = 'aaron';
$server = 'Graceland';
```

With this user information, we are ready to connect to the server. The call to the ct_connect method uses the generic Sybase::CTlib object. The call then returns a specific object for the connection that was opened.

```
$ctlib = Sybase::CTlib->ct_connect($user, $pass, server);
```

Using our active connection, we will execute a select command, as shown below:

```
$ctlib->ct_execute("select * from sysusers");
```

Displaying the Results of the Select Command

To process the results from the select command, we will loop through all the result sets and display an HTML table for any of the returned rows (or fetchable rows).

The ct_results call determines the result type for each set, and stores the result type in the argument $restype. As long as this call returns CS_SUCCEED, there will be result sets waiting to be processed. If the result type doesn't contain row results, we will continue to loop; otherwise, we'll pull down all the column names using the `ct_col_names` function and display the column names as header cells in the table. After that, we'll look through all the rows and display them as data cells. Remember that we don't need to worry if any of the cells are special numeric, money, or date types, as these will automatically be converted to strings in the `print` call.

```
#Inspect the result type, stop looping if there are no more result sets.
while( $ctlib->ct_results($restype) ==CS_SUCCEED) {

#Loop if it is not a fetchable result type.
        next if(!$ctlib->ct_fetchable($restype));

#Open up an HTML table.
        print "<TABLE BORDER=BORDER>";

#If we have column names, loop to print each one as header information.
        if(@names = $ctlib->ct_col_names()) {

#Print a table row.
                print "<TR>";

#Print each name as a column header.
                foreach (@names) {
                        print "<TH>",$_;
                }
        }

#Loop over all the rows (fetching them incrementally using ct_fetch).
        while(@dat = $ctlib->ct_fetch) {

#Open a new table row for each row of data.
                print "<TR>";

#Loop to print each row element.
                foreach (@dat) {
                        print "<TD>",$_;
                }
        }
}
```

We could have used `ct_sql` to pull the entire result set down into an array, but we used `ct_execute` and `ct_fetch` because they have smaller memory requirements. At any one time, only one row is in memory with `ct_fetch`. Use `ct_sql` when you know that you will be returning a small number of rows that can be held in memory, and for commands that do not return data.

Following is the code for the two standard Sybase callbacks, server and client. These callbacks generate obscure messages that when translated may be helpful to users. You should take steps to hide the messages you don't want users to see and make the messages that would help users more intelligible. One way to hide messages from users is to place the callback inside of an HTML comment. We will only show one callback here, as there is very little difference between server and client callbacks.

```
#Set up a callback to print all the Open Client messages.

sub msg_cb {
        my($layer, $origin, $severity, $number, $msg, $osmsg) = @_;
        printf STDERR "\nOpen Client Message: (In msg_cb)\n";
        printf STDERR "Message number: LAYER = (%ld) ORIGIN = (%ld)
",$layer, $origin;
        printf STDERR "SEVERITY = (%ld) NUMBER = (%ld)\n",$severity,
$number;
        printf STDERR "Message String: %s\n", $msg;
        if (defined($osmsg)) {
                printf STDERR "Operating System Error: %s\n", $osmsg;
        }
    CS_SUCCEED;
}
```

Using CGI Scripting and SybPerl to Build an Internet Application

In this section, we're going to show you two applications for processing a customer order from an Internet shopping site to illustrate how CGI and Sybase work together. These applications contain many of the interactions between the Web client and a server that you will most likely want to use in your own applications. Figure 4-2 shows the form containing the order information we'll be processing in this section. For more information about creating forms, see Chapter 2, "Creating Forms."

The first application processes the information in the order form above using two Perl CGI scripts. One script generates a form on the fly to confirm the order and get pertinent customer information. The other script commits the order information to the database. The second application implements a drill-down report that shows summary information when a user first displays the form, then allows the user to selectively expand items on the report to show more detailed information. We'll create the report using a single CGI script, and utilize the `GET` method and its associated argument-passing abilities to dictate how deep to drill.

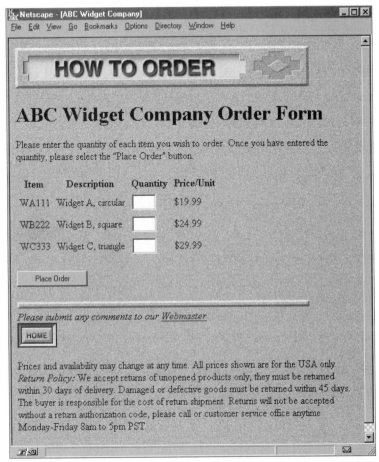

Figure 4-2. The Internet shopping form

Processing the Customer Order

The first task is to calculate the total cost of the order. To do this, we need to find the prices of all the products and multiply the number of each product ordered by the appropriate price. After we display the total cost, we'll display a new form for collecting customer information. We want to make the HTML generated by the form dynamic so we won't have to edit it if the ABC Widget Company starts carrying different inventory.

In this section, we'll show you how to use two powerful commands in CT-Lib: `ct_execute` and `ct_sql`. The `ct_execute` command is useful for manipulating large result sets, and the `ct_sql` command is useful for SQL commands and selects that generate small result sets. Please refer to the WebExtra Web site for complete source code.

Displaying the Total Order Cost and Collecting Customer Information

The CGI script begins by setting up the environment to allow the CGI script to talk to Sybase. CGI scripts usually execute with very few privileges and a sparse environment. As a programmer, you're probably used to having environment variables such as `$SYBASE` tell the operating system where to look for the parts it needs: CGI programs don't have this capability.

We discussed the `%ENV` variable earlier in the "Perl's Search-and-Replace Engine" section of this chapter. You can also use `%ENV` to set environment variables. `%ENV` is an associative array, so all you need to do is reference the variable name you want to set, and supply it with a value. You need to set two variables to make the environment Sybase-aware: `LD_LIBRARY_PATH` and `SYBASE`.

If you built SybPerl with dynamic linking, you need to set up the `LD_LIBRARY_PATH` environment variable to tell the runtime linker where to look for shared libraries. You need to set this to point to the directory containing the Sybase shared libraries. Assuming that your Sybase home directory is /antelope/sybase/1002, you would place the libraries in /antelope/sybase/1002/lib using the following command:

```
$ENV{'LD_LIBRARY_PATH'}="/antelope/sybase/1002/lib";
```

You also need to set up the `SYBASE` environment variable using the following code. Notice in the code below that we are setting the `LD_LIBRARY_PATH` and `SYBASE` variables in a special block. The `BEGIN BLOCK` syntax guarantees that the block runs immediately before anything else, ensuring that the environment is properly set up.

```
#Set up environment.

BEGIN {
$ENV{'LD_LIBRARY_PATH'}="/antelope/sybase/1002/lib";
        $ENV{'SYBASE'}="/antelope/sybase/1002";
}
```

The program you're going to create uses the CTlib package to communicate with Sybase SQL Server, and the `cgisub` package to access form information. The following code references the packages.

```
#Use necessary packages.

use Sybase::CTlib;
use cgisub
```

It is important to do some kind of error trapping. In the application, we're going to show you how to display the errors as HTML comments, which allows you to see the messages without confusing the customers. In your own application, you will want to rewrite some of the more informative errors and make them available to the customer. The following lines set up the server and customer callback routines.

```
#Add callbacks which print their messages as HTML comments.

ct_callback(CS_CLIENTMSG_CB, \&msg_cb);
ct_callback(CS_SERVERMSG_CB, "srv_cb");
```

The following code initiates interaction with the customer's browser. The first message from the CGI program needs to be a valid HTML header, so we'll show you how to instantiate a form object, then display an HTML header.

```
#Instantiate a form object.
$form = new cgisub;

#Display the html header.
$form->showHeader();
```

After sending the HTML header, you need to connect to the server using the `ct_connect` command and begin manipulating data. The `ct_connect` command takes an optional number of arguments. If you don't supply any arguments, it uses default arguments. You need to supply arguments for the username, password, and Sybase server as shown below, but leave the application name empty so the command will use the default value null instead. The `ct_connect` command returns an object reference that you will use to call the CTlib methods.

```
#Connect to server.
$ctlib=Sybase::CTlib->ct_connect($user,$pass,$server);
```

Next, you need to print a summary of the items the customer has selected and the total cost of those items, and allow the customer to decide if they want to continue with the order. To do this, you need to select all the products from the product table and loop through them. If you find a valid order (the customer placed an order for one or more products) you need to display a line in your order table showing how many products were ordered and the total cost.

Use `ct_execute` to send a request to the server and begin executing your query. The `ct_execute` command does not return the data by itself: you have to call `ct_fetch` to fetch your results. This is good for cases when you are unsure how many rows you will return, and if you think that there is a possibility that you will not be able to hold all the rows in memory at one time. You cannot begin another transaction until all the result sets have been dealt with and the open customer layer has signaled that the command is done. You can check the status of result sets using `ct_results`.

The `ct_results` command returns `CS_SUCCEED` if there are result sets waiting to be processed. It returns the type of result set in the argument passed to it, which can be used to test if the result set contains fetchable data. In this example, you have control over the SQL, so you know that if the command succeeded, it will return a result set. In the example in the "Using Perl to Create CGI Scripts" section, we showed you a generic method for handling result sets and any query. That method was more robust than you need here, so for speed and simplicity, you can use your knowledge to your advantage. The following code executes a query and displays the query results.

```
#Select all the products.
$ctlib->ct_execute("select * from product");

#If the command didn't succeed, signal an error and exit.
$ctlib->ct_results($restype) == CS_SUCCEED || die "Select error: Unable to
load products!\n";
```

Having determined that you have a valid result set, you need to fetch each row individually and display it in an HTML table. You need to give fetch a non-null value as its first argument, causing fetch to return an associative array instead of a regular array. The associative array uses the column names as its keys.

```
while(%dat = $ctlib->ct_fetch($ReturnAssoc)) {
```

To actually reference elements of this associative array, you need to treat it like any other associative array. At this point, the row from the database has become just another Perl variable, except for the fact that the date, time, and numeric data types are actually Perl objects. These objects automatically convert themselves to strings when you print them, so you don't need to worry about the fact that they are Perl objects for this example. If you want to do some calculations for your own form, use methods that act upon the Sybase data types so that you don't lose any precision due to differences in Sybase's representation and Perl's. If you don't, the objects are converted to the corresponding Perl data type, and you are subject to Perl's rounding errors and precisions. Figure 4-3 shows the result of the CGI script so far.

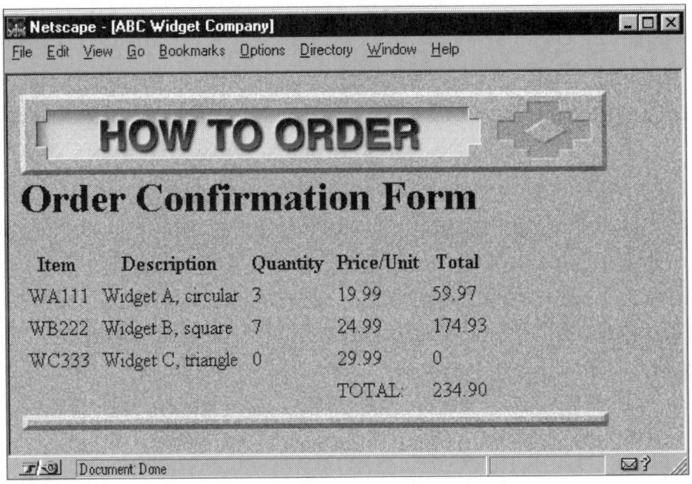

Figure 4-3. The form resulting from processing the customer's order

After you process each row, you need to check for other result sets and handle them until all the rows are processed. Unless something unexpected happens, you only need to call ct_results one more time to retrieve the command done message. After checking the result set, you need to check if the result type returned is fetchable. If it is fetchable, that means that the server sent some unexpected results back, and that you need to signal an error. Note that we don't tell you to check if the result type is command done; instead, we expect the ct_results call to fail when you have handled all the result sets.

After you finish displaying the rows, you should have the following code:

```
while($ctlib->ct_results($restype) == CS_SUCCEED) {
        next if(!$ctlib->ct_fetchable($restype));
        print "Extra Fetchable Results!\n";
}
```

Next, we'll show you how to use a set of print calls to display a form in which customers can enter personal information. Your next task, assuming that the customer decides to place their order, is to pass the order information to the database.

Passing the Customer's Order to the Database

In this section, we'll show you how to write a CGI script to connect to the Sybase server and then pass the customer's order to the database. To do this, you'll need to generate the customer ID and the order ID values, and send the SQL insert commands to the server. You also need to signal to the customer that their order was processed. As before, we will concentrate on the interesting portions of the source code for this discussion. Please refer to the WebExtra Web site for a complete listing of related code.

After you set up your environment and return the proper HTTP headers, you need to connect to the Sybase server using the ct_connect command, as shown in the following code:

```
#connect to the server
$ctlib=Sybase::CTlib->ct_connect($user,$pass,$server);
```

The order has a timestamp, so you need to get the current time and create a new Sybase DateTime object. There are some caveats with using date objects. For a description of these, see Appendix E, "The CT-Lib API." We'll show you how to use the built-in function localtime to get the local time, and then use the result to initialize a date object. The localtime function returns its results as an array value, so you'll use Perl's special ability to assign an array to a list of scalar variables, and then use these to supply a string representing the current date and time to the newdate method. There's an easier way to do this using the curdate Transact SQL command, but we are using this example to expose you to Sybase native data type handling using SybPerl.

```
($sec,$min,$hour,$mday,$mon,$year,$wday,$yday,$isdst) = localtime();

#Create a sybase datetime object, initialized to today.

#We increment the month because localtime begins at 0 instead of 1.
$date=$ctlib->newdate($mon+1)."/".$mday."/".$year."
".$hour.":".$min.":".$sec);
```

Now that you have the customer and order IDs and the timestamp, you can begin a transaction and commit the customer information to the database. You need to start by beginning a transaction using the ct_sql statement, shown below. The ct_sql command is similar to ct_execute except that it handles the result processing for you by automatically reading in all the results from the command and returning them as an array of reference arrays.

```
$ctlib->ct_sql("begin transaction");
```

Next, you need to select from the customer table to generate a unique ID. You will want to do this differently in a production system, as the holdlock in this statement causes problems in a busy system. Once again, you're going to use ct_sql to get the results of the select. You're only expecting one row back, so you don't have to worry about the memory issues associated with a larger select.

```
@custid=$ctlib->ct_sql("select max(customer_id)+1 from customer HOLDLOCK");
```

After obtaining your unique id, you need to generate a SQL insert command and store it to a variable. We'll show you how to use the getArg accessor method from the cgisub form object to get the values that the customer entered in the form, and use the values to populate the table. Having generated the SQL, you need to use ct_sql to execute the command. As you insert data into the table, you will give the customer feedback showing that each product was successfully ordered. Figure 4-4 shows the visible result of this CGI script.

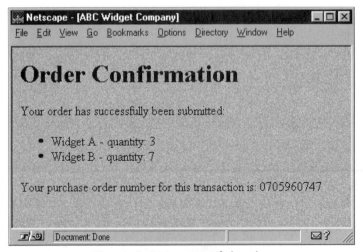

***Figure 4-4.** A successful order*

```
#Set up the sql to insert into the customer table.

$insertcust="insert into
customer(customer_id,last_name,first_name,phone_number,address,city,state,z
ip) values (".$custid[0][0].",\'".$form->getArg('last')."\',\'".$form-
>getArg('first')."\',\'(".$form->getArg('ac').") ".$form-
>getArg('ph')."\',\'".$form->getArg('add1').$form-
>getArg('add2')."\',\'".$form->getArg('city')."\',\'".$form-
>getArg('state')."\',\'".$form->getArg('zip')."\')";

#Actually insert the row.

$ctlib->ct_sql($insertcust);
```

Next, you need to use the same mechanism above to generate a unique ID for an order ID, then generate an array of SQL `insert` commands for each product that the customer ordered. After you have completed that command structure, you will execute the `insert` commands. Note that you can't use the same connection for more than one SQL command at once. We could have shown you how to allocate more than one connection to handle the inserts, but that requires creating a new method for generating IDs.

In this example, we showed you how to use two powerful commands in CT-Lib: `ct_execute` and `ct_sql`. You saw how `ct_execute` is useful for manipulating large result sets, and how `ct_sql` is useful for SQL commands and selects that generate small result sets.

Creating a Drill-down Decision Support Tool

Assuming that you've successfully sold many widgets to your customers, you're now ready to create a drill-down tool enabling the company managers to view sales figures. We'll show you how to display an overview of an entire year, then drill-down through the quarters, months and orders, down to a single specific order.

We'll show you how to build a single CGI script that branches to the appropriate snapshot of sales figures based on an argument supplied as part of a GET method. From each snapshot, the manager will be able to choose another snapshot that shows more detail, until finally reaching a single order.

Choosing the Depth to Drill

You'll use a CGI GET argument to supply the depth to drill. You'll take a blank value for this argument as a signal that the starting point for the drill should be the yearly figures. Use the LABEL BLOCK syntax to create a switch statement similar to what you have in C. This switch statement will then call separate subroutines to display the current levels information.

```
#Branch to a particular subroutine based on the type.

SWITCH: {
    do {drillMonth(); last SWITCH;} if $type eq "month";
    do {drillQuarter(); last SWITCH;} if $type eq "quarter";
    do {drillOrder(); last SWITCH;} if $type eq "order";
    drillYear();
}
```

We could have implemented the above code using an if..elsif structure, but we are particularly partial to the somewhat more confusing method shown previously. Some people feel that the switch-like construct is more confusing, and in fact can be dangerous if the last clause is omitted. The following snippet is just as valid, and may prevent some of the potential pitfalls of the switch style statement:

```
if ($type eq "month") {
    drillMonth();
} elsif ($type eq "quarter") {
    ...
```

Drilling Down

The drill-down CGI script presents the user with a simple form containing a radio group prompting the user to choose a quarter. After the user chooses a quarter, you will present the months in the quarter with their corresponding sales, and accompany the information with a form allowing them to view sales for a particular month. If the user decides to view the month detail, you'll present a form allowing them to view information about particular orders. Figure 4-5 shows the first page presented to the user.

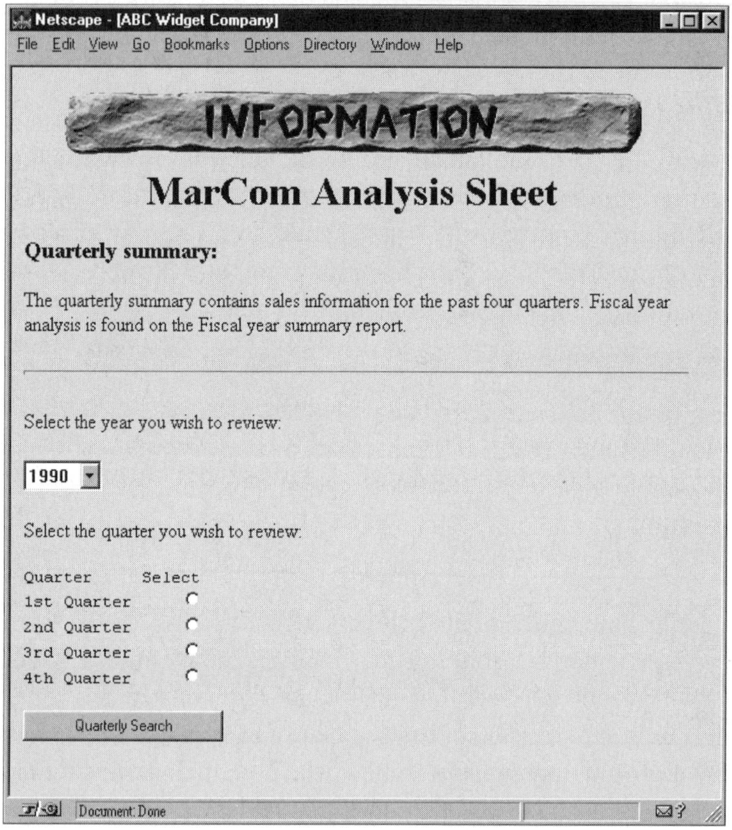

Figure 4-5. *The form that prompts the user to select a quarter*

To break the data out into quarters or months, you need to use the Sybase `datepart` call to return a number representing the quarter or month. You will use this number to select only the records for the period the user selected.

Using this call, you can select a finished table and only use Perl to display the results and maintain running totals. This allows each of these drill-down problems to fit nicely into our toolbox of execute, fetch, and display routines that we have developed so far.

Summarizing a Quarter

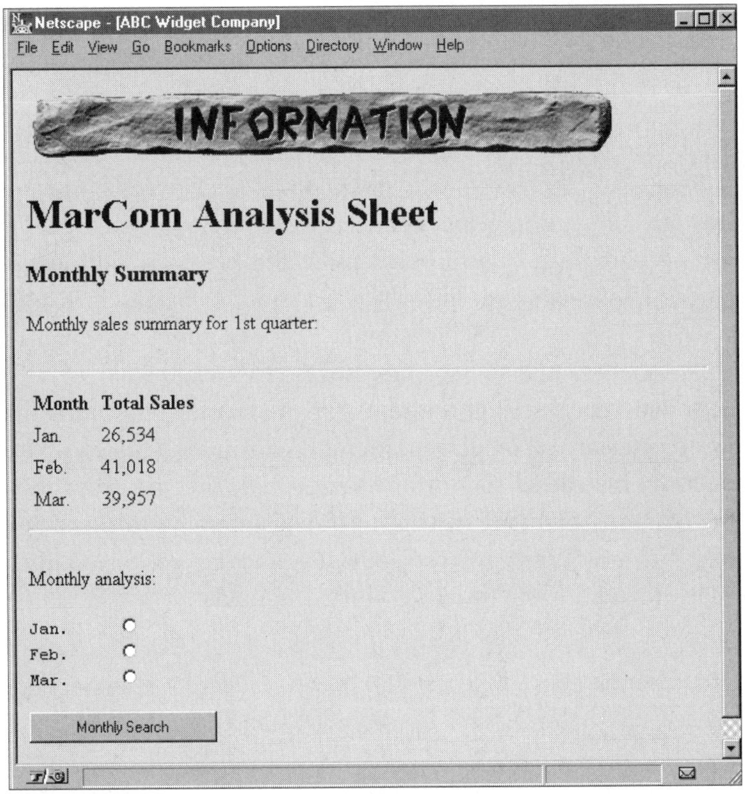

***Figure 4-6.** The Monthly summary and a form for drilling down*

The subroutine drillQuarter displays the appropriate HTML headings and queries the database for monthly totals. Figure 4-6 shows the desired output. This subroutine is a good example of using `ct_sql` to return results from a `select` query. In this example, you're pulling back only three rows and firing them off to the screen, so you don't need to worry about memory issues. You can also use the `row` function to display the values. To do this, you need to declare an anonymous function `inline` to print the proper information. The following code illustrates the anonymous function.

```
$ctlib->ct_sql($select,sub { print
"<TR><TD>",$q{$_[0]},"</TD><TD>",$_[1],"</TD></TR>";});
```

After displaying the month summaries, you display a form that allows the user to select a month for more detail. The code for doing this is shown in the WebExtra Web site. You'll notice that we use a hidden INPUT element in the form to tell the CGI script handling the form's results which form it should expect to handle. We did it this way so we could have the entire drill-down portion of the application in a single file. This makes maintaining the code and your Web space easier, as you are less likely to lose a portion of your code.

Summarizing a Month

The drill month subroutine displays a one-line summary of all orders in the current month, as shown in Figure 4-6. Unlike the previous subroutine, you are handling an unknown amount of records. Memory becomes an issue with large volumes, so instead of using the simple ct_sql approach, you need to use ct_execute, ct_results and ct_fetch to process the result set.

The following code selects the rows for the month and loops through the result set until they are all displayed. Using the form of ct_fetch that returns an associative array instead of the form that returns a normal array allows you to refer to the columns by name instead of order. Referring to them by name not only makes the code easier to read, but also allows you to modify the select without worrying about the order in which the fields are listed.

```
$select="select order_id,order_date,sum(cost) cost from cust_order where
datepart(mm,order_date)=".$theMonth." group by order_id,order_date";
#Execute the select statement.
    $ctlib->ct_execute($select);

#Check to make sure we got good results. If we didn't, signal an error
and quit.
        $ctlib->ct_results($restype) == CS_SUCCEED || die "Select error:
Unable to load Order information!\n";

#Print an html table tag, and set up the title headings.
    print "<TABLE>";
    print "<TR>";
    print "<TH>PO</TH><TH>Date</TH><TH>Amount/TH>";
    print "</TR>";
        while(%dat = $ctlib->ct_fetch($ReturnAssoc)) {
    print "<TR><TH><A
HREF=\"drill.cgi?type=order&o=",$dat{'order_id'},"\">",$dat{'order_id'},"</
A></TH><TD>",$dat{'order_date'},"</TD><TD>",$dat{'cost'},"</TD></TR>";
    }
```

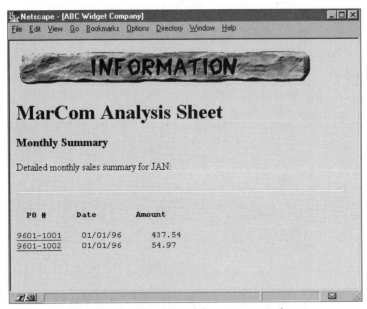

Figure 4-7. The Monthly summary sheet

Displaying Customer Information

The drill order subroutine shows the customer information and the products they ordered. You will use `ct_sql`, `ct_execute`, `ct_results`, and `ct_fetch` in this subroutine. The customer information is a good candidate for `ct_sql` as it represents only one row, while the order information is a candidate for the other three methods.

Instead of using a row function to display the customer information, you need to return the results as an array. This allows you to more precisely control how the information is displayed instead of presenting it in one big table. Figure 4-8 shows how the information will be displayed.

For the order information, you need to use the standard execute, loop, and fetch paradigm you have used previously. As you loop, you need to keep a running total of all the sales so that you can display the total as the last row in the table.

You now have a complete application that supports order entry and reporting. As we built this application, we used several approaches that can be used in your own applications. With the skills you've developed and the sample code found in this chapter, you have a well-supplied toolchest for building SQL Server applications over the World Wide Web.

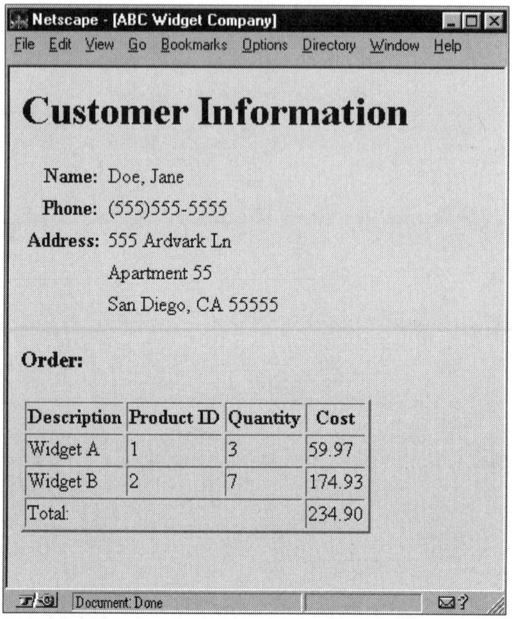

Figure 4-8. The order summary

Tips and Tricks

The following tips will help you use Perl more effectively:

- Learn the meaning of $, @, and %

- When debugging, keep an eye on your WWW server's error log

- When referencing the value of an array, use the scalar notation `$array[6]`, not `@array[6]`

- When reading in a file, make sure you use scalar notation unless you really want to read the entire file into an array

- The `-w` flag to Perl tells you all kinds of interesting things about your code

- You can handle all database requests by pulling all the rows down at once and using them as a simple Perl array, or by pulling them down one at a time

- The `ct_sql` command is useful for small result sets, while `ct_execute`, `ct_results`, and `ct_fetch` are useful for large results sets

- Turn your code into a Perl module using the object extensions whenever possible so that you can re-use and extend yesterday's work for tomorrow's tasks

- Read the documentation that comes with the distribution. It has lots of useful examples.

Useful Internet Sites

General index of Perl information:
http://galaxy.einet.net/galaxy/Engineering-and-Technology/Computer Technology/Programming-Languages/Perl.html

Perl FAQ:
http://www.sra.co.jp/public/doc/perl-faq/perl-FAQ.html#TOC

Larry Wall's talk on Perl 5:
http://www.khoros.unm.edu/staff/neilb/perl/VHLL/slide01.html

Perl Resources:
http://www.ee.pdx.edu/~rseymour/perl/

Searchable Hotlinked Perl Documentation:
http://www.cs.cmu.edu/htbin/perl-man

Tips for using PERL on the WWW:
http://WWW.Stars.com/Vlib/Providers/perl.html

Everything you could want:
http://www.perl.com/

Summary

Perl's object extensions allow you to make useful libraries of code that you can re-use to solve multiple problems. Its regular expressions allow you to detect patterns and act upon them, and pull apart data and examine it.

After you know what you want from Sybase, it is easy to pull the data down and allow Perl to manipulate it. You have two approaches: use `ct_execute`, `ct_results`, and `ct_fetch` to pull each record down one at a time, or use `ct_sql` to execute a command and pull the entire result set down at once. These two approaches give you the tools you need to handle almost any request.

5

Creating CGI Scripts Using Tcl

The Tool Command Language, Tcl (pronounced either tickle or tee-see-ell) is one of several scripting languages currently available for creating CGI scripts that access a database or other interactive programs. Tcl's many string-handling features allow you to create Web pages in a straightforward manner from data retrieved from a database. This chapter shows you how to use Tcl and several of its extensions to create CGI scripts that access and update data in Sybase SQL Server, and create new HTML documents and forms.

The development of Tcl began in the late 1980's in John Ousterhout's lab at University of California at Berkeley. Ousterhout's original goal was to create a general-purpose scripting language as a C library package. Tcl can be embedded in C programs, or it can stand on its own as a scripting language. In this chapter, we will focus upon using Tcl as a scripting language, not embedding it in C programs.

You can extend Tcl as needed by defining new commands or using one of the many available extensions written by other programmers. In this chapter, we will cover two extensions: Sybtcl, written by Tom Poindexter, and Expect, written by Don Libes.

Tcl was originally developed under UNIX, but has been ported to the Macintosh and to PCs running Windows. As of this writing, Expect and Sybtcl have not been ported to Windows. There is a port of Sybtcl underway for the Macintosh, but it is not yet released.

The applications in this chapter are developed around the requirements of The ABC Widget Company. We'll show you how to create a sales reporting application to illustrate how to generate reports from user input. We'll also show you a reporting application that demonstrates how to link reports together in a drill-down report in which summary lines in one report are linked to other reports that display the detail. These reports are all generated on the fly by accessing the data in a Sybase SQL Server and then using the Tcl script to generate the necessary HTML statements to create a complete Web document or form. Finally, we'll show you a simple widget ordering application to demonstrate how to use Tcl to accept input from an HTML form, generate another HTML form, update a Sybase SQL Server, and return status information to the user.

We begin the chapter by covering basic information for writing scripts with Tcl, then cover using Sybtcl and Expect to create CGI scripts. If you are already familiar with Tcl and its extensions, you may want to skip to the "Tcl and the WWW Server" section, where we discuss making the connection between Tcl and a Web server.

This chapter contains the following sections:

- Tcl Basics

- Using Sybtcl to Communicate with a Sybase SQL Server

- Using Expect to Handle Interactions between Tcl and Other Programs

- Tcl and the WWW Server

- WWW Applications using Tcl and Sybase

- More Tcl Resources.

Tcl Basics

Planning and writing Tcl scripts is relatively straightforward. The basic parts of a Tcl script are the full path to the Tcl interpreter `tclsh` (this path will vary from machine to machine), the function declaration, and the main section of your script. The full path to `tclsh` is preceded by a `#!`, and should be the first line of your script. For example:

```
#! /usr/local/bin/tclsh
```

Except when used in the very first line in your Tcl script, the # (pound sign) is the comment character.

In Tcl, you need to declare procedures before they are called. These declarations usually occur at the beginning of the script. You do not have to declare variables before you use them, but it's a good idea to declare global variables at the beginning of the script. Variables created (by declaration or use) inside a procedure are available only to that function. Variables created outside procedures are global and can be accessed in a function with the global declaration. Variables in Tcl are denoted by the dollar sign $.

This section contains the basic information you need to begin writing Tcl scripts.

Tcl Programming Constructs

All Tcl programming blocks, procedures and tests are enclosed in curly braces {}. The basic layout of a Tcl script is: the path to tclsh; global variable declarations; function declarations; and the main body of the program. Procedures are defined with the statement:

```
proc function_name { param1 param2 ...} { Programming Block }
```

Values are returned from a procedure using the return statement.

Tcl offers the following ANSI C looping and branching programming constructs:

if...elseif...else

```
if { Boolean Test } { Programming Block }
elseif { Boolean Test } { Programming Block }
else { Default Programming Block }
```

switch

```
switch $var { Test Values
        TestValue1 { Programming Block }
        TestValue2 { Programming Block }
        TestValue3 { Programming Block }
}
```

for

```
for { Set Variable } { Test Variable } { Change Variable }
    { Programming Block }
```

foreach

```
foreach var_name $list_name { Programming Block }
```

while

```
while { Boolean Test } { Programming Block }
```

break

Break causes the innermost loop to terminate immediately.

continue

Continue causes the current iteration of the innermost loop to terminate immediately.

A typical Tcl script might look something like the following:

```
#! /usr/local/bin/tclsh
#Set Global Variables
set var1 ""
set list1 {}
#Procedure Declarations
proc foobar { param1 } {
        global var1
        set locvar1 $param1
        if { $var1 == $locvar1 } {
                set var1 [expr $locvar1 + 1]
        } else {
                set var1 $locvar1
        }
        return $locvar1
}
#Main
set var1 [lindex $argv 0]
lappend list1 [ foobar $var1 ]
puts $list1
exit 0
```

Tcl Expressions, Operators and Operands

In Tcl, the `expr arg1 arg2...` command concatenates all of its arguments, evaluates the result as an expression, and returns a string corresponding to the expression's value. This is most commonly seen with arithmetic operators such as the plus sign (+). For example:

```
expr 5 + 7
```

returns the value 12.

Precedence and operators in Tcl work in a similar fashion to ANSI C except that some of the operators allow strings. Tcl supports the arithmetic operators +, -, *, /, and %, which can be used as binary or unary operators. Table 5-1 summarizes the Tcl operators.

Table 5-1. *Summary of the Operators Allowed by Tcl*

Syntax	Result	Operand Types
x*y	Multiply x and y	int, real
x/y	Divide x by y	int, real
x%y	Remainder after dividing x by y	int
x+y	Add x and y	int, real
x-y	Subtract y from x	int, real
-x	Negative of x	int, real
!x	Logical NOT: 1 if x is zero, 0 otherwise	int, real
~x	Bit-wise complement of x	int
x<<y	Left-shift x by y bits	int
x>>y	Right-shift x by y bits	int
x<y	1 if x is less than y, 0 otherwise	int, real, string
x>y	1 if x is greater than y, 0 otherwise	int, real, string
x<=y	1 if x is less than or equal to y, 0 otherwise	int, real, string
x>=y	1 if x is greater than or equal to y, 0 otherwise	int, real, string
x==y	1 if x is equal to y, 0 otherwise	int, real, string
x!=y	1 is x is not equal to y, 0 otherwise	int, real, string
x&y	Bit-wise AND of x and y	int
x^y	Bit-wise exclusive OR of x and y	int
x|y	Bit-wise OR of x and y	int
x&&y	Logical AND: 1 if both x and y are non-zero, 0 otherwise	int, real
x||y	Logical OR: 1 if either x is non-zero or y is non-zero, 0 otherwise	int, real
x?y:z	Choice: if x is non-zero then y, else z	x:int, real

Expression operands are normally integers, real numbers or strings. Tcl evaluates an expression to see if it makes sense numerically. If not, it continues to treat the operands as strings. If the operand starts with a 0, Tcl reads it as an octal (base 8) number. If it starts with a 0x, Tcl treats the operand as a hexadecimal (base 16) number.

If you need to treat an integer with a leading zero as a decimal number, append a .0 to the end of it, as shown below. Perform the calculations, but always remember to convert the operand back to an integer.

```
set prefix [string range [lindex $argv 0] 0 2]
set suffix [string range [lindex $argv 0] 3 7]
append $suffix .0
set newnum [expr int($suffix + 1)]
set newdoc $prefix$newnum
return $newdoc
```

Tcl Arrays and Lists

Tcl implements only one-dimensional arrays, but because Tcl supports associative arrays, you can simulate multidimensional arrays by concatenating multiple indices. The following example illustrates this. *Peach* is the output of the program.

```
set arr_var(1,1) "Apple"
set arr_var(1,2) "Peach"
set arr_var(2,1) "Broccoli"
set x 1
set y 2
puts $arr_var($x,$y)
```

Peach

Tcl also offers a data structure known as a *list*. Tcl lists can serve many of the same functions as structures in C. The elements in a list can be any valid Tcl data type or other lists or arrays. To denote a list, you need to enclose the elements in braces and separate them by white space. Lists are indexed starting with element zero.

Tcl treats many elements as lists, such as command-line arguments and rows from Sybase SQL Server. Table 5-2 shows the Tcl commands specifically related to lists.

Table 5-2. *A Summary of List-oriented Tcl Commands*

TCL COMMAND	DESCRIPTION
lindex *list index*	Returns the *index*'th element from *list*.
linsert *list index value#1...*	Returns a new list formed by inserting all of the *value* arguments as elements of *list* before the *index*'th element of the original *list*.
concat *list#1 list#2...*	Joins multiple *lists* into a single list and returns a new list.
join *list joinstring*	Concatenates *list* elements together with the *joinstring* as the separator between the elements. *Joinstring* defaults to space and returns the result.
lappend *list value#1...*	Appends each *value* to the end of *list*. Creates *list* if it did not already exist.
list *value#1 value#2...*	Returns a list with elements comprised of the *value* arguments.
llength *list*	Returns the number of elements in *list*.
lrange *list first last*	Returns a list consisting of the *first* through *last* elements of *list*.
lreplace *list first last value#1...*	Returns a new list form by replacing the *first* through *last* elements that are inclusive of *list* with 0 or more *values*.
lsearch *list pattern*	Returns the index of the first element in *list* that matches *pattern* or -1. The default pattern matching technique is *glob*, but you can change the technique to *-exact* or *-regexp*. These pattern-matching techniques are discussed later in this section.
lsort *list*	Returns a new list formed by sorting the elements of *list*. The default order is *increasing*, and the default comparison function is ASCII. Other comparison functions include: *-integer*; *-real*; and *-command*. You can reverse the order using the *-decreasing* option.
split *string splitChar*	Returns a list form by splitting *string* on *splitChar*.

String Handling in Tcl

Tcl offers an assortment of commands for manipulating strings. Format strings in Tcl are specified in the same manner as they are for C. They start with a leading percent sign followed by the an optional dash to left-justify them, and then are followed by the length and the type of field. For example, `%11.2f` specifies a float data type with eleven total places and two decimal places. `%-15.15s` indicates a string with a length of 15 characters that are left-justified. The .15 indicates that the string will be padded or truncated appropriately to equal exactly 15 characters. Table 5-3 shows the available Tcl string commands.

Table 5-3. *Summary of Tcl String Commands*

`string compare string#1 string#2`	Returns a -1, 0 or 1 if `string1` is lexicographically less than, equal to, or greater than `string2`.
`format format_string value#1 value#2...`	Returns a result equal to `format_string` except that the `value` arguments replace the % sequences in the `format string`.
`string first string#1 string#2`	Returns the index in `string#2` of the first character in the left-most substring that exactly matches `string#2`, or returns a -1 if there is no match.
`string last string#1 string#2`	Does exactly what `string first` does except that it matches to the right-most substring.
`string index string index`	Returns the character in `string` specified by `index`. The `index` of the first character in `string` is 0.
`string length string`	Returns the number of characters in `string`.
`string match pattern string`	Returns 1 if `pattern` matches `string` using glob style pattern-matching.
`string range string first_index last_index`	Returns the substring of `string` that lies between the `first_index` and the `last_index`.
`string tolower string`	Converts all uppercase values in `string to lowercase` and returns the new string.

Table 5-3. *Summary of Tcl String Commands (cont.)*

string toupper *string*	Converts all lowercase values in *string to uppercase* and returns the new string.
string trim *string [char]*	Trims all leading and trailing *chars* from *string* and returns the new string.
string trimleft *string [char]*	Same as *string trim* except that only leading *chars* are trimmed.
string trimright *string [char]*	Same as *string trim* except that only trailing *chars* are trimmed.

Glob-style Pattern-matching

Tcl offers two pattern-matching styles: *glob* and *regular expression*. Glob-style pattern-matching is useful in simple pattern-matching cases because it allows only absolute, wild card, and simple range or series matching. Table 5-4 shows the special characters allowed in glob-style pattern-matching.

Table 5-4. *Special Characters Allowed in Glob-style Pattern-matching*

*	Matches any sequence of zero or more characters.
?	Matches any single character.
[chars]	Matches any single character in *chars*. If *chars* is a sequence, like A-Z, any character between A and Z will be matched.
x	Matches *x* literally. Provides a way to match special characters like * and ?.

Regular Expressions for Pattern-matching

Regular expressions are more complex and powerful than glob-style patterns. Tcl's regular expressions are based on Henry Spencer's publicly-available implementation. Regular expressions use the concept of an atom, which can be a single character or a group of characters surrounded by the special matching characters. Table 5-5 shows the special characters allowed by regular expression pattern-matching.

Table 5-5. *Special Characters Permitted by Regular Expression Pattern-matching*

.	Matches any single character.
^	Matches the null string at the start of the input string.
$	Matches the null string at the end of the input string.
\x	Literally matches x (escapes special characters).
*	Matches a sequence of 0 or more of the preceding atom.
+	Matches a sequence of 1 or more of the preceding atom.
?	Matches either a null string or a single match of the preceding atom.
[chars]	Matches any single character from chars, or matches a sequence like A-Z.
(regexp)	Matches anything that matches regexp. Is used for grouping pieces of matching substrings.
regexp1 | regexp2	Matches regexp1 or regexp2.

The following example uses the regular expression pattern-matching command `regexp` and a special command called `regsub` (regular expression substitution) to clean up the input from an HTML form.

```
foreach pair $in_vars {
        regexp {(^.*)=(.*$)} $pair all name val
        regsub -all {\+} $val { } val
        regsub -all {\%0A} $val \n\t val;
        regsub -all {\%2C} $val {,} val
        regsub -all {\%27} $val {'} val
}
```

String Conversions

Because Tcl allows you to declare variables on the fly, it does not require that you declare data types for variables. Tcl treats all data as strings except during numerical operations. To keep precision for floating point numbers during these conversions between string and various numerical data types, you must set the `tcl_precision` variable at the beginning of the program. Setting the `tcl_precision` variable to 17 on a machine that uses IEEE floating point guarantees that you won't lose information during string conversions.

Tcl Error Handling

Errors that occur in Tcl cause the current command to abort. If the current command is called in the context of a script, the script is also aborted. Sometimes, these aborted scripts can cause Web Server errors to occur if they are not trapped and handled properly. One way to trap Tcl errors and the messages they generate is with the Tcl `catch` command. The `catch` command enables the program to trap errors without aborting the script, and, depending upon the error, allows the program to take appropriate action. The syntax for the `catch` command is:

```
catch {Tcl_command} [var_name]
```

`Var_name` catches normal and abnormal returns from `Tcl_command`, and then can be tested to see if the script should continue or gracefully exit.

For more complete coverage of the Tcl language, we recommend *Tcl and the Tk Toolkit* by John Ousterhout, or *Practical Programming in Tcl and Tk* by Brent Welch.

Using Sybtcl to Communicate with a Sybase SQL Server

Tcl provides you with tools for manipulating and formatting data in order to create a Web document. *Sybtcl* allows you to communicate with a Sybase SQL Server within a Tcl script and extends Tcl's capabilities by making Tcl commands available that utilize Sybase's CT-Lib/DB-Lib calls. Sybtcl opens a connection to a Sybase server, changes databases on that server, pipes SQL statements to the server, and returns data and error messages. If your Sybase server is on a different machine than your Web server and Tcl scripts, you need to make sure that the Sybase Open Client package is installed on the Web server machine in order for Sybtcl to work.

In this section, we'll show you how to use Sybtcl commands to open a connection to a Sybase SQL Server, select a database and send SQL statements, return status and error messages, and retrieve data from Sybase SQL Server. Table 5-6 summarizes the basic Sybtcl commands for retrieving data from a Sybase SQL Server.

Table 5-6. *Summary of Sybtcl Commands*

sybconnect *syb_userid syb_password syb_server*	Returns a connection (*db_conn_id*) to a Sybase SQL Server (much like an open returns a file descriptor), then uses it in subsequent commands.
sybuse *db_conn_id db_name*	Returns the name of the database selected if the command is successful.
sybsql *db_conn_id sql_statements [asynch]*	Sends *sql_statements* to the server. It returns the following: REG_ROW to indicate normal execution and that the data is now available; NO_MORE_ROWS to indicate normal execution and that no data is available; or PENDING if the asynch flag is used to indicate that the query is still executing.
sybnext *db_conn_id tcl_statements*	Fetches the next row of data available from the last executed SQL statement. Returns a row of data for manipulation by Tcl. Sets the global array sybmsg element nextrow to REG_ROWS or NO_MORE_ROWS.
sybpoll *db_conn_id [timeout] [all]*	Polls an executing query to see if it has finished. Returns a NULL if queries are still executing, or returns the *db_conn_id* of the queries that have finished. *[all]* checks all available *db_conn_id*'s.
sybclose *db_conn_id*	Closes a connection to Sybase.

Opening a Connection to a Sybase SQL Server

You can open a connection to a Sybase SQL Server using the sybconnect command: it returns an identifier that acts much like a file identifier after you have opened a file. Use this database connection identifier any time you want your program to interact with the database through this connection. The following code shows an example of setting some variables with the necessary information to establish the connection to Sybase SQL server, and then executing the sybconnect command to establish the connection.

```
set sybuser "youruser"
set sybpwd "userpwd"
set sybsrv "yourserver"

if { [catch {sybconnect $sybuser $sybpwd $sybsrv} dbcon] } {
  append err_msg $sybmsg(dberrstr)
  do_exit
}
```

Selecting a Database and Sending SQL Statements

Many times, you may want your program to open several connections to a database at once for different purposes. It is often convenient to have one connection for querying the database, and another for updating or inserting data. After you use `sybconnect` to connect to the database, you can use the `dbuse` command to select the database, then use the `sqlres` command to send SQL statements to the database connection. The following code shows this process.

```
set sybdb "company_x"

#Choosing the Database

set dbuse [sybuse $dbcon $sybdb]

#Check to see that the database got set properly

if { $dbuse != $sybdb } {
  append err_msg "Could Not Use Proper Database"
  do_exit
}
set sql_cmd "select last_name, first_name,
phone_number, address, city,  state, zip
                        from customer
                        where
customer_id = $cust_id"

if { [catch {sybsql $dbcon $sql_cmd} sqlres] } {
  append err_msg "QUERY ERROR $sybmsg(dberrstr)"
  do_exit
}
```

If your SQL statement does not fit on one line, you need to escape the newline characters with a backslash so that Tcl treats the entire string as the variable `sql_cmd`.

Returning Status and Error Messages

After Sybase processes the SQL statement, it returns a status message that is the return value of the sybsql command. The status message indicates if no data was returned, if data was returned, or if the query failed.

Sybtcl also provides an associative array called sybmsg for handling status and error messages. Some of the most common indices into sybmsg are dberrstr, nextrow, and coltypes. The dberrstr array element contains error messages from Sybase; nextrow supplies information about the status of the next row in the Sybase buffer; and coltypes returns data type information for the various columns.

Getting the Data

Sybase does not return the data automatically. The data from the query is stored in a buffer on the Sybase server. You need to retrieve it one row at a time using the sybnext command. You have two options for looping through all of the data returned by a query: you can use a Tcl looping construct such as a while loop, or you can use the sybnext command itself. When the sybnext command is executed as a standalone command, it returns the row of data as a Tcl list. Using sybnext as a looping construct allows you to use the @ notation to access the entire row of data with @0, or access the individual columns using @ and the number of the column. The example below illustrates using sybnext to process the individual columns from the row that is being returned:

```
sybnext $dbcon {
    set lnm @1
    set fnm @2
    set phone @3
    set addr @4
    set city @5
    set state @6
    set zip @7
}
```

There are times when you don't want sybnext to use looping. In the code below, a Tcl list variable is set to a single row of data returned from the Sybase server. You can control how the data is retrieved from Sybase using a while loop that tests the value of sybmsg(nextrow).

```
set data_row [sybnext $dbcon]
while { $sybmsg(nextrow) != "NO_MORE_ROWS" } {
  set mo [lindex $data_row 0]
  set pid [lindex $data_row 1]
  set prod [lindex $data_row 2]
  set ttl [lindex $data_row 3]
  set qtr_ttl [expr $qtr_ttl + $ttl]
  puts [format "%-8.8s  %4d  %-35.35s  %11.2f" $mo $pid $prod $ttl]
  set data_row [sybnext $dbcon]
}
```

Using Expect to Handle Interactions between Tcl and Other Programs

Expect is an extension to Tcl that provides a way to automate the interaction between Tcl and interactive programs such as ISQL. Use Expect to communicate with a Sybase SQL Server when Sybtcl is not available on the computer you are using, or when you require interaction with the server that is not covered by Sybtcl.

Expect uses both glob and regular expression pattern-matching, operating on the basis of pattern action pairs. Expect looks for certain patterns coming from a process and then initiates actions to that process. Table 5-7 shows the commands used by Expect to initiate and interact with a process.

Table 5-7. *Summary of Commands Used in an ISQL Expect Script*

spawn *program_name*	Starts *program_name* and returns a spawn_id that is used for other commands.
send [*-i spawn_id]* *text_string*	Sends a *text_string* to a process. If the -i and *spawn_id* is not specified, it sends the *text_string* to the most recently spawned process.
expect *text_string* [{ *action* }]	expects *text_string* back from a process. If the *action* is used, it executes upon matching the *text_string*.

The following sections show you how to use Expect within a Tcl script to start an ISQL process, send SQL commands to the ISQL process, and return the results of a query.

Invoking ISQL from an Expect Script and Sending a Command

The example below shows you how to invoke ISQL from an Expect script. `$isql_cmd` is the path to the Sybase ISQL command; `$srv` is the name of the Sybase server to which the connection is made; `$usr` is the Sybase user ID; and `$pwd` is the Sybase password.

```
#Open connection to sybase server via isql.

  spawn -noecho $isql_cmd -S $srv -n -w 2056 -U $usr
  expect {
        -re "^Password: "
               { send "$pwd\r\n"; exp_continue }
        -re "\r\n" {}
        -re "Login failed" {
             puts "ERROR 13 login failed to $srv"
             return  0
        }
        timeout
             { puts "Server ERROR 14 Timed out starting $srv"; return  0 }
             eof { puts "Server ERROR 15 eof on $srv at startup"; return  0 }
  }
```

After the ISQL process is invoked, SQL commands can be sent to that process. The following example shows how to send a simple SQL statement to the open ISQL connection.

```
send -i $spawn_id
"select last_name, first name
from company_x..customer\n\go\n";
```

Interpreting the Command Results and Parsing the Data

After the SQL command is sent, Expect needs to interpret the results and parse out the data. The `expect` command gets data from the input buffer, performs pattern matching, and takes the action indicated when there is a match. When a match is made, it fills the different elements of the `$expect_out` array with various pieces of the data from the input buffer, and takes the indicated action. If there are any more matching statements in the `expect` block, Expect attempts to use those to match the remaining data in the input buffer. The `exp_continue` command has the effect of causing the `expect` command to act like a loop. When a pattern is matched that has the `exp_continue` command as its action, the current `expect` command is executed again.

The following example shows Expect looking for data and discarding the header lines and other extraneous information that it gets back from ISQL.

```
expect {
-i $sql_id
-re "^\r\n" { exp_continue }
-re "^ —.*- \r\n" { exp_continue }
-re "^ *\r\n" { exp_continue }
-re "^.\[0-9]+ rows? affected.\r\n$" {exp continue }
-re "^select.*\r\ngo\r\n" { exp_continue }
-re "^ \[^\r\n]+\r\n" { exp_continue }
```

The next example is still within the `expect` statement, and illustrates how Expect handles data that it wants to keep. `$sep` is the separator character with which ISQL was invoked, and `reslist` is the name of the list variable in which the data is returned to the calling program.

```
-re "^$sep\[^\r\n]*$sep\r\n" {
        regsub -all "\[\r\n]" $expect_out(buffer) "" tempstring
        regsub -all "^$sep" $tempstring "" tempstring
        if { $tempstring != "^$" } {
            lappend reslist $tempstring
        }
            exp_continue
}
-re "^Msg.*\r\n" {
        set tempstring $expect_out(buffer)
        if { $tempstring != "^$" } {
            set err_msg $tempstring
            set errs 1
        }
}
```

You may need to experiment with matching patterns and the order of pattern matching within the `expect` block to produce the results you want. However, you will find that Expect is a useful tool for creating a communication link between an HTML form and an interactive program like ISQL.

Tcl and the WWW Server

Regardless of the type of server you are using (for example, NCSA's HTTP server or Netscape server), it must be configured to run Tcl as CGI scripts. Configuring Tcl to do this usually involves telling the server two things: first, to allow executables with a Tcl extension; and second, the location of the executables. The typical location for executables is the CGI-bin directory, but you can use any directory as long as you set the proper permissions.

In this section, we'll tell you about some considerations for linking Tcl and the WWW Server, which include the environment variables for creating a communication link between HTML forms and Tcl CGI scripts, and issues related to data integrity.

Creating a Communication Link Between HTML Forms and Tcl CGI Scripts

The environment variables provided by the Web server are the key to creating a communication link between an HTML form and Tcl CGI script. Tcl stores environment variables in an associative array called env in which the names of the environment variable are the indices into the array. Most Web servers provide the following environment variables:

```
AUTH_TYPE
CONTENT_LENGTH
CONTENT_TYPE
HTTP_ACCEPT
PATH_INFO
REMOTE_ADDR
REMOTE_HOST
SCRIPT_NAME
SERVER_NAME
SERVER_SOFTWARE
GATEWAY_INTERFACE
QUERY_STRING
REMOTE_USER
SERVER_PORT
REQUEST_METHOD
SERVER_PROTOCOL
```

See Appendix C, "CGI Environment Variables and Return Codes" for descriptions of the environment variables.

The environment variables that handle how data is passed between HTML forms, documents, and the CGI script are: CONTENT_LENGTH, QUERY_STRING, and PATH_INFO.

HTML forms using the POST method pass the variables NAME and VALUE to a CGI script in the CONTENT_LENGTH environment variable. If the form utilizes the

GET method, the NAME and VALUE variables are passed in the QUERY_STRING environment variable. An HTML form that utilizes the POST method and contains the following elements:

```
<P>
Select the year, month and product you wish to review:
</P>
<SELECT NAME="YR" SINGLE SIZE=5>
<OPTION VALUE="1994"> 1994
<OPTION VALUE="1995"> 1995
</SELECT>
<SELECT NAME="MONTH" SINGLE SIZE=5>
<OPTION VALUE="January"> January
<OPTION VALUE="February"> February
            .
            .
            .
<OPTION VALUE="December"> December
</SELECT>
<HR>
<PRE>
Product     Select
Widget A    <INPUT TYPE="RADIO" NAME="PROD" VALUE="1"\ ALIGN="TOP">
Widget B    <INPUT TYPE="RADIO" NAME="PROD" VALUE="2"\ ALIGN="TOP">
Widget C    <INPUT TYPE="RADIO" NAME="PROD" VALUE="3"\ ALIGN="TOP">
</PRE>
```

. . . could be parsed with the following Tcl code:

```
set in_vars [split [read stdin $env(CONTENT_LENGTH)] &]
foreach pair $in_vars {
  regexp {(^.*)=(.*$)} $pair all name val
  regsub -all {\+} $val { } val
  regsub -all {\%0A} $val \n\t val;
  regsub -all {\%2C} $val {,} val
  regsub -all {\%27} $val {'} val
  switch $name {
        #Year comes from a scrolling list of all available years
        YR {
                if { $val != "" } {
                        set year $val
                }
        }
        #The months are a scrolling list
        MONTH {
                if { $val != "" } {
                        set mo $val
                }
        }
```

```
PROD {
        if { $val != "" } {
                set prod $val
        }
}
}
}
```

If the form utilized the GET method instead of POST, the only difference in the Tcl would be in the line that splits the input. Instead of reading:

```
set in_vars [split [read stdin $env(CONTENT_LENGTH)] &]
```

the Tcl code would read:

```
set in_vars [split $env(QUERY_STRING) &]
```

HTML text variables work the same way. Whatever the user types in the text area gets passed as the value for that variable.

The PATH_INFO environment variable provides a way to pass information from an HTML document or form to a CGI script without using form elements. The information being passed is appended to the end of the path to the CGI script. The HTTP server loads that information into the PATH_INFO environment variable, which can then be accessed by the CGI script. Drill-down reports provide one example of how you might use this capability. The initial report may be generated by some user input to a form that calls a CGI script. The report that is generated is not an HTML form, but a document. Portions of the document can then be hotlinked to other CGI scripts that generate other related reports.

Below is an example of some HTML that passes information to a CGI script in the PATH_INFO environment variable.

```
<A href="http://sales_dtl.tcl/January:1995:1">January   WIDGET A
$300.00</A>
```

The last item in the path is the information stored in the PATH_INFO environment variable. The Tcl code that would parse out that information for use by a script could look like this:

```
set in_vars split $env(PATH_INFO) ":"

set mo [lindex $in_vars 0]
set yr [lindex $in_vars 1]
set prod [lindex $in_vars 2]
```

The use of the colon to separate fields is arbitrary. You could use another character, or none at all if the information is fixed in length. If the information is fixed in length, you could use the `string range` command to substring it out.

Checking Data Integrity

After the data is received from the HTML form and parsed by the Tcl CGI script, it must be checked for integrity. Checking the integrity of the data coming into a CGI script is extremely important when using the Web as an interface to Sybase. Clever hackers find ways to do things like sending your password files to themselves if the parameters for your scripts are not carefully checked to make sure that they are what the program was expecting.

With Tcl, this checking must take place on the server. There is no way to limit what someone can put into an HTML text field except for its length. To avoid having the server do a lot of work just to return errors to the user, the most efficient thing you can do is check the data up front using Tcl's pattern-matching tools. Below is an example of checking a value coming from an HTML form to make sure that it is an integer.

```
if { $val != "" } {
        set QtyA $val
        if { [regexp {^[0-9]+$} $QtyA] != 1 } {
            append err_msg "Quantity for Widget A "
            append err_msg "must be an integer"
            do_exit
        }
}
```

To return error messages to the user and avoid having trivial messages cause server errors, you must identify the output to the HTTP server as being HTML. A good way to do this is to place the following lines at the beginning of your Tcl CGI script. These lines output a basic HTML header and then flush the standard out buffer to make sure that the HTML header is the first output that the HTTP server gets from the CGI script.

```
set Hdr "Content-type: text/HTML\n\n<HTML>\n<HEAD>\n"
append Hdr "<TITLE>SCRIPT TITLE report:</TITLE>\n</HEAD>\n<BODY>"
puts $Hdr
flush stdout
```

The reason you want to flush the standard out buffer is that sometimes the output of a `puts` statement gets stored in the standard out buffer, which gives other output streams the chance to reach the HTTP server before the HTML code does. If this happens, the HTTP server may not know how to interpret what it is receiving, and an error will occur.

CGI scripts should have an exit procedure to deliver any error messages and perform any cleanup. Sometimes, it is helpful to deliver certain error messages to a system administrator as well as the user via e-mail. Below is an example of an exit procedure:

```
proc do_exit {} {
  global err_msg
  global msg_file
  if { $err_msg != "" } {
        puts [format "<PRE> %s </PRE></BODY>"
  $err_msg"
  }
  if { file exists $msg_file } {
        [eval exec /usr/bin/mailx sysadmin <
  $msg_file]
        [eval exec rm $msg_file]
  }
  exit
}
```

WWW Applications Using Tcl and Sybase

Applications involving forms and databases can be divided into two general categories: 1) applications that report information based on a user's request initiated by a click on a hotlink in an HTML document, or by a CGI script generated when a user fills out an HTML form; and 2) applications that update a database based on some input from the user. In this section, we'll show you how to use HTML forms and Tcl CGI scripts to generate reports and update a Sybase SQL Server.

Generating Reports from the Database

You have two options for generating reports using Sybase SQL Server and the Web. If you generate only a few reports and the data does not change very often, you can run reports in batch mode and store them as standard HTML documents. This method provides very fast access to the user, but can become unmanageable if the data changes often or if you generate many different reports. (We're not going to cover batch mode in this section.)

If the latter is the case, your second option is to provide the user with *parameterized* reports that are generated on the fly using Tcl CGI scripts. You can create parameterized reports and then allow the user to input the parameters via an HTML form, or allow hard-coded parameters to be passed to a CGI script as part of the path to the CGI script (using the PATH_INFO environment variable). In this section, we'll show you how to create both types of parameterized reports.

Creating Parameterized Reports with User-defined Parameters

When a user inputs parameters into an HTML form to specify the report they want, the form calls the Tcl CGI script to generate the appropriate HTML along with the data. An example of this is the quarterly sales report from the ABC Widget Company. The user specifies in an HTML form the year and quarter they want to view. The form passes these parameters to a Tcl script that queries the database for the information, and then formats the information with the appropriate HTML. The following examples guide you through getting the parameters from a form, parsing the data, querying the database, and returning a report. Figure 5-1 shows the qsum.html form used to request specific quarters.

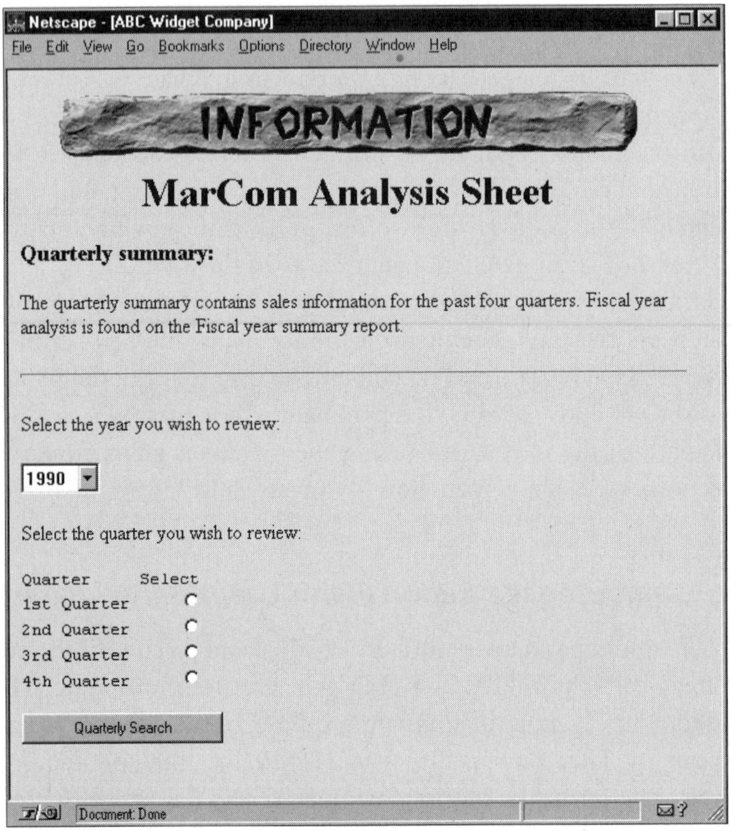

Figure 5-1. *A qsum.html form for inputting parameters*
to the quarterly report

In the qsum.html form, the user chooses radio buttons and pick lists to indicate the year and quarter from which they want information. The form passes the user request to the qtr_report.tcl script in the CONTENT_LENGTH environment variable. Because the form presets the values of the variables, minimal checking is required. The qtr_report.tcl script parses this information and sets variables to build the query, as shown below:

```
set in_vars [split [read stdin $env(CONTENT_LENGTH)] &]
foreach pair $in_vars {
  regexp {(^.*)=(.*$)} $pair all name val
  regsub -all {\+} $val { } val
  regsub -all {\%0A} $val \n\t val;
  regsub -all {\%2C} $val {,} val
  regsub -all {\%27} $val {'} val
```

```
  switch $name {
        #Year comes from a scrolling list of all available years.
        YR {
              if { $val != "" } {
                    set year $val
              }
        }
        #The quarters are radio buttons on the form.
        QRTR_SUM {
              if { $val != "" } {
                    set qtr $val
              }
        }
  }
}
switch $qtr {
  1 {
        set title "First Quarter "
        set begmo "1"
        set endmo "3"
  }
              .
              .
              .
  4 {
        set title "Fourth Quarter "
        set begmo "10"
        set endmo "12"
  }
}
```

After the year and the month ranges have been set, you can build the query statement, as shown:

```
set syb_cmd "select datename(month,o.order_date), p.produce_id,
p.description, sum(o.cost)
from cust_order o, product p
where datepart(month,o.order_date) >= $begmo and
      datepart(month,o.order_date) <= $endmo and
      o.product_id = p.product_id
group by datename(month,o.order_date), p.description"
```

The rows returned by the query can then be formatted with HTML statements to produce a report, as shown:

```
set data_row [sybnext $dbcon]

while { $sybmsg(nextrow) != "NO_MORE_ROWS" } {
  set mo [lindex $data_row 0]
```

```
set pid [lindex $data_row 1]
set prod [lindex $data_row 2]
set ttl [lindex $data_row 3]
set qtr_ttl [expr $qtr_ttl + $ttl]
set sumline [format "<STRONG>%-8.8s    %-40.40s
%11.2f</STRONG>" $mo $prod $ttl]
set data_row [sybnext $dbcon]
}
```

Figure 5-2 shows the report generated by the query.

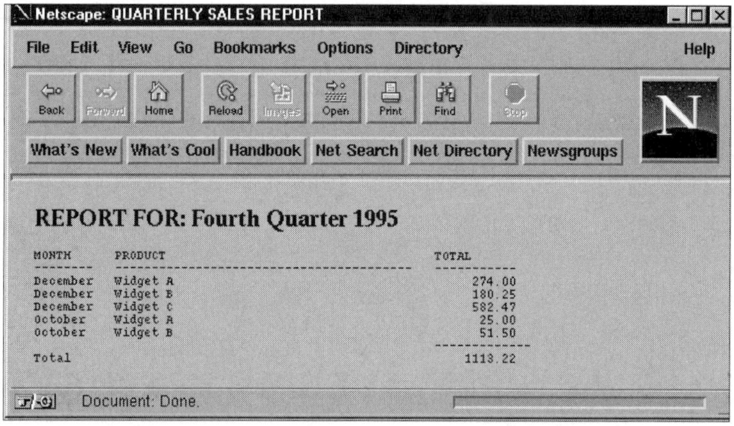

Figure 5-2. *Output of the quarterly report*

Creating Parameterized Reports from Hard-coded Input

In static Web documents, relationships between reports are expressed in the form of hotlinks that link one topic in a document to another document containing related information. You can use the same concept to create drill-down reports that allow interactive Web reporting. The drill-down reports covered in this section are examples of calling a parameterized report in which the parameters are not directly generated by the user.

At the same time that you're gathering data to create a simple report based on user input, you can also gather data to create links to any related reports using HREF parameters. These parameters are passed to the next level of CGI script in the PATH_INFO environment variable. In the report displayed in Figure 5-2, only the month, product name, and the total for the product are printed, but other data is gathered by the query that can be used to create the parameters to feed another report. The following code shows how to create a hotlink to another report that can be called from the first report.

```
set sumline [format "%-8.8s    %-40.40s    %11.2f" $mo
$prod $ttl]
set href [format "<A href=\"http:sales_dtl.tcl/
%s:%s:%s\">%s"
          $mo $yr $pid $sumline]
append href "</A>"
puts "$href\r"
```

Figure 5-3 shows the quarterly sales report with a hotlink to a report that contains the detail behind the summary information.

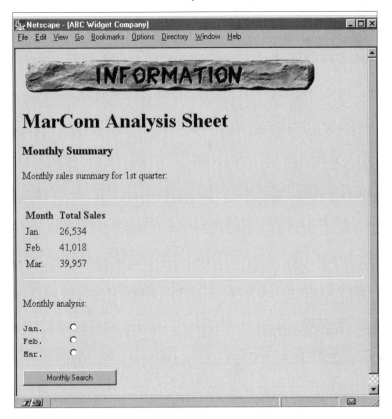

Figure 5-3. *Quarterly sales report with drill-down to sales detail report*

If a user were to click on the January line for Widget A, they would get the following detail report.

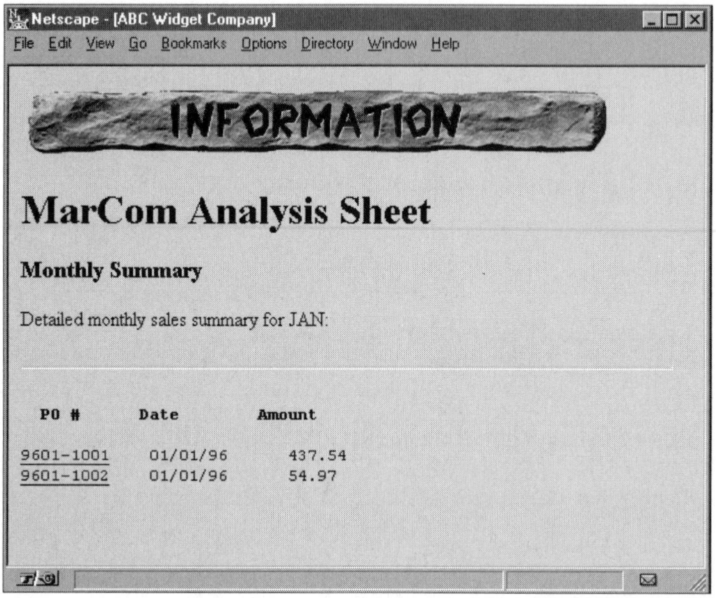

Figure 5-4. *The sales detail report "drilled-down" from quarterly sales report*

You can create as many links as you want (keeping in mind that there's a sensible limit) to create a system of reports that provide the highest level of summary down to the lowest possible level of detail.

Updating the Database

Interactions with databases are typically not based on reporting alone: there has to be a way to get the data into the database. Figure 5-5 shows a form used for ordering Widgets from our famous ABC Widget Company. The information the user enters into the form is parsed and checked for content integrity, then sent to the database through a SQL call.

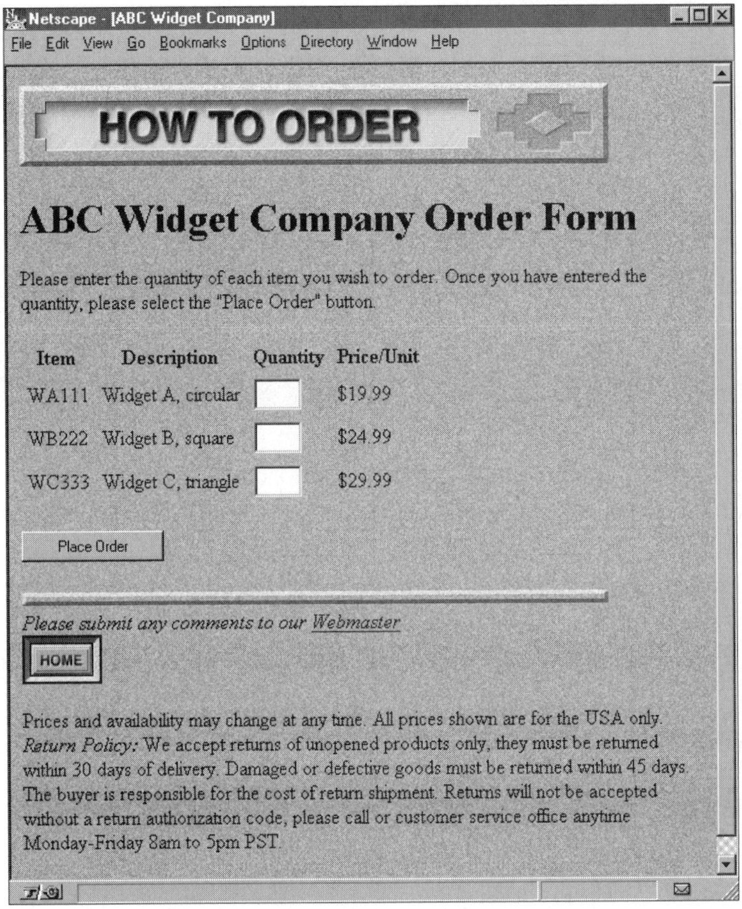

Figure 5-5. The widget order entry screen

More specifically, when the user fills in the order entry screen, the form calls the enter_order.tcl script that queries the database and builds the confirmation form, which is a new HTML form. The confirmation form shows the user what will be inserted into the database, and asks for a confirmation. The confirmation form also prompts existing customers to update their address if necessary, and prompts new customers to add their address information to the database. Below is an example of some of the Tcl code that prints the new form based on values from the database, and values from the previous form.

```
puts "<FORM METHOD=\"POST\" ACTION=\"http:update_order.tcl/$params\">"
if { $cust_id != "NOID" } {
  puts "<PRE>"
  puts "Customer Information"
  puts "$fnm $lnm $phone"
  puts "$addr"
  puts "$city, $state, $zip"
  puts "</PRE>"
  puts "<INPUT TYPE=\"RADIO\" NAME=\"CUSTSTAT\"\ VALUE=\"C\">Has your
address changed?"
} else {
  puts "<INPUT TYPE=\"RADIO\" NAME=\"CUSTSTAT\"\ VALUE=\"N\">Are you a new
customer?"
}
```

When the user selects the Place Order button, the order information is added to the database, and the customer information is updated if required. This form passes information to the update_order.tcl form in the CONTENT_LENGTH and PATH_INFO environment variables. The variable $params, built earlier in the script, consists of a string with no white spaces and no special characters that contains the customer number and the quantity and cost of the widgets ordered. The fields are separated by colons and are then parsed using the split command in the update_order.tcl script. The CONTENT_LENGTH environment variable contains the information from the radio buttons and the address fields. The Tcl code below shows how the PATH_INFO information is parsed and assigned to variables.

```
set var_list [split $env(PATH_INFO) :]
set cust_num [string trimleft [lindex $var_list 0]\ "/"]
set prod_list {}
set widget_list {}
lappend widget_list "1"
lappend widget_list [lindex $var_list 1]
lappend widget_list [lindex $var_list 2]
lappend prod_list $widget_list
```

From the CONTENT_LENGTH and PATH_INFO environment variables, the update_order.tcl script generates the SQL necessary to update the database. The script adds new records to the cust_order table and updates, inserts, or ignores the customer table. The Tcl code below generates the SQL calls necessary to perform the update.

```
foreach prod $prod_list {
  set prod_id [lindex $prod 0]
  set qty [lindex $prod 1]
  set cost [lindex $prod 2]
  if { $qty != 0 && $cost != 0 } {
      set syb_cmd "insert into cust_order(order_id, customer_id, product_id,
          order_date, quantity, cost) values($nu_order_id, $cust_num,
          $prod_id, '$odt', $qty, $cost)"
  if {[catch {sybsql $dbcon $syb_cmd} sqlres]} {
      append err_msg "NEW ORDER FAILED FOR $prod_id"
          append err_msg " $sybmsg(dberrstr)"
      }
  }
}
```

After the database is updated, the script retrieves the information from the
database and generates HTML output to display to the user what was actually
put into the database. Figure 5-6 shows an example of a Web page returned
from the database.

Figure 5-6. *A generated Web page with data returned from the database*

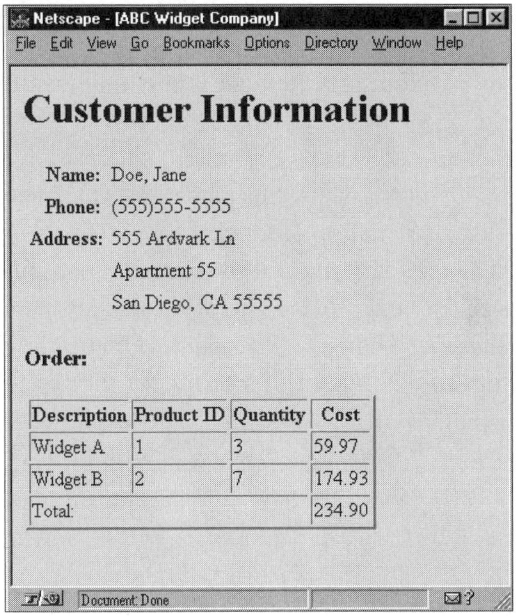

One disadvantage of doing data entry from an HTML form is that there is no way to give the user feedback about the validity of the data entry until the data is sent to the server. This problem is minimized by making intelligent use of scrolling pick lists and radio buttons, and by doing as much data integrity checking as possible in the script. See "Checking Data Integrity" earlier in this chapter.

Creating Flexible Applications

Creating flexible user applications with Sybase SQL Server, Tcl, and the Web requires some planning up front. Always remember that when using the Web, you basically sacrifice knowing how and where users will enter your application. This provides some challenges for programming, but it frees the user from having to rely on a programmer's preconceived notions about how they go about their job and the order in which they do things. A good example of different user approaches is how users access reports. Some users access them by drilling-down from other reports, while others want to select a report menu item. This section shows you how to create a flexible reporting system that can accommodate both approaches.

The first step in developing a flexible reporting structure is developing a core program for the report that takes a number of command-line arguments and produces the appropriate HTML document. There are two feeder scripts for this core program. The first feeder script parses the information coming from a user form and gets its information from the CONTENT_LENGTH environment variable. This script has to do a fair amount of data integrity checking, especially if there are text fields on the user form. The other feeder script handles the drill-down situation and parses the PATH_INFO environment variable. Minimal data integrity checking has to be done in this script because this data is not coming directly from user input. Figure 5-7 shows a schema for feeder and core scripts.

Figure 5-7. Schema for feeder and core scripts for reporting system

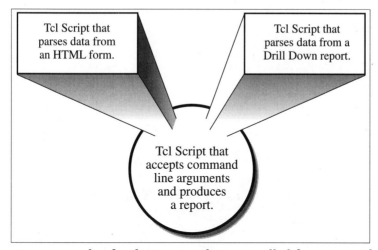

Below is an example of a short script that gets called from a user form that in turn calls the sales_dtl.tcl script with the appropriate arguments.

```
#! /opt2/local/bin/tclsh
set Hdr "Content-type: text/HTML\n\n<HTML>\n<HEAD>\n"
append Hdr "<TITLE>SALES DETAIL REPORT</TITLE>\n</HEAD>\n<BODY>"
puts $Hdr
flush stdout

#This section parses and cleans up the variables
#coming in from the input
#form using regular expression pattern matching.

set in_vars [split [read stdin $env(CONTENT_LENGTH)] &]
foreach pair $in_vars {
        regexp {(^.*)=(.*$)} $pair all name val
        regsub -all {\+} $val { } val
        regsub -all {\%0A} $val \n\t val;
        regsub -all {\%2C} $val {,} val
        regsub -all {\%27} $val {'} val
        switch $name {
                #Year comes from a scrolling list of all available years
                YR {
                        if { $val != "" } {
                                set year $val
                        }
                }
                #The months are a scrolling list
                MONTH {
                        if { $val != "" } {
                                set mo $val
                        }
```

```
                    }
                    PROD {
                            if { $val != "" } {
                                    set prod $val
                            }
                    }
            }
}

set progdir "/full_path /cgi-bin"

puts "[eval exec $progdir/sales_dtl.tcl $mo $year $prod]"
```

For the drill-down report, the feeder script is even shorter.

```
#! /opt2/local/bin/tclsh


set in_vars [split $env(PATH_INFO) ":"]

set mo [string trimleft [lindex $in_vars 0] "/"]
set yr [lindex $in_vars 1]
set prod [lindex $in_vars 2]

set Hdr "Content-type: text/HTML\n\n<HTML>\n<HEAD>\n"
append Hdr "<TITLE>ABC WIDGET COMPANY:</TITLE>\n</HEAD>\n<BODY>"
puts $Hdr
flush stdout

set prog_dir "/full_path/cgi-bin"


puts "[eval exec $prog_dir/sales_dtl.tcl $mo $yr $prod]"
```

Both of the feeder scripts output the HTML header, but the rest of the page building is done by the reporting script. The reason for this is that if there are any errors along the way, there is a reasonable chance that they will get output to the user and not cause a server error.

More Tcl Resources

Tcl and Sybtcl are available via anonymous ftp from: ftp.aud.alcatel.com. Expect is available via anonymous ftp from ftp.cme.nist.com. Below is a list of some other good sources of information about Tcl, Sybtcl and Expect:

- D.A. Clark's WWW page http://www.ucolick.org/~de

- http://sybase.pnl.gov.2080/Sybase/Sybase_interface_builder_ Sybtcl_abstract

- The Internet news group comp.lan.tcl

- *Tcl and the Tk Toolkit* by John Ousterhout

- *Expect* by Don Libes.

Summary

With Tcl, Sybase, and a Web server, you can quickly develop flexible, platform-independent applications for reporting and data entry. In this chapter, we showed you how to use Tcl and several of its extensions to create CGI scripts that access and update data in Sybase SQL Server, and create new HTML documents and forms. With this knowledge, you're on your way toward developing flexible and platform independent applications at a fraction of the cost of similar cross-platform development tools.

6

Using Java for Client-side Programming

In April, 1995 Sun Microsystems posted an experimental Web browser named HotJava on the Web. This browser was written in an object-oriented language named Java, also developed at Sun. HotJava supported extensibility to HTML features by automatically loading compiled Java programs from the Web server back to the Web client, and executing them through the Web browser. By January, 1996, Netscape provided commercial support for Java within their Navigator 2.0 browser, and Spry, IBM, and Oracle had announced plans for Java support in future releases of their Web browsers. Java development tools and Java-enabled Web browsers are now available on Windows NT, Windows 95, MacOS, and UNIX platforms.

In this chapter, we'll present a summary of the Java programming language and demonstrate Java's features by showing you how to implement a *smart* order-entry system. The application creates a spreadsheet-like interface on a Web page that interacts with Sybase SQL Server through a Perl script running on any machine with network access to the Web client and the machine running Sybase SQL Server. This application differs from those in the previous chapters in the following ways:

- The HTML forms code that runs on the browser is replaced by the Java program we create. The resulting entry form is *smart* because it checks for valid data and computes order totals on-the-fly on the client-side versus performing those functions on the server-side. All of the user interaction for selecting items and placing the order is compressed into one Web page.

- The CGI script that runs on the Web server is replaced by a Perl script that accepts a network socket connection from the Java program. Interaction with Sybase SQL Server proceeds across this connection rather than through the Web server.

Because we use object-oriented programming in our application example, you will find this chapter easier to follow if you are already familiar with object-oriented concepts and the basic syntax of C or C++. However, we have organized the material into the following sections so an experienced programmer who is unfamiliar with these concepts should be able to understand them.

- The Java Language

- The Java Run-time Environment

- Writing a Simple Java Program

- Writing a Java Applet

- Building a Java Graphical User Interface

- Connecting Java to Sybase SQL Server

- Tips and Tricks.

The Java Language

Java was designed to be a compact, machine-independent, and object-oriented programming language. Its basic syntax and language constructs are very similar to those in C and C++. Java has a small and well-defined set of primitive data types and the means to create *classes* of programmer-defined *objects*. Java source code is compiled to an abstract machine code called *bytecodes* that was originally defined for a *virtual computer*. Java programs require a run-time environment that simulates the virtual computer by interpreting the bytecodes.

Two primary goals of the Java design were simplicity and removing redundancy. Temptations to add powerful, expressive features were offset by the desire to create relatively small and robust compilers and interpreters. Although not as minimalist as Nicholas Wirth's *Oberon* language, Java is often first viewed in terms of the features it *doesn't* have. The most prominent features found in C and C++ that are missing in Java include:

- The Preprocessor. Java eliminates the preprocessor compiler found in C and C++, thus eliminating the `#include`, `#define`, `#ifdef`, and related constructs.

- Structures and Unions. Both of these C features relate to how the programmer controls memory representation. As you will see in the following sections, part of Java's portability and security model is its limitation on defining how programs and data are stored into memory. Like Structures, Java Classes (described later) allow you to logically group variables, but there is no guarantee of how the variables are physically grouped. Unions have no meaning in a language that doesn't concern itself with memory representation.

- Goto Statements. Java provides a rich set of control structures and a powerful exception control mechanism, eliminating the temptation to write "spaghetti code."

- Operator Overloading. Operator overloading allows the programmer to define methods within classes that *overload* the standard operators like + and - with special meaning. Operator overloading places a significant burden on the compiler and has the potential to confuse those who later have to maintain code containing conflicting definitions for a commonly-used operator. Java makes one special exception: it supports the + operator for string concatenation.

- Pointers. Java eliminates user-accessible memory pointers, forcing the programmer to consider alternate programming tactics such as using arrays of objects. Although it is often shocking to C and C++ programmers, programmers of other languages including Visual Basic and Smalltalk have prospered without pointers.

Basic Java Syntax

This section provides an overview of the basic Java syntax for the Java language. The sections "Writing a Simple Java Program," "Writing a Java Applet," and "Connecting Java to Sybase SQL Server" build upon the basics learned in the example code throughout this section. For the complete syntax, refer to the *Java Language Definition* found at the following location on the Java Web server:

```
http://www.javasoft.com
```

The basic unit of compilation is a text file, typically with a name extension of .java. The text file can contain a statement that declares the *package* to which all of the symbols defined in the text file belong, and statements that import symbols from other packages. The body of the text file then has declarations of classes or class interfaces. The basic structure of a java file is:

```
<Package Declaration>
<Import Statement>
.
.
.
<Class or Interface Declaration>
.
.
.
```

Unlike C++, Java strictly enforces object orientation: all procedures (called *methods*) and variables must be encapsulated within class declarations.

Naming Conventions

Java is case-sensitive. There is a difference between the symbols "java," "Java," and "JAVA," which is the same as in C and C++, but may be a new twist for FORTRAN or COBOL programmers.

Java provides great flexibility in defining names for classes, methods, and variables. Names have the following characteristics:

- No arbitrary length limit (usually naturally limited by the patience of the programmers)

- Cannot start with a number

- Cannot have any of the normal code delimiters or separators, such as ; or }

- Cannot be one of the Java reserved words listed in Table 6-1.

Table 6-1. *Java Reserved Words*

abstract	do	implements	package	throw
boolean	double	import	private	throws
break	else	inner	protected	transient
byte	extends	instanceof	public	try
case	final	int	rest	var
cast	finally	interface	return	void
catch	float	long	short	volatile
char	for	native	static	while
class	future	new	super	
const	generic	null	switch	
continue	goto	operator	synchronized	
default	if	outer	this	

Java Statements

Java statements are delimited with the semicolon. You can include more than one statement per line (Java doesn't impose a limitation on the length of lines), but experience and common sense has convinced most programmers of any language to limit lines to a page width of 60-79 characters.

You can code comments in two ways: you can follow the classic C convention and enclose them within /* and */ anywhere in the file, or you can precede them with double slashes (//). We use the latter method throughout this chapter.

Blocks of Java statements are delimited by curly braces ({}). A *block* of statements includes an entire class declaration, an entire method declaration, and all of the statements bounded by the language control constructs.

Data Types

Java supports a very limited and basic set of data types and does not provide mechanisms such as operator overloading to create user-defined data types. There are two families of data types in Java: primitive types and objects. The primitive data types consist of integers, characters, floating point numbers, and booleans. Objects include arrays, strings, and programmer-defined classes. We'll describe each of these in this section.

Integers

Java supports only signed integer types in four sizes: byte (8-bits), short (16-bits), int (32-bits), and long (64-bits). Unlike C and C++, Java specifies the size of its primitive types, eliminating one frequent source of machine incompatibility.

Characters

Characters, `char`, are represented as 16-bit Unicode values to accommodate different languages. This is a significant departure from languages such as C and FORTRAN, which use 8-bit characters.

Floating Point Numbers

Java supports both single- and double-precision floating point numbers in conformance with the IEEE 754 standard: `float` (32-bit) and `long` (64-bit).

Booleans

There is a boolean type called `boolean` that can be `true` or `false`. Java does not allow you to cast integer values to booleans, or vice versa. Although this restriction may require a little more code, it results in safer code and eliminates any questions or portability issues as to which integers are equivalent to `true` and `false`.

Arrays

Arrays are special objects that contain ordered sets of other primitive types or objects. Elements of an array are indexed by a non-negative integer. Arrays have only one dimension, but you can easily declare and use arrays of arrays. An array variable is actually a reference to an array object: after you declare the variable, you must create the array object using `new`, as shown below:

```
int testarray[];
testarray = new int[100];
```

For convenience, you can declare and initialize an array in one line:

```
int testarray[] = new int[100];
```

Arrays are dynamic and aren't created until runtime, a benefit of a dynamic language. You can't resize arrays after you create them. Arrays always have their indices checked: you cannot turn off this feature.

Strings

Strings are objects in their own right: they are *not* arrays of characters. Java provides the + operator to concatenate two strings. String literals can't span two lines, but can be concatenated:

```
String VeryLongString = "This string won't fit" +
"on one line!";
```

In this example, the string initializer is used by the compiler to provide the appropriate object allocation.

Classes

We live in a world of hierarchies. When we talk about an *instance* of a human being, we know that he or she has certain attributes and behaviors common to the general *class* of humans. In fact, we know that humans inherit the attributes of mammals, which in turn inherit the attributes of animals, which in turn inherit the attributes of life forms.

This is an important analogy. When we say that humans are mammals, we automatically know that certain attributes exist: they are warm blooded, bear their young, and so on. Humans can be considered a *subclass* of mammals. When we talk about other *subclasses* of mammals, we only need to describe how they are different from other subclasses of mammals: knowing that they are mammals eliminates the need to fully describe them.

Without such class hierarchies, we would have to waste a lot of effort fully describing everyday objects. As it is, when someone tells us they have a Rolls Royce, we recognize that they are referring to a class of automobile and we immediately infer many things about it, even assuming that we could drive one: all we really need to know is how it is different from other automobiles.

Class hierarchy is the basis of object-oriented programming. The success of this programming methodology results from the efficiencies of inheritance: we can re-use the software of a parent class, only adding or modifying code unique to our new subclass. Designing software classes to encourage and sustain software reuse is by no means trivial. It is usually easier to think of all the programming elements as stand-alone functions. Traditionally, this means defining a main program and supporting procedures and functions, and possibly throwing in a few global variables to tie everything together. As we will see later, Java doesn't allow this programming method.

In Java, like other object-oriented programming languages, a class definition has both data and code. Code is included in methods that, when called, may have arguments passed to them, and may return a single result. You will see a special type of method in our examples called a *constructor*. A constructor method has the same name as the class in which it is defined, and is called when an object is first created. We use constructors to create initialized instances of classes.

The basic syntax for a class includes the declaration of the class name, its parent class (if any), and declarations of its variables and methods, as shown in the following code:

```
class ClassName extends ParentClass {

    // This class will have only one additional
    // class variable in addition to what is
    // already in ParentClass.

    boolean ClassVariable;

    // A constructor method has the same
    // name as its class.  In this case, it
    // will initialize the class variable,
    // "ClassVariable", based on the boolean
    // parameter passed to it when the
    // constructor is called, as in:
    //    ClassName c = new ClassName(true);

    void ClassName (boolean Usefulness) {
        ClassVariable = Usefulness;
    }

    // We will define only one method which
    // returns the value of the instance
    // variable:

    boolean IsUseful() {
        return ClassVariable;
    }
}
```

Classes are only definitions of *objects*, which are said to be an *instance* of a class. Declaring a variable as a class type provides a way to reference an instance of the class, but does not create the instance. This can be confusing at first, so perhaps it is best to think of the variable as being the *handle* for an object (a class instance), and not the object itself. You create objects using the new operator, as shown in the following code:

```
. . .
// Declares the object:

ClassName C;

// Now create an actual instance of the object:

C = new ClassName(true);
```

It is common to see objects declared and allocated in the same statement, as shown in the following code:

```
ClassName C = new ClassName(true);
```

We have already seen this syntax with arrays. You might be wondering what happens to an object's memory when its reference variable is re-used for a new object:

```
// The following declaration also demonstrates
// array initialization syntax, which can
// only be used the first time the object is
// declared. It is equivalent to:
//
//    int ChangingArray[] = new int[4];
//    ChangingArray[0]=1;
//    ChangingArray[1]=2;
//    ChangingArray[2]=3;
//    ChangingArray[3]=4;

int ChangingArray[] = {1, 2, 3, 4};

// Create a new integer array and reference it.
// We can't use an initializer this time, fill
// in the array contents one cell at a time.

ChangingArray = new int[2];
ChangingArray[0] = 5;
ChangingArray[1] = 6;
```

What happens to the first integer array {1, 2, 3, 4}? The answer is that the Java run-time system's *garbage collector* periodically finds objects that are not referenced by a variable and automatically reclaims that memory. This is a great convenience for the programmer and helps eliminate memory leaks, a common source of software bugs.

Operators and Expressions

Java provides a rich set of operators for primitive data types, matching those found in C and C++. The +, -, *, and / operators all perform the expected addition, subtraction, multiplication, and division operations, and % performs an integer modulus operation. The operators >> and << shift integer values right and left, and the bitwise operators, |, ^, &, and ~, indicate ORs, exclusive ORs, ANDs and NOTs.

Java supports the convenient unary operators of C and C++: ++ and -/ increment and decrement integer values, respectively. You will see i++ in our example code, which indicates that the integer variable should increment itself.

Comparison operators include <, <=, >, and >= for less-than, less-than-or-equal to, greater-than, and greater-than-or-equal to. The == operator compares for equality and != compares for inequality. Comparisons always return a boolean result.

Finally, the logical operators || and && are analogous to their bitwise cousins for ORs and ANDs. The ! operator serves as the logical negator.

The expressions in this chapter's example are all very simple, so we won't try to discuss the complexities of operator precedence and type conversions.

Class Interfaces

A Java object can call a method in another object as long as that object has already been compiled, making its definition information available to the Java compiler. What happens if the referenced object needs to call a method in the referencing object? We have a "chicken-and-the-egg" problem: one object must logically be compiled before the other, and therefore can't access the definition information it needs to be sure that the appropriate interfaces exist.

Java provides a special class definition called an *interface*. An interface declaration creates a *template* for method declarations. Any class that *implements* an interface must complete the definition of the methods defined in the interface.

Classes that implement interfaces can be referenced by other objects using their implemented interface name rather than their actual class name as long as the referencing objects only reference the methods in the interface. This makes it possible for two objects to reference each other without circular definitions.

For example, we will see the following definition in the code we develop in the section, "Connecting Java to Sybase SQL Server."

```
class OrderEntry
    extends java.applet.Applet
    implements UpdateApplet;
```

The interface `UpdateApplet` contains the following declaration:

```
interface UpdateApplet {
    public void Update();
}
```

The class `OrderEntry` *must* define a method named `Update` with the same parameters (none, in this case) and return value (`void`, in this case). Thereafter, other objects may reference the `OrderEntry` class as if it were an `UpdateApplet` class as long as they only reference the one method, `Update`, declared in the class interface. In fact, only `UpdateApplet` has to be compiled before other objects that will call the `Update` method. This eliminates any circular definitions.

Packages

When you want to create a final program image, traditional static languages require you to explicitly tell the linker program whether the code and variables are in object files or libraries. Java takes a different approach. All compiled classes residing in one of the standard locations can be seen by the compiler and run-time system (by default, the standard locations are the built-in libraries, the current directory, or all of the directories listed in the `CLASSPATH` environment variable). How do you manage such a large namespace? For example, how would you provide your own definition of a class method `println` if you don't want to use the one provided by the system?

Java solves the problem by organizing classes into *packages*. All classes belong to a package, if not explicitly, then to a single, unnamed package. By default, all names of classes, their methods, and variables must be *fully-qualified*, meaning that the name must include the base name of the class or class component and the name of the package in which they are defined. Packages are hierarchical: you can organize packages within packages so that the resulting fully-qualified names, which include the hierarchy of packages, begin to look like Internet addresses:

```
java.awt.Button myButton;
```

Classes are declared as belonging to a package by the first statement in the file in which the class is declared:

```
package SQLserverProject;
```

Although fully-qualified names ensure that you can always determine where a class originates, repeatedly using classes with long qualified names such as `java.awt.Button` can become tedious. Using Java's `import` statement, you can direct the compiler to recognize names without their package path. You can import specific names, or all of the names in the package. For example, a Java source file that contains the following statement at the head of the file:

```
import java.awt.Button;
```

thereafter recognizes `Button` by itself. If you wanted to use a wildcard to import all of the names in the java.awt package, you would enter:

```
import java.awt.*;
```

Visibility Specification

Declarations of classes, methods and variable declarations in Java can specify their visibility to other objects. If a class, method, or variable is "visible," it can be referenced, called, or accessed. Controlling visibility can prevent programmers from using unpublished interfaces. Java has four levels of visibility:

- Private. Only methods within the defining class can reference private methods or variables. Private classes have no practical use.

- Protected. Protected is like private except that any methods that might extend the parent class can access protected methods and variables.

- Public. Visibility is unrestricted to public classes, methods, and variables.

- Public to package. By default, all classes and methods within a package have visibility to other classes, methods, and variables belonging to the same package.

Control Statements

Java supports all of the control statements found in C and C++. If you want to execute more than one statement based on a condition, you must delimit the block of statements with { and }. This section covers some of the more common control statements.

if/else

Unlike C and C++, the if/else conditional statement in Java requires a boolean parameter. Like C and C++, there is no then keyword: the block of code following the condition is executed if the condition is true. The else block is optional. The following code executes a single statement if the stated condition is true and a block of statements if the stated condition is false.

```
if (a < 5) a = 5;
else {
   a = a - 1;
   System.out.println("Continuing...");
}
```

for

The for statement provides iterative looping. The head of the statement has three parameters separated by semicolons. The first parameter is an initialization statement in which a local looping integer variable is set to a starting value. The second parameter is the condition to execute the statement or block of statements. The third parameter provides a final action to be performed at the end of the loop. For example,

```
for (i=0; i < 100; i++) System.out.println(i);
```

prints the first hundred integers. Note that the variable i is not defined before the for statement: it is automatically assumed to be an integer and cannot be used outside the for statement. This example also introduces the increment operator ++, which increments integer variables by one.

while

The `while` statement provides iteration based on a boolean condition checked *before* the iteration is executed. Using the `while` statement to print the first hundred non-negative integers requires you to explicitly declare a looping variable that must also be explicitly incremented during each iteration, as shown below:

```
int i = 0;
while (i < 100){
    System.out.println(i);
    i++;
}
```

do/while

The `do/while` statement is similar to the `while` statement except that the boolean condition is checked *after* the iteration is executed. To implement the previous `while` example using the `do/while` statement, you must modify the condition as follows:

```
int i = 0;
do {
    System.out.println(i);
    i++;
} while (i < 101);
```

switch

The `switch` statement uses the value of an expression as the basis for transferring control within the statement to one of several statements tagged by the keyword `case`, or to `default` if no matching value is found enclosed.

```
switch(value) {
    case constant-value: statement;
    case constant-value: statement;
    default: statement;
}
```

The case tags themselves are only markers used by the compiler to create a jump table. After control is passed to one of these markers, execution continues until the end of the switch statement unless the compiler encounters the `break` or `return` statements, discussed in the following sections.

break

The `break` statement can occur only inside one of the iteration statements (`for`, `while`, or `do/while`) or inside the `switch` statement. This statement immediately terminates execution within the enclosing control statement, allowing control to fall outside, and is used most often within the `switch` control statement to terminate execution within a case, as in the following example:

```
switch(i) {
    case 1:    System.out.println("One");
               break;
    case 100:  System.out.println("Hundred");
               break;
    default:
        System.out.println("Neither 1 or 100!");
}
```

This example prints one of three strings depending on the value of the variable `i`. If the value of the variable `i` is 1, all three strings are printed without the above `break` statement.

continue

The `continue` statement can only occur inside one of the `for`, `while`, or `do/while` iteration statements. This statement immediately passes control to the end of the statement.

return

The `return` statement immediately terminates execution within a method and optionally returns a value if the method returns a value. This statement immediately terminates any of the control structures.

Exceptions

An exception is a definable event that requires some type of action. The most common exception is a response to an error condition. There are many exceptions already defined by the run-time system, such as division by zero and I/O errors. Exception events are initiated by the `throw` statement, which has an object type that is a subclass of `exception` as an argument. You can handle exceptions that occur within a `try` block using an accompanying `catch` block, as shown next:

```
try {
    intvalue = java.lang.Integer.parseInt(string);
} catch (NumberFormatException e) {
    intvalue = 0;
}
```

The method `java.lang.Integer.parseInt(string)` returns an integer value for `string` unless it does not parse correctly as an integer. In that case, a `NumberFormatException` is thrown and we assume the value is 0.

The Java Run-time Environment

Java is a dynamic, interpreted language built around a *virtual machine* that can be simulated on any computer. This virtual machine defines not only the machine code that drives the computations, but also the run-time system that provides the fundamental resources such as I/O, a graphical user interface, and run-time utilities.

Java programs are compiled from text files, typically with the filename extension .java. The result of the compiler is a bytecode file named *class-name*.class that contains the virtual machine code for each of the classes. Although you can define more than one class in a source file, the compiler creates a separate bytecode file for each class.

Executing (or, if you prefer, interpreting) a Java program is a multi-step process. First, you must use the *class loader* (like the linker for native machine code compilers) to load the individual compiled classes in order to make instances of the classes. Because the entire run-time system is dynamic and object-oriented, what would prevent someone from loading a class with the same name as one of the fundamental, trusted run-time classes with the intent of bypassing built-in security measures? The class loader takes care of this possibility by distinguishing between the built-in classes and those that are loaded from the local disk or over the network from a Web server. Not only does this prevent the built-in classes from being spoofed, it prevents conflicts between applets from different sources.

The compiled bytecode file actually contains much more than just the execution steps: it contains full symbolic information for the class, and additional information to provide additional run-time and pre-run-time checking. Before a method is executed, the *bytecode verifier* does some basic checking to make sure that the method doesn't unbalance the stack (one traditional way of cracking into the system) and that methods always pass the right number and types of parameters.

Following bytecode verification, the bytecodes are executed through an interpreter that simulates the virtual computer. Another approach to run-time interpretation is "Just in Time" compilation: the verified bytecodes are compiled to the native machine code of the computer running the Java program. Although this results in a delay the first time the class is encountered, the machine code is saved, or cached, and subsequent calls to the class methods can execute the cached machine code with significant improvements in execution speed.

In addition to the bytecode verifier, class loader and interpreter, the Java run-time system provides a number of predefined or built-in supporting classes that we will discuss in the next section.

The System Class Libraries

Java consists of three definitions: the language, the virtual machine, and the system class libraries. The language defines the syntax and semantics of Java programs. The virtual machine defines what the compiled bytecode files look like and how the interpreter executes them. The system class libraries define a specific set of services for all Java run-time systems. Currently, six major service categories exist:

- Language primitives. These are included in the package `java.lang`, and contain the definitions for `Object`, the root of *all* objects, `Class`, the parent of all classes, `String` and `Stringbuffer`, the string classes, and class wrappers for all of the primitive types.

- Networking. The package `java.net` contains the classes for Internet addressing, URLs, and network socket connections. We will visit this package in a little more detail when we show you how to open a socket connection between a client applet and the Perl script communicating with SQL Server.

- Stream I/O. The package `java.io` contains classes for opening, closing, reading, and writing files. `System.out.println`, mentioned earlier, uses this package to print to the standard output device, which is the controlling terminal or window that activates the Java run-time system.

- Basic run-time utilities. The package `java.util` contains general-purpose utilities including definitions for *container classes* (as introduced by Smalltalk) such as `Dictionary`, `Hashtable`, `Stack`, and `Vector`. Also included are frequently used classes such as `Date`, which handles dates and time in a system-independent fashion, and `Random` for generating integer or floating point pseudo-random numbers.

- The Abstract Window Toolkit. `java.awt` provides a system-independent 2D windowing environment, including support for objects such as buttons and menus, and layout managers for simplified GUI development. We will explore this package in some detail when we create the graphical user interface.

- Applets. An applet is a network Java program that runs under the Java Abstract Window Toolkit. All Web applets must be a subclass of the class `Applet`, which is defined in the package `java.applet`.

The Java development team chose to keep the number of system classes small by design to allow Java to grow from small to moderate instead of from large to huge. The Java development team is already exploring extensions to the system classes.

Java Security

While writing Java applets, you will run into some things that you might have been able to do with a more traditional language, but simply can't do in Java. These limitations stem from Java's security model, which discourages features used to exploit security loop-holes at a variety of levels. For example:

- The language is strongly typed, and does not allow the programmer to determine how memory will be laid out, and most importantly, does not support pointers.

- The bytecode verifier ensures that the stack is not unbalanced, that the correct number and types of parameters are passed to a method, and that arrays are indexed within their bounds.

- The class loader ensures that security-sensitive functions such as networking cannot be replaced.

- Java-enabled browsers restrict the path to which the applet can read or write files, thereby preventing applets from reading sensitive system files and passing them back over the network, destroying important files, or planting files with embedded viruses in locations where they may be inadvertently executed.

- You can configure Java to restrict networking privileges. For example, you can prevent your Java browser from opening a socket connection to another connection within your firewalled network when the applet source is a server outside the firewall. This eliminates one possible class of covert channel from outside a firewalled network.

Writing a Simple Java Program

In this section, we are going to show you how to write a very short, *standalone* Java program to demonstrate the basics of writing a standalone program and using the compiler. This program is not an applet, and will not run on a Web page. (We show you how to write an applet in the next section, "Writing a Java Applet.") Instead, it is executed via the Java interpreter *java*, and simply reads and writes to the command terminal or window from which java is run. The program is shown below:

```
// File: hello.java

class hello {
  public static void main(String arg[])
    if (arg.length < 1)
      System.out.println("Hello, there!");
    else
      System.out.println("Hello," +
                         arg[0] + "!");
  }
}
```

When it is run without any arguments, this program simply prints "Hello, there!" to the window or console from which the java interpreter is run. If there are any arguments provided when the program is run, this program chooses the first argument and prints that instead of "there."

For this program, we will create a class named `hello` that has only one method named `main`. The declaration of `main` has three modifiers that proceed it:

`public`	Declares the visibility of the method to exist outside the scope of the class, so that we can "see" it to run it.
`static`	Declares the method to be a *class method*. Class methods don't require an instance of the class to be created, and the Java interpreter counts on this to start the program.
`void`	Declares that the method does not return a value.

The Java interpreter passes `main` arguments as an array of strings, and we declare this by including the argument list within parentheses: `main(String arg[])`. We can tell if there are any arguments by checking to see if the size of the array is less than 1:

```
if (arg.length < 1)
```

If there are arguments, we print the first, `arg[0]`, ignoring any others (if they exist).

Assuming the test program above was in the file "hello.java," you first compile the program using *javac*, then run the program using the standalone interpreter *java* by passing it the name of the class you want it to view. The following is a sample that compiles and runs the program as seen on a UNIX system (user input is in **bold**):

```
joe% javac hello.java
joe% java hello
Hello, there!
joe% java hello Trudy
Hello, Trudy!
```

Writing a Java Applet

A Java *applet* is a special category of the Java program that uses the Java Advanced Window Toolkit (AWT) to create a Graphical User Interface, or GUI. Applets are important, not only because they provide a way to create graphical applications, but because they provide the framework for Web-based applications.

Programming an applet consists of writing setup and housekeeping code and writing customized responses to five categories of events:

- Mouse events. When a user presses a mouse button, there is an expectation that something is going to happen: the user will press a button, select a menu item, or draw something where the cursor was positioned. *Dragging* the mouse, that is, holding a button down and moving the mouse, usually draws lines or moves objects.

- Keyboard events. The keyboard is used for entering data in the form of characters, navigating with the arrow keys, and even for controlling program execution, such as when a function key is used to activate a task. Keyboard events at their lowest level are generated when a key is pressed, and when it is released.

- Paint events. Everything, including text, is actually drawn in a GUI. When a closed window is opened, or a when a portion of a previously-covered window is uncovered, a paint event is generated, signaling that the program must draw all or part of the application window.

- Component events. A component is an object that includes any of the user interface items, including buttons, menus, scroll bars, and text input areas. Components usually have generalized responses to mouse events. For example, clicking the mouse anywhere inside a button selects the button. A button event supersedes mouse events when the mouse is clicked inside the button, so the programmer doesn't have to figure out *when* the mouse cursor is inside the button to respond to the click.

- Activation/deactivation events. Some windows need to know when the cursor is inside or outside of it, or when it has *input focus* or not. Java applets need to handle special events such as when the Web page containing the applet is no longer being viewed, or when that page is viewed again. For example, an applet may include sounds that play when the user does a particular function: you would probably want to turn off the sounds when the user leaves the page, and turn the sounds back on when the user returns.

This approach to programming is called *event-driven programming*. In event-driven programming, you write the code that responds to the various events applied to the affected objects. The beauty of Java's AWT is that all components of the GUI are objects, and default behaviors have been assigned to the events for these components. Your job is four-fold:

- Understand the GUI components. Obviously, you want to know what the built-in AWT components can do. If they don't provide what you need, you can create your own components, although that is not necessarily a trivial task.

- Understand the events that have meaning for the GUI components you want to use.

- Write code that creates instances of the GUI that you want for the application.

- Write code that changes the default responses to the various events for each component.

Of course, let's not ignore the fundamental law of accelerated GUI programming: find code for an applet that is similar to what you want, then modify it.

Now that you have some background, we're ready to create a trivial applet to demonstrate many of the default event responses that form the starting point for more meaningful applications.

All applets are derived from the Applet class, which is found in the package `java.applet`. The following code creates a *subclass* of Applet:

```
// file: TrivialApp.java

public class TrivialApp extends java.applet.Applet{
}
```

The Java compiler *javac* expects to see source files for an applet with the same name as the applet with the .java extension, so that in the above example the source file for the applet TrivialApp must be named TrivialApp.java. We compile this program using the compiler program, *javac*:

```
javac TrivialApp.java
```

To test the applet with the *appletviewer* program or a Java-enabled Web browser such as Netscape Navigator 2.0 (or later), you must embed a reference to the compiled applet in an HTML file, and provide a default applet width and height. Following is a very minimal HTML file that does the job.

```
<APPLET CODE="TrivialApp.class" WIDTH=100 HEIGHT=100>
</APPLET>
```

After we have compiled the program and created the HTML file named trivial.html, we can run the program by typing `appletviewer trivial.html` from a command window. Figure 6-1 shows the resulting window:

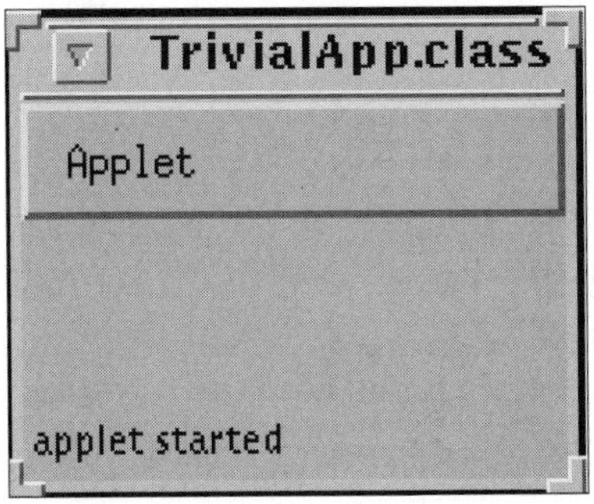

Figure 6-1. *Trivial applet*

The following messages appear in the window where you started the appletviewer.

```
status: applet loaded
status: applet initialized
status: applet started
```

These messages come from the default handlers for applet events. When you close the applet window then reopen it, you will see the messages:

```
status: applet stopped
status: applet started
```

Finally, if you quit the applet by selecting Applet/Quit from the menu, you will see three more messages:

```
status: applet stopped
status: applet destroyed
status: applet disposed
```

Again, these messages are generated by the default Applet event methods. All but the first and last messages (loading and disposing) can be replaced by your own code.

The purpose of this exercise was to give you a basic feel for the life-cycle of an applet. You can customize the actions taken during these events by providing your own definitions for the following four methods:

init()   This method is called when the applet is first created. You do all of your one-time setup here.

start()   This method is called whenever the applet becomes active. This happens when the applet first starts, and whenever the user returns to the applet after leaving it, such as going to another Web page and returning, or opening and closing the Applet window from the appletviewer.

stop()   This method is called whenever the applet becomes inactive, such as when the user leaves the Web page. This is where you clean up after yourself: for example, you might turn off any audio playing.

destroy()   This method is called when the appletviewer or the Web browser is terminated. This is where you would release critical resources and do any final cleanup.

Another important event to be aware of is the paint event. Let's extend our trivial applet just a little to demonstrate how (and when) to paint a simple string:

```java
// file: Paint.java

public class Paint extends java.applet.Applet{
    public void paint(Graphics g) {
        g.drawString("Java!", 10, 25);
        System.out.println("status: paint");
    }
}
```

In this example, we created a new paint() method that overrides the default in the class Applet. A graphic object is passed to paint(), which is the canvas that you can paint by calling the canvas' methods. In the above code, we draw the string "Java!" (using the default font) 10 pixels over and 25 pixels down from the top left corner of the canvas, then print a status line to the console that is similar to those printed by the other default event handlers.

All that's left to do is modify the HTML file to reference the `paint` class instead of TrivialApp. Figure 6-2 shows the result of running the extended applet from the appletviewer.

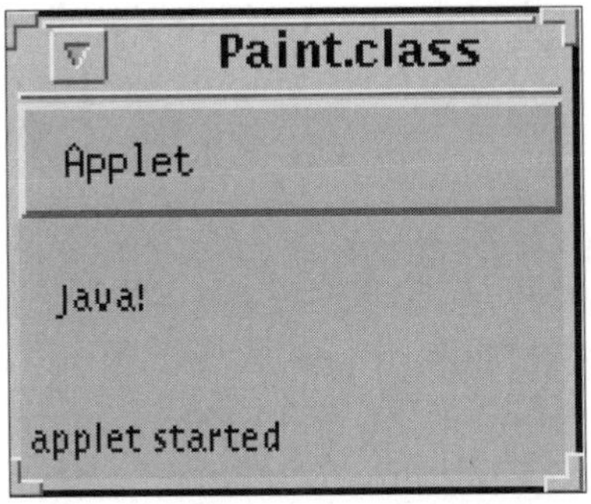

Figure 6-2. An Applet that paints

Building a Java Graphical User Interface

You create Java user interfaces by adding *components* to *containers*. Components are objects that comprise a user interface, such as buttons, menus, scroll bars, and text input areas. There are two classes of containers: *Panels* and *Windows*. Panels are used to group components, and Windows are used to manage and display components. Windows provide two subclasses to manage and display components: *Frames* and *Dialogs*.

Components consist of the following object categories:

- Containers. As you will see, you can group components into Panels, then group the Panels into the Applet, Frame, Dialog, or even another Panel.

- Basic Controls. All GUI frameworks provide objects to control the actions of a program. The Java AWT supports Buttons, Checkboxes, Choices, Lists, Menus, and TextFields.

- Miscellaneous objects. These provide the other amenities of a GUI, including Scroll bars, Labels, Text Areas, and Canvases.

Creating a powerful, flexible user interface is surprisingly easy in Java thanks to the *Layout Manager* classes. These five classes provide standardized layouts based on five patterns. We will use two of these: *GridLayout*, which organizes components of equal size into rows and columns to create a spread-sheet, and *GridBagLayout*—the most complex Layout Manager—allowing dif-ferent-sized components.

All containers use a default Layout Manager. Panels and Applets use the *FlowLayout*, which simply positions components from left to right. Frames and Dialogs have the *BorderLayout*, which positions components relative to North, South, East, West, and Center.

Not only do Layout Managers free you from having to know the exact pixel position for each component: when you resize the containers, each component is appropriately resized and repositioned.

All containers add components using an add() method. Let's extend our simple application to add a Button and a Label.

```
// file: TwoComponents.java

import java.awt.*;

public class TwoComponents extends java.applet.Applet {
    public void init() {
        add(new Button("Hot"));
        add(new Label("Java"));
    }
}
```

Remember, you need an HTML file that includes the following lines:

```
<APPLET CODE="TwoComponents.class" WIDTH=150 HEIGHT=50>
</APPLET>
```

Figure 6-3 shows the results when you run this applet from the appletviewer.

This simple example demonstrates many important points that will help you in the next section, "Connecting Java to Sybase SQL Server," in which we start building a *real* applet.

First, we took advantage of the fact that the applet has a default Layout Manager, FlowLayout, and a method, add(), for placing components according to that Layout Manager: in this case simply from left to right.

Figure 6-3. *The applet with two components*

Second, we showed you how to create components on-the-fly by simply creating new instances of their respective classes. In the case of Buttons and Labels, you can pass a string that is displayed as a part of the component. These classes know how to respond to events such as painting themselves. Because of this, and because we aren't going to do anything else with the components, you can create and add each component within the add method, such as:

```
add(new Button("Hot"));
```

Third, all applets use a start-up initialization method called init() where you typically create the various containers and components for an applet. It is not unusual for init() to be one of the longer methods in an applet: after all of the components are in place, they typically handle their own events. Before we launch into the real application, let's change the previous example so that the Button label alternates between "Hot" and "Cold" when the button is pressed. This involves creating a subclass of Button called MyButton that changes the component constructor and the action event handler.

```java
// file: SmartButton.java

import java.awt.*;

class MyButton extends Button {
    private String original;
    private final String alternate = "Cold";
    private boolean flag;

    public MyButton(String label) {
        super(label);
        original = label;
```

```
            flag = true;
    }

    public boolean action(Event evt, Object obj) {
        if (flag) setLabel(alternate);
        else setLabel(original);
        flag = !flag;
        return true;
    }
}

public class SmartButton extends java.applet.Applet {
    public void init() {
        add(new MyButton("Hot"));
        add(new Label("Java"));
    }
}
```

Note that the only change we made in the init() method was to substitute MyButton for Button. In subclassing Button, we first created some local variables. These are all private because nothing outside this class needs to see them. The first string saves the original label (which we know will be "Hot"). The second string saves the alternate string, which we denote as final to indicate that the variable is a constant and will never change: it won't even reference another string. The flag variable is a boolean that tells us which string to apply to the Button label when the user presses the button.

Fourth, we also defined a new constructor (remember, constructor methods have the same name as the class) that does everything the parent constructor does by calling super(label), saving the original label, and setting flag, which we will toggle every time the user presses the button.

Finally, all of the real work happens in the method action(), which is called whenever the button is selected with the mouse. This method must be defined with the given parameters (even though we will ignore them) so that it supersedes the Button action method. In this method, we simply change the button's label based on the flag, then toggle the flag.

Figure 6-4 shows the two states of the applet.

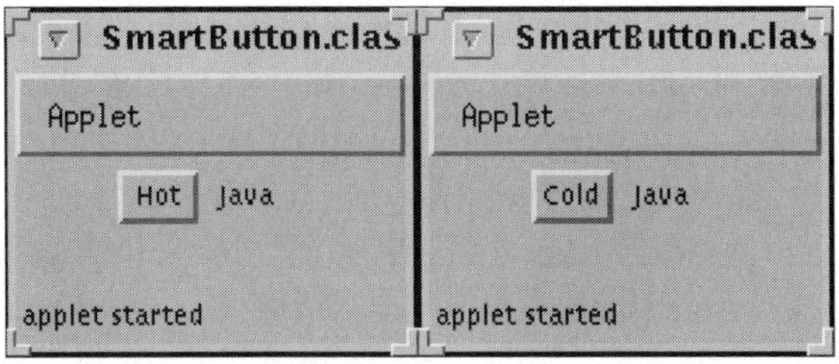

Figure 6-4. *The applet with custom button*

Connecting Java to Sybase SQL Server

Now that you have been introduced to the Java language and Java's run-time environment and have experimented with Java programs and applets, you're ready to implement a real application. This section shows you how to create an order entry application using Java. In particular, this section focuses on using Java to create a user-friendly interface on the client side.

In the previous chapters, we relied on two HTML forms to present a series of pages. The first form presents the user with the list of items and quantity of each to be ordered, and the second form prompts the user for shipping information.

What happens when the user returns the first form with a non-numeric entry in one of the quantity fields, such as the word "one" instead of the numeral "1"? The form is blindly sent back to the server and the server must respond by sending a *new* page with an error message and the original form for submission.

How does the user calculate the total cost of his or her order? The user must either manually calculate totals on the side, or wait for the server to calculate the total and return it via *another* page. Suppose the user decides that they have spent too much money: they have to start all over, resulting in *more* pages, which means more strain on the server.

This is a fine example of pages proliferating pages and the inherently weak interactivity of HTML. We're going to fix this by writing a Java program that presents the user with only *one page* containing an interactive spreadsheet that ensures that the user enters only positive numeric values, and calculates the item totals and the order total on-the-fly. When the user submits the order, they are presented with a separate pop-up window for entering their shipping information instead of another page. Figure 6-5 shows an example of the two windows using the Netscape Navigator 2.0 browser. Note that the window for the shipping information is labeled "Untrusted Java Applet Window." This label is provided by Netscape Navigator on all pop-up windows resulting from Java applets to make it clear to the user that the window is associated with a program that has been loaded over the network. Hopefully, if such a window prompts the user to enter their system password, they will think twice!

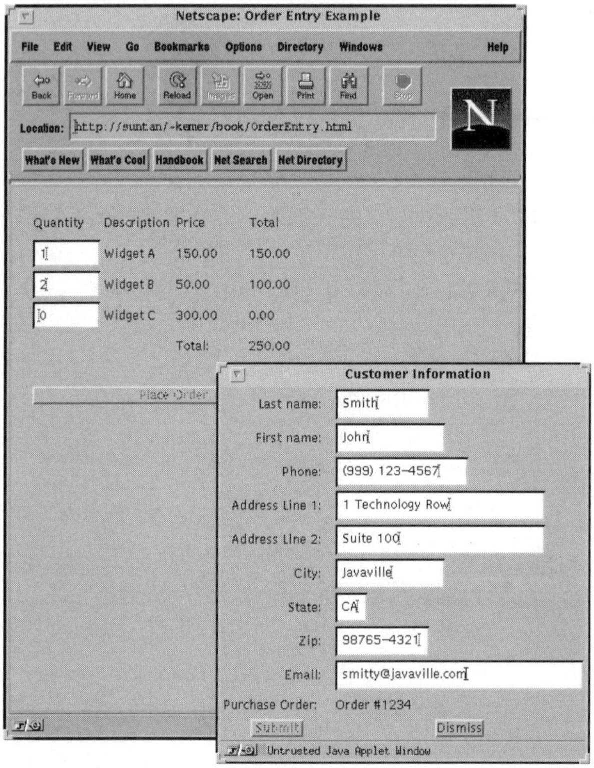

Figure 6-5. *The client example using Java*

We're going to split the application into two pieces: the user interface and a class that provides the interface to Sybase SQL Server. Putting all of the Sybase SQL Server interface code into one class isolates the interfaces, providing greater flexibility for implementation. We will also take advantage of Java's dynamic object linking by putting the code for each class into a separate file. By doing this, we have to recompile *only* the file for the class when we change or enhance it. Table 6-2 provides a summary of the classes we will develop. The WebExtra Web site contains these source files as well as the Perl script that provides the interface to Sybase SQL Server.

Table 6-2. *Classes Used in the Order Entry Application*

Classes	File	Purpose
UpdateApplet	UpdateApplet.java	This defines the class interface that makes it possible for the classes OrderEntry and IntField to reference each other.
OrderEntry	OrderEntry.java	This is the applet. It gets the items from the database and creates and updates the spreadsheet.
Dollars	Dollars.java	This is a supporting class that represents dollar amounts without any rounding errors. It provides methods to multiply dollars by an integer and to add two dollar objects together. We need this class to handle updating the ordered totals in the spreadsheet.
IntField	IntField.java	This is a subclass of the standard TextField component. It allows the entry of only integer values and calls the Update() method in Project when a field changes.
CatalogEntry	CatalogEntry.java	An array of CatalogEntry objects is used to represent the spreadsheet. Each object has an item name and price, retrieved from the database, plus the quantity entered by the user and references to the components on the spreadsheet for use by the GUI.
Entry OrderForm	Entry.java	These classes are used to represent the shipping information entered by the user.

Table 6-2. Classes Used in the Order Entry Application (cont.)

Classes	File	Purpose
OrderButton SubmitButton CancelButton	OrderButton.java	These classes are all derived from the standard component Button. OrderButton creates the separate frame for entering the shipping information.
DBinterface DBConnection DBResult	DBinterface.java	DBinterface provides an interface to the database; DBConnection manages the network socket connection between the applet and a Perl "relay" to Sybase SQL Server; and DBResult handles the SQL results.
	DBdummy.java	DBdummy.java contains an alternate implementation that simulates the database with fixed data and responses.

Creating the Graphical User Interface

The Graphical User Interface is handled by two classes: OrderEntry, which is the controlling applet, and OrderButton, which is subclassed from the Button component. OrderEntry creates an order entry spreadsheet and OrderButton creates the customer information form. We will discuss each of these classes separately with comments on their supporting classes. The complete code is located on the WebExtra Web site. The following discussions group some statements differently than the actual source to underscore their relationship.

The OrderEntry Class

The OrderEntry applet has only two methods: init(), which is called when the applet is first created, and Update(), which is called from the IntField class whenever a value in an IntField component changes. Most of the work performed in init() involves creating a panel and a button: init() creates a top panel with the order entry spreadsheet, and a bottom Place Order button.

Creating the Panel and Button

In order to place the panel at the top and place the button at the bottom, we explicitly set the Layout Manager for the applet to be a BorderLayout using the following statement:

```
setLayout(new BorderLayout(5,5));
```

Incidentally, the parameters set the horizontal and vertical gap to five pixels to provide space around the components. After we finish creating `topPanel`, we'll create an instance of `OrderButton` (a subclass of `Button` that we will discuss in more detail in the next section), and add them both to the applet, as shown in the following code:

```
add("North", topPanel);
OrderButton placeOrderButton =
    new OrderButton("Place Order");
add("South", placeOrderButton);
```

The spreadsheet we'll create is a four-column table, so we want the top panel to have a GridLayout. We create the panel and set it to be a GridLayout using the following code:

```
Panel topPanel = new Panel();
topPanel.setLayout(new GridLayout(0, 4));
```

When you create a GridLayout, you have the option of setting the number of rows and columns. You can, as we have here, set the number of rows to zero, which allows you to keep adding rows until you are finished inserting data. Note that our `topPanel` is a separate object from the applet itself, so you must qualify actions performed on it with its name (that is, `setLayout()` sets the Layout Manager for the applet, and `topPanel.setLayout()` sets the Layout Manager for `topPanel`). After you have set a GridLayout, you simply add components sequentially from left-to-right, four components per row. The top row usually has the column descriptions, so we add these as four Label components:

```
topPanel.add(new Label("Quantity"))"
topPanel.add(new Label("Description"))"
topPanel.add(new Label("Price"))"
topPanel.add(new Label("Total"))"
```

Because we aren't going to change the column header labels, we can use the generic Label class and not save a reference to it.

Filling in the Spreadsheet

We then fill in the rows of data retrieved from the database. The data is retrieved and stored in another object called `Catalog` using the following code:

```
Catalog = DBinterface.getInitialData();
```

We put all of the database interface code into one separate class, DBinterface, and provide a simple interface to it using two methods: one to read the database, and the other to update it. This logical partitioning makes it easy to create a test implementation that doesn't require Sybase SQL Server for testing. We'll discuss the actual implementation in the next section, "Creating the Sybase SQL Server Interface."

The array `Catalog` contains `CatalogEntry` objects. Each object has six variables, which we may think of as fields. Table 6-3 shows the six variables, their data type, and use.

Table 6-3. Fields for CatalogEntry Objects

Field	Type	Purpose
Description	String	A description of the product displayed in the spreadsheet.
ProductID	String	The database key for the product used by the database for queries and updates.
Price	Dollars	The unit price for the product. We created a Dollars object to provide a representation of dollar amounts that could be manipulated without rounding problems.
Qty	int	The number of this product being ordered by the user. This is extracted from the QtyField.
QtyField	IntField	This is a reference to the spreadsheet component that has the user-entered quantity. We will use this in the Update() method to extract the Qty field and update the totals.

Table 6-3. Fields for CatalogEntry Objects (cont.)

Field	Type	Purpose
TotalField	Label	This is another reference to a spreadsheet component, this time a Label with the total dollar cost for the number of ordered items of the product. This reference is updated in Update(), and is simply the product of Price and Qty.

Three of the fields in the CatalogEntry are provided when we call DBinterface.getInitialData(): Description, ProductID, and Price. We will fill-in QtyField and TotalField when we create the body of the spreadsheet. We do this in a for-loop with one iteration for each product in the database. We need to add four columns for each product corresponding to the heading.

The first column is the field in which the user selects the quantity to be ordered. This component is going to be a special subclass of the TextField we write called IntField, which we'll discuss a little later. We want to save a reference to this field as shown in the following code, because we'll use it later on to update the spreadsheet:

```
Catalog[i].QtyField = new IntField(5, this);
topPanel.add(Catalog[i].QtyField);
```

The second column is the product description that we have already extracted from the database and is in the Catalog. This will never change, so we don't need to save a reference to this object:

```
topPanel.add(new Label(Catalog[i].Description));
```

The third column is the product price. This has already been retrieved by the database and is being saved as a Dollars object in the Price variable. When we create the Label, we need to pass a String to it: we provided a conversion method, toString(), which we use when we create the Label. This is another unchanging field, so we don't need to save a reference to its component:

```
topPanel.add(new Label(Catalog[i].Price.toString()));
```

The final column is the total. This is initially zero dollars, so we'll create a Label with that string. We'll be updating it later, so we want to save a reference to that component:

```
Catalog[i].TotalField = new Label("0.00");
topPanel.add(Catalog[i].TotalField);
```

We're almost done with the spreadsheet: we need to add the grand total, which we will calculate later, so we'll want to save the reference to that field in a class instance variable, GrandTotal. The GridLayout needs four components for the final row: we will give it two empty Labels, a static label with the String "Total:", and the GrandTotal label with the initial value of "0.00."

Handling User Input

The setup for the GUI is complete. To make the form interactive, we need to have some things happen when the user enters values into the Quantity column. This is handled by the class IntField, a subclass of TextField. First, we have modified the constructor to initialize the field to zero and to save a reference to the object creating it (which is the OrderEntry applet) in the instance variable Parent. We need to save this reference so that later on we can call the Update() method to update the spreadsheet:

```
public IntField(int width, OrderEntry parent) {
    super(width);
    setText("0");
    Parent = parent;
}
```

At this point, the user can enter any text into the field. We want to make sure that the value is an integer, then update the spreadsheet. There are two events that we want to trigger the update: when the IntField loses its input focus (that is, when the mouse is moved to another component or outside the applet), and when the user presses the ENTER or RETURN key.

Fortunately, both events have default event handlers, lostFocus(), and action(), respectively. We can handle the event first in lostFocus():

```
public boolean lostFocus(Event evt, Object what) {
    int intvalue;
    try {
        intvalue =
```

```
            java.lang.Integer.parseInt(getText());
    } catch(NumberFormatException e) {
        setText("0");
    }
    Parent.Update();
    return true;
}
```

The method `getText()`, which is defined in the parent class TextField returns the value of the field as a String. We want to make sure that this String is an integer value, so we take advantage of the class method `java.lang.Integer.` `parseInt()` to attempt to convert the value to an integer. By calling this method inside a try-catch exception block, we can catch the `NumberFormatException` that is raised if the String parameter doesn't parse into an integer: in that case, we immediately change the IntField value to "0."

After we have made sure the field is an integer, or have changed it to "0," we want to update the entire spreadsheet. We do this by calling the parent applet's `Update()` method. We saved the reference to this object so that we could do just that: `Parent.Update()`. We'll talk about that method in a minute.

We need to be sure to declare `lostFocus()` exactly as shown, even though we don't use the parameters `evt` or `what`, and return a boolean value of true so that we become the event handler.

We want `action()`, which is called when the user presses ENTER or RETURN, to do exactly the same thing, so we simply call `lostFocus()`:

```
public boolean action(Event evt, Object what) {
    return(lostFocus(evt, what));
}
```

Whenever an IntField changes, we update the entire spreadsheet. This is actually pretty easy: we want to update the order total for each Product, which is the product of the Quantity field and the Price. We get the quantity as an integer value by calling IntField's method—which is why we saved a reference to it—and we save it in the Catalog's Qty field:

```
Catalog[i].Qty = Catalog[i].QtyField.getIntValue();
```

We don't want to accept negative quantities, so as a refinement we make sure it is non-negative, making the field zero otherwise:

```
if (Catalog[i].Qty < 0) {
    Catalog[i].Qty = 0;
    Catalog[i].QtyField.setText("0");
}
```

We retrieve a copy of the price, which is a Dollars object, and calculate the subtotal as the product of the Price and Quantity:

```
subtotal = new Dollars(Catalog[i].Price);
subtotal.Times(Catalog[i].Qty);
Catalog[i].TotalField.setText(subtotal.toString());
```

One final task remains for the Update() method: to calculate the grand total. We do this by:

1. Creating a zero Dollar object using the following statement:

    ```
    Dollars total = new Dollars(0);
    ```

2. Adding the subtotal for each row. and

    ```
    total = total.Plus(subtotal);
    ```

3. Updating the grand total field.

    ```
    GrandTotal.setText(total.toString());
    ```

The OrderButton Class

In the OrderEntry applet, we created a Button with the label "Place Order." Now, we want to create a separate window that is displayed when the user selects the Place Order button to collect customer information. We'll create two additional buttons for this window: a Submit button that is selected when the user is ready to submit the order, and a Cancel button that allows the user to cancel the pending order. We do this by creating three subclasses of Button:

OrderButton	Creates a frame with a GridBagLayout for the customer information form and the two buttons when the Place Order button is selected (resulting in an action event).
SubmitButton	Responds to being selected by calling the OrderButton's Submit() method.
CancelButton	Responds to being selected by calling the OrderButton's Cancel() method.

The OrderButton class involves rather complex behavior. When the user selects the Place Order button, we don't want to make any changes to the original spreadsheet until the user fills in the new window: to do this, we need to disable the button. When the user selects the Cancel button, we want to destroy the window, re-enable the button, and continue with the applet. When the user selects the Submit button, we want to disable that button so the user can't submit the order again, then update the form with a purchase order identification and convert the Cancel button to a Dismiss button, which destroys the window and returns to the applet.

When the user selects the Place Order button on the applet, the `action` event handler disables the button so the user can't select it again until we have all the information we need, and then builds the frame that collects customer information, as shown in the following code:

```
public boolean action(Event evt, Object what) {
    disable();
    buildFrame();
    return true;
}
```

Formatting the New Window

All of the setup for the new window is done in `buildFrame()`. In essence, we create a new frame container, give it a GridBagLayout Layout Manager, add components to the frame, then *pack*, resize, and display it. Window containers, that is, Frames and Dialogs, must be *packed* to position all the added components using `pack()` before they are displayed using `show()`. We could have given the window an absolute dimension, but the method `preferredSize()` returns an optimal dimension just big enough to hold the components, providing a convenient way to automatically allocate the correct amount of space. These steps are summarized in the following code:

```
f = new Frame("Customer Information");
GridBagLayout g = new GridBagLayout();
f.setLayout(g);
// Add the components
f.pack();
f.resize(f.preferredSize());
f.show();
```

Handling the Order Information

The customer order information can be represented as a table of fields consisting of the customer's last name, first name, address, and other personal information. We build this table by creating an array of objects that are of a class we define called `Entry`. `Entry` contains variables for the field name (or descriptor), its value (provided by the user), the character width of the input field, and finally a reference to the TextField component for the input field so we can extract the information entered by the user.

The class `OrderForm` contains `OrderInfo` and an array of `Entry` objects, one for each field in the customer information order form. We create an instance of `OrderForm` in `buildFrame()`, and save it in the variable `form`.

Creating the Order Information Entry Form

We are ready to create the customer order entry form consisting of pairs of components using the information in `form`: a Label with the field description, and a corresponding TextField for the customer to enter the information described by the field description.

As we mentioned earlier, we have attached a GridBagLayout Layout Manager to the Frame to build the entry form. The GridBagLayout uses another object, GridBagConstraints, to tell it *how* to place components. We place form components in pairs: the first half is the field description (as initialized in `form.OrderInfo.[i].name`), and the second half of the pair is a TextField component for entry of the field text (which we create and save in `form.OrderInfo.[i].field`). We right-align the first component and want the second component positioned next to it, so we initialize a GridBagConstraint instance, `c`, to:

```
c.gridwidth = GridBagConstraints.RELATIVE;
c.anchor = GridBagConstraints.EAST;
```

We then create the label, which we must save in a variable because we need to pass it along with the GridBagConstraints to the GridBagLayout before actually adding it to the frame:

```
label = new Label(form.OrderInfo[i].name);
g.setConstraints(label, c);
f.add(label);
```

We want the next field to be left-aligned because it is the last field in this row, so we initialize the GridBagConstraint object, c, to:

```
c.gridwidth = GridBagConstraints.REMAINDER;
c.anchor = GridBagConstraints.WEST;
```

We want to save this field in the OrderInfo array because we will retrieve its value in Submit() when the form is submitted:

```
field = new TextField(form.OrderInfo[i].size);
g.setConstraints(label, c);
f.add(field);
```

After we've added a row for each entry in OrderInfo[], we add another row for the Purchase Order number. Because the Purchase Order number won't be received until the user submits the form, we initialize its value to asterisks and update the field later in Submit().

The Submit and Cancel Buttons

Finally, we add a row containing the two buttons for submitting or canceling the order. Each of these Button subclasses save a reference back to OrderButton so that they can call its Submit() and Cancel() methods.

After the user presses the Submit button, we call the Submit method and fill in all of the value fields in form.OrderInfo[] using the references to the TextField components we saved in field:

```
form.OrderInfo[i].value =
    form.OrderInfo[i].field.getText();
```

We submit the completed form to the Sybase SQL Server interface method, which returns the purchase order number in the variable ID:

```
ID = DBinterface.submitData(form);
```

Later, we update the form with the purchase order number:

```
POlabel.setText(ID);
```

The variables sb and cb contain references to the Submit and Cancel buttons. We disable the Submit button to avoid confusing the system with a second submission before this one is complete, and we change the label on the Cancel button from Cancel to Dismiss. We want to display the completed form long enough so that the user can see the updated purchase order number:

```
sb.disable();
cb.setLabel("Dismiss");
```

The `Cancel()` method holds the final piece to this puzzle. This method is called by the CancelButton component, either to cancel the transaction or to dismiss the completed form after the transaction is complete. Either way, there are two things to do: re-enable the Place Order button on the applet spreadsheet, and dispose of the customer information frame using the following commands:

```
enable();
f.dispose();
```

We have completed our discussion of the Java code that creates the user interface for our application. In the next section, we will discuss the Perl code that connects the server to Sybase SQL Server and the Java class `DBinterface` that completes that connection to the server.

Creating the Sybase SQL Server Interface

As we mentioned in the last section, we have isolated all of the Sybase SQL Server interaction to one class, DBinterface. Not only does this lend itself to portability, it also makes the applet easier to test. Two versions of the class are provided on the WebExtra Web site: one that simulates the Sybase SQL Server response, and one that actually interacts with Sybase SQL Server.

The implementation makes a significant architectural modification to our earlier approaches. Instead of communicating with the Web server through CGI, the applet opens a network socket to a Perl script that resides on a server. The Perl script, which we will refer to as the "SQL Server Relay," interacts with Sybase SQL Server and handles packaging and unpackaging of information coming to and from the applet. With this approach, the Sybase SQL Server, SQL Server Relay, and Web Server can be (and often should be) on separate computer systems.

In this section, we will implement a server application, the relay server, and Java classes to communicate with that server. The relay server implemented in SybPerl communicates directly with Sybase SQL Server. We will develop a standard API to communicate with the relay server using Java's networking API's, allowing us to build Java applets that can communicate with Sybase SQL Server. In the final section of this chapter, we will pull all these pieces together and enable the applet we've created in this chapter to communicate with Sybase SQL Server.

Communicating with Sybase SQL Server

The code for communicating with Sybase SQL Server is split between the Web client and the relay server. The Web client handles the communication with any Java applications, and the relay server communicates between the Web client code and the Sybase SQL Server.

The first step in developing the code for communicating with Sybase SQL Server is to define a protocol for the relay server and the Web client. We will make the protocol as simple as possible, but still powerful enough to handle any application. Our protocol will be used to pass SQL code to the server, and then to respond with the results. There will be three kinds of results: failure, success, and success with result rows. Failure will signify that the SQL code could not be executed for some reason. Success will signify that the SQL code was executed without a problem, but that it did not return any results. The final result type will tell the client that the command completed successfully, and that we will also be returning result rows. When we have success with result rows, we will need to transmit the column names and the individual row values. For simplicity and to facilitate testing, we will transmit all of our results as character values.

Now that we know what we plan to say in our protocol, let's explicitly define it. The first action from the relay server after receiving an SQL request will be to tell the Web client the type of results being returned. Our protocol will signal an error by returning a -1, signal success by returning 1, and signal success with results by returning a 2. We'll follow the results with a newline character. The next block will be the column names, with each column on its own line. The column names will be terminated by a blank line, which will serve not only to tell the client the names of the columns, but also the number of lines to read for each row. Following the column names will be the row values. These will be in column name order, and there will be a line for every row. The entire result will be terminated by a blank line. We don't need individual row terminators because we can count the columns based on the number of column names.

Following is a result set from a successful query with results. You can test this on your own by starting up the Perl server and issuing a SQL command to select all the data from the product table. This can be done by telneting (which is a remote connection to the server) to the port where the server is running and issuing the SQL statement `select * from product`.

```
2
product_id
description
price

1
Widget A
24.99
2
Widget B
29.99
```

The Sybase SQL Server Relay

The server connection is written in Perl, as Perl already has a robust set of tools for communicating with Sybase SQL Server called SybPerl. We will do a cursory explanation of the server code here. For a more in-depth description, see Chapter 4, "Creating CGI Scripts Using Perl" in this book.

The server where the Perl script resides (which we'll call the Perl server) will wait for new connections and fork a new process when one comes in, leaving the original process to listen for and handle future connections. When it receives a connection, the Perl server will then connect to Sybase SQL Server, maintaining a separate server connection for each client connection. It will then relay any messages from the client to Sybase SQL Server. The Perl client will then extract any data sets generated from the server and send them over the network to the client. The server will then continue reading from the client until the socket is closed.

We will describe portions of the server code that differ from the code presented in the Perl chapter. The main difference between the Perl server code and the other Perl code presented in this book is that this code is interacting with a socket instead of with a Web server.

To communicate with the Java client code, the Perl server needs to use the Perl socket libraries. We will use the platform-independent versions of the socket libraries delivered with Perl5. Platform independence allows our code to run on any system that can run Perl5 and SybPerl. Code that doesn't use the Perl5 socket implementation will break on some systems such as Solaris. To use the Perl5 socket implementation, we will need to import the Socket module. We import modules with the `use` command.

```
use Socket;
```

We will then read the port to start the Perl server from the command-line arguments, defaulting to port 2345. Following this, we will create a TCP socket, bind it to the port, and begin listening for new connections. Perl4 programmers may notice that the arguments to the socket and bind calls are different than the ones they're used to seeing because we are using the Perl5 symbols that hold these values instead of the Perl4 variables. The Perl5 symbols will work on any machine where Perl4 style calls are not portable.

```
my $port = shift || 2345;
#Initialize Socket Datastructures.
my $proto = getprotobyname('tcp');
socket(SERVER, AF_INET, SOCK_STREAM, $proto)         || die "socket: $!";
 setsockopt(SERVER, SOL_SOCKET, SO_REUSEADDR, 1)     || die "setsockopt:
$!";
bind(SERVER, pack_sockaddr_in(AF_INET,$port, INADDR_ANY))  || die "bind:
$!";
listen(SERVER,5)                                     || die "listen: $!";
```

Now we are ready to begin accepting client connections. We will display a message to `STDOUT` stating that the SQL relay server and port are ready. The server will then loop indefinitely, accepting new client connections. When a new client connection comes in, we will fork a new process to handle the request, leaving the original process free to listen for new client connections. This allows our code to handle many connections without bogging down a single process. We will use a `for` statement to loop indefinitely, as shown in the following code:

```
for ( ;
    ($addr = accept(CLIENT,SERVER)) ;
    close CLIENT)
{
```

Within the `for` statement we will fork a new process and connect to the Sybase SQL Server. We will then set up the client socket to feed `STDOUT` and read from `STDIN`. This is mainly for convenience to avoid having to explicitly state the file to which we're sending our data, and from which we're reading requests. We fork using the Perl command `fork`. All the code that follows the `fork` call is executed as a new process.

```
if (($child = fork()) == 0) {
```

Within the child process, we will initialize CT-Lib and connect to the server. In this example, we set the login information explicitly. If you want to use client-side login information, this is a good place to read it in. It would be easy to extend the protocol to require the user name, password, and server name as the first three arguments to a new connection, but we're not using that method here because we're assuming that all security is handled by the Sybase SQL Server. Either approach is good: the one you choose depends upon your application. If you decide to go with the route we use here, you must make sure that it is safe to give free access to the server with the login you use, as anyone can telnet to the Perl server and issue their own SQL.

Now, we will initialize `STDIN` and `STDOUT` and set `STDOUT` to be command-buffered. We set `STDOUT` to be command-buffered so that results are passed back immediately, instead of after a buffer is full.

```
#Set the STDIN and STDOUT to the socket for ease of use.
        open(STDIN,  "<&CLIENT")   || die "can't dup client to stdin";
        open(STDOUT, ">&CLIENT")   || die "can't dup client to stdout";
        $|=1;
```

Now that our connection is established, we will loop over all the input and execute each command as it comes in using the CT-Lib `ct_execute` command. After this, we will check the result set we have, and output the result type. This is done using a simple `if` statement along with a `print` statement. If the result type has fetchable rows, we will send down the names of the columns and the row values. We will read these in using the standard CT-Lib calls. For more information on using these statements and other CT-Lib calls, please see Chapter 4, "Creating CGI Scripts Using Perl" in this book.

Implementing the Java Client

In this section, we will look at the Java code to connect to our relay server. We will begin by building two support classes that you can use in any Java application. Then, using these classes, we will build a specific interface for the order application. Breaking with the pattern of the earlier Java code, we will encapsulate all the communications classes in a single file for two reasons: first, their functionality is so closely tied that if we were not concentrating on making our tools reusable, we could be sorely tempted to make them all one class; second, placing all the communications classes in a single file allows us to make the raw interface to our server private, preventing any unauthorized access from Java clients. Only the public class DBinterface will be able to access the two support classes, making it the only class other Java applications can use to interact with the database.

The two support classes we will develop will handle all the interaction with the server and its return values. We will need a class to handle the connection to the relay server, and another class to handle the results returned by the server. These classes together with the Perl server give you all the tools you need to handle any application that needs to communicate with Sybase SQL Server.

Connecting to the Perl Server

We will begin by creating a class called `DBConnection` to connect to the server and execute a SQL command. The `DBConnection` constructor, using the host and port as arguments, will open the socket to the Perl server. The following is the beginning of our `DBConnection` declaration:

```
DBConnection (String Host,int thePort) {
```

The first thing the constructor will do is store the host and port as instance variables so that they can be retrieved at a future date. Then, using the try/catch syntax to handle any I/O exceptions, it opens a new socket. As we have seen earlier, exceptions are Java's way of making sure that any error conditions are handled. After opening the socket, we will set up two instance variables: input and output to communicate with the Perl server. We store them as instance variables for easy access.

```
try {
//Open the connection.
        server = new Socket(Host, thePort);
        input = server.getInputStream();
        output = new PrintStream(server.getOutputStream());
    } catch(Exception exception) {
```

If an exception is thrown, we will attempt to handle it gracefully by closing the connection and outputting the exception to the error stream. If this fails, we will exit the applet. The following code handles any exceptions that may occur:

```
System.err.println("Exception:\n"+exception);
        try {
//Try to close the connection.
            server.close();
        } catch(Exception e) {
//If there was another error, signal the exception and exit.
            System.err.println("Exception:\n"+e);
            System.exit(1);
        }
    }
```

We now have an active connection to the relay server. Next, we want to issue commands. We will define a method, execute, that will take a SQL command as a string parameter, and send the command to the server. This method will also create a result object and return the results. We will talk more about result objects shortly. Execute's first order of business is to get the SQL command in a format that it can send down the socket. Java sends bytes down a socket, so we will create a byte array the length of our command by taking advantage of the fact that Java doesn't require array bounds to be known at compile time, just at execution time. We will dynamically allocate our array with the following declaration:

```
byte bytes[] = new byte[SQL.length()];
```

Now that we have an appropriately-sized byte array, we will populate it with the 8-bit representation of the SQL string. This is necessary because Java strings are stored as 16-bit Unicode values. The string class has a method called getBytes that returns the bytes that make up a Unicode string. We will use the following code to convert the string to a byte array and send it to the relay server.

```
SQL.getBytes(0,SQL.length(),bytes,0);
output.write(bytes);
```

Next, we will read in any results returned from the SQL command. The exe-cute method will return a null value if any exceptions are thrown: otherwise, we will use a new class to store and manipulate the results called DBResult. Like DBConnection, we will use DBResult's constructor to do work for us. When DBResult is constructed, it will read the results waiting from the last SQL com-mand. The following code creates a new DBResult instance and returns it from the execute method:

```
res = new DBResult(this);
return res;
```

Handling Results

We will hold any results from the Perl server in the class DBResult. DBResult will start by reading any waiting result set, and store the values in its three instance variables. DBResult will track the result type, the column names, and the row values. We will use the utility class Vector to hold the varying number of field names and rows. Vector allows you to dynamically add objects, handling low-level details like memory allocation behind the scenes for you.

The DBResults constructor does all the work. It relies on a method in DBConnection called readln, which reads a newline terminated string from the relay server and is the basis of our protocol. We are implementing this ourselves instead of using the DataInputStream class so you can choose your own termi-nator if the newline character is unacceptable for your applications. The con-structor uses readln to read in the result type, followed by a blank line. Then, if the result type is 2, it reads all the column names and terminates when an empty line is reached. It uses the vector method addElement to dynamically add each column name to the FieldNames instance variable. The following loop reads in all the field names:

```
while ((curline=ServInt.readln()).length()>0) {
//Add each column name to the FieldNames Vector
  FieldNames.addElement(curline);
}
```

We can now loop over the remaining results. For each row, we know the number of columns to read, which is simply the number of elements in the

`FieldNames` vector. We will loop until we hit an empty line, reading an array of strings for each row. We will dynamically create the array, allocating the number of columns as follows:

```
currow=new String[FieldNames.size()];
```

For each row, we will use a `for` loop to read the correct number of columns. The following simple loop pulls in all the columns for a specific row.

```
for (int i=0; i<FieldNames.size(); i++) {
  curline=ServInt.readln();
  currow[i]=curline;
}
```

With these two classes, you now have a toolbox that you can use as the foundation of any application you choose to develop in the future. There are some places where you can extend this foundation. First, the `execute` method is only designed to handle a single result set. You could easily execute to return a vector of results. Also, the classes are not prepared to handle newline characters. If you want to do this, you can encode them when they are transmitted from the relay server.

Using the Application Interface

Now that we have a foundation, we are ready to implement the next level. We will build `DBinterface` on top of `DBConnection` and `DBResults`. `DBinterface` will show how easy it is to use the lower-level classes for simple and complex problems.

`DBResults` uses two methods. The first, `getInitialData`, queries the server for all the products and places them in an array of `CatalogEntry` objects by:

1. Creating a connection to the relay server.

2. Calling the `execute` method on the connection object to execute a SQL command.

3. Storing the results returned from the call to execute in the `DBResults` variable products.

Here is the code to select all the products:

```
products=theConnection.execute("select description,
product_id,price from product\n");
```

We then loop over the rows in the products result set and populate the catalog object. When that is done, we return a new `catalog`, and we have completed our first query to the Sybase SQL server!

`DBInterface`'s next method, `submitData`, takes the information from the form and commits the data entered into the database. Once again, for an in-depth discussion of the SQL used to do this, refer to Chapter 3, "Using ISQL to Connect to Sybase SQL Server," and Chapter 4, "Creating CGI Scripts Using Perl." This method uses the same paradigm as the above method, but it also checks the result values. The `submitData` method needs to issue several commands wrapped in a SQL transaction. If any of these fail, we should roll back the transaction. We maintain a Boolean variable called `commit` that holds `true` if all the execute calls return a result type of success or success with rows, and `false` if any of them fail. We use the following code, substituting a 1 or a 2 depending on the expected result type. You will notice the use of the self-referencing conjunction assignment operator, `&=`. This creates a logical AND between the value on the left and the right of the operator.

```
commit&=(Result.resultType.equals("1"));
```

At the end, we test `commit` to determine if we should issue a `commit` transaction SQL call or a rollback call. We set the `order_id` field to the string "Error!" at the end if we were unable to commit the transaction to the database. Otherwise, we use the value that is set at the beginning of submitData using the following code:

```
Result=theConnection.execute("select max(customer_id)+1 from customer HOLD-
LOCK\n");
cust_id=((String[])Result.Rows.elementAt(0))[0];
```

Finally, we return the `order_id` value so the user can retain a reference to their order. In this function, we use a return value to signal an error. You could also use an exception.

```
if (commit) {
  theConnection.execute("commit transaction\n");
} else {
  theConnection.execute("rollback\n");
  order_id="Error!";
}
        return order_id;
```

Tips and Tricks

There are many opportunities for refinements in this applet. This applet is representative of much of the client/server interaction that occurs with Sybase SQL Server applications, and thought should be given to creating reusable classes for later work. As we commented earlier, the IntField class is a good example: forms entry often requires input of integer and non-negative integer values, and a hierarchy of reusable classes to handle such components speeds the development of intelligent forms.

In fact, we didn't check *any* of the fields in the customer information form. It would make sense to have some intelligence checking for reasonable phone numbers and zip codes. You could even check the "State:" field for correct input of the two-character abbreviation.

Generically, smart forms need classes that parse a variety of fields, including dates and monetary amounts. The value of object-oriented programming is directly proportional to the number of reusable classes that exist. Completed libraries of smart form components could make the development of custom forms trivial.

One issue we didn't consider was what should happen to the standalone window for customer information when the user leaves the page containing the applet. Our implementation keeps the window visible, even if the applet is nowhere in sight. In fact, it probably makes sense to hide the frame using the `hide()` method when the applet is stopped, which invokes the applet event method `stop()`. You would then display the frame using `show()` when the user returns to the applet, which invokes the event method `start()`.

Useful Internet Sites

The Official Java site
`http://www.javasoft.com/`
Java Database Connectivity API
`http://splash.javasoft.com/jdbc/`

Gamelan, A comprehensive collection of Java information
`http://www.gamelan.com/`

Database Information at Gamelan
`http://www.gamelan.com/frame/Gamelan.programming.db.html`

Java World, an Online Magazine

`http://www.javaworld.com/gamelan.index.html`

Summary

In this chapter, we have shown that Java is a versatile cross-platform language that has strong ties to the World Wide Web. We discussed how Java allows you to create small programs called applets that process data at the client side, instead of simply transmitting information back to the server to be processed. This allows you to free the server from handling numerous CGI requests, and it allows you to create a more versatile interface for the client.

Using other robust tools, we showed you how to control input to text fields, use Java's class libraries to interface with other programs over the Internet, and communicate with a database server. With Java, you can create robust Web pages containing client/server applications.

7
Using Web.sql to Streamline Data Flow

Web.sql is, at this writing, a brand new Sybase product—in fact, this chapter is based on a beta version. Web.sql is a tool for accessing databases through the Web, specifically databases that can be reached via Sybase's Open Client architecture. The obvious choice for such a database is Sybase SQL Server, but many types of databases can be reached using connectivity tools or data replication. This chapter begins with a 50,000-foot view of web.sql and a broad explanation of how it works. Next, we use an example Web site to illustrate web.sql constructs one by one, and to show how to use them to build a Web site.

We'll do this in the following sections:

- Getting a Feel for Web.sql
- Developing a Web Site
- Winding Up
- Tips and Tricks.

Getting a Feel for Web.sql

The Web is a good place to search for information about web.sql. Begin by looking at the Sybase home page at `www.sybase.com`, where you can find a variety of information about web.sql including web.sql documentation, example Web sites, and a mailing list to which you can add yourself.

What Web.sql Does for You

You can make two general observations about web.sql as you look around. First, you may notice that web.sql code itself is not sent over the Internet. If you bring up a site that is built using web.sql and view the document source, you will see only HTML—no web.sql code. The only time you will see web.sql code is if you happen to look at a site that has supplied a button for the specific purpose of displaying the code. Some of the examples of web.sql supplied by Sybase have this.

Second, web.sql code takes the Perl, SybPerl, CGI code, and HTML that normally are part of building a Sybase Web site and lets you combine them into a single document file. Thus, you can combine the techniques that you have used so far in this book in a file that is shorter, and easier to write and maintain. For example, let's see what it takes to build one of the examples used previously.

In Chapter 2, "Creating Forms," we created a form for the ABC Widget Company's quarterly report (shown in Figure 2-20). We discussed the CGI script that produced that report in Chapter 4, "Creating CGI Scripts Using Perl." To provide a comparison, you can implement the form in web.sql using the following single document source file, qrtr.hts:

```
<HTML>
<HEAD>
<TITLE>ABC Widget Company</TITLE>
</HEAD>

<BODY>
<BODYTEXT>
<H1>MarCom Analysis Sheet</H1>
<H3>Monthly Summary</H3>
<P>Monthly sales summary for Q$QRTR_SUM
<HR>

<BR>
```

```
<SYB TYPE=SQL>
select Month = datename(mm,order_date),
    "Total Sales" = sum(cost)
    from cust_order
    where datepart(qq, order_date) = $QRTR_SUM
    group by datename(mm, order_date),
        datepart(mm, order_date)
    order by datepart(mm, order_date)
</SYB>

<BR>
<BR>
Monthly analysis:
<FORM ACTION="drill.hts" METHOD="POST">
<INPUT TYPE = "HIDDEN" NAME="type" VALUE="month">
<TABLE>

<SYB TYPE=PERL>
if ($QRTR_SUM eq "1") {
    %q = "'1', 'January', '2', 'February', '3', 'March');
}
if ($QRTR_SUM eq "2") {
    %q = "'4', 'April', '5', 'May', '6', 'June');
}
if ($QRTR_SUM eq "3") {
    %q = "'7', 'July', '8', 'August', '9', 'September');
}
if ($QRTR_SUM eq "4") {
    %q = "'10', 'October', '11', 'November', '12', 'December');
}

foreach (keys(%q)) {
    print "<TR><TD>$q{$_}</TD><TD><INPUT TYPE=RADIO NAME=MONTH_SELECT
VALUE=$_ ALIGN=TOP></TR>"; }
</SYB>

</TABLE>
<INPUT TYPE="SUBMIT" VALUE="Monthly Search" ALIGN="TOP">
</FORM>

</BODYTEXT>
</BODY>
</HTML>
```

To invoke qrtr.hts, the code that used to call the CGI script qrtr is replaced by a reference to qrtr.hts. The line:

```
<FORM ACTION="http://www.abcwidget.com/cgi_bin/qrtr">
```

is replaced by:

```
<FORM ACTION=qrtr.hts>
```

All of the code in cgi-bin—qrtr, the drillQuarter subroutine, and all of the supporting Perl code—is no longer needed.

At this point, you may want to study the on-line web.sql documentation available on the Sybase home page (follow anything referring to *Web.sql Programmer's Guide*). Or read on, as we're going to provide a different approach. We will explain a little bit about how web.sql works at a high level, then use an example to illustrate most of the web.sql constructs. You may then want to go back to the *Web.sql Programmer's Guide* for full documentation.

How It Works

Essentially, web.sql works by placing a wrapper around an HTTP server that preprocesses web.sql queries, formats the output in HTML, and sends the resulting HTML code to the user's browser. That is an oversimplification, but that's essentially what web.sql does. Web.sql can bypass the CGI interface completely (a CGI version is also available), allowing database connections to stay open between pages, which greatly reduces the overhead of interacting with a database. This bypass is possible because when web.sql is installed, the HTTP server is linked with library code that can recognize and interpret web.sql code. The Netscape API (NSAPI)—which is itself a sort of "open server" application—is used to accomplish this bypass of CGI.

Web.sql code takes the form of .hts files that replace HTML files in a URL. HTS files are HTML files with the web.sql extensions enclosed between <SYB> and </SYB> tags. When a user initiates a request, the code between the <SYB> and </SYB> tags is preprocessed and replaced by the resulting HTML code, allowing the HTML page to be built by the server "on the fly." No database queries are sent over the wide area network, which helps protect database security by preventing users from seeing the table and column names being accessed, as well as any code that might be used to log in to the database.

Between the <SYB> and </SYB> tags, your web.sql code will include some combination of SQL, Perl, or Client Library API calls to access the database and format the results as HTML. Use SQL to run simple database queries and output the results in a default format. This requires minimal programming effort on your part and is useful when SQL constructs are adequate to handle the program logic and the default output format is acceptable. Following is an example of SQL code in a web.sql script:

```
<SYB TYPE=SQL>
  select "Message of the Day" = motd from motd
</SYB>
```

Use Perl together with API calls in all other situations, especially when the desired output format is too complicated to be handled by the default. Perl is a widely-accepted, interpreted, and full-featured language providing data structures, flow control, and the ability to invoke other programs. When used with web.sql, its power lies in submitting database queries and processing the output in many flexible ways, including producing HTML code from retrieved row values. Web.sql also allows Perl global variables to appear outside the <SYB> tags, thus providing a way to pass data between <SYB> blocks and hence between database queries.

We should also note that Perl is available for use in HTS files even when there are no database queries. This way, you can keep your Perl code in the same file as the HTML.

You use a set of API calls embedded in your Perl code between the <SYB> and </SYB> tags to access the database. These calls look very much like the Sybase Open Client API calls, except that they are embedded in Perl, not C, and Perl variables are typically used to collect the output and manipulate it as desired.

Actually, there are two types of API calls: *convenience* routines, which begin with ws_, and *Client Library* routines, which begin with ct_. The convenience routines are a little easier to use, but less flexible. The Client Library routines are more flexible, but require you to write a little more code. An example of the previous statement follows, written both ways.

Using the convenience routines:

```
<SYB TYPE=PERL>
$sql_stmt = qq!select "Message of the Day" = motd from motd!;
ws_sql($ws_db, $sql_stmt);
</SYB>
```

Using the Client Library API:

```
<CENTER>
<P> Message of the Day
<P>
<SYB TYPE=PERL>
$sql_stmt = qq!select motd from motd!;
$ret_val = ct_sql($ws_db, $sql_stmt);
while (($rval = ct_results($ws_db, $results_type)) == CS_SUCCEED)
{
    RESULTS:
    {
        if ($results_type == CS_ROW_RESULT)
        {
```

```
        while (@motd = ct_fetch($ws_db)) {
            print @motd;
        }
        last RESULTS;
    }
  }
}
</SYB>

</CENTER>
```

This can seem confusing at first because web.sql combines several types of languages and calls. Your source files will include HTML, SQL, Perl, ws_ API calls and ct_ API calls. However, mixing languages is already typical of Web programming, and once you understand the differences and appropriate uses of the several techniques, web.sql can really seem quite simple. The advantage of using web.sql is that you can use the several techniques together in a single HTS file. In addition, there are not too many API calls, so if you know HTML, Perl and SQL (which you should if you have gotten to this point in the book), putting it all together is not that difficult.

Developing a Web Site

The following example Web site uses almost all of the web.sql constructs and illustrates many of the reasons for using a database in building a Web site:

- To parameterize a site

- To provide a context-sensitive site

- To fill template pages from a database

- To provide forms for data entry

- To provide conventional, complex database queries.

In this section, we will walk through the example site and illustrate the web.sql constructs along the way.

Define the Application

We're going to walk you through an example of building a Web site for a company that specializes in custom software development on a consulting basis.

The company wants the Web site to contain information about the services offered, the types of projects the company specializes in, and the names of the company's consultants. The Web site will:

- Be parameterized so that company employees can show new projects and updated technical information without redoing the Web pages

- Direct users to other related pages based on the types of projects in which they show an interest

- Show biographical pages for individual consultants by building a template page, then filling it with information from the database

- Allow the consultants to modify their own bio page on the Web

- Let consultants enter their own hours for billing purposes on the Web.

The Database

For the example, you will use the database shown in Figure 7-1.

The tables are as follows:

Technologies	Keeps a list of the technical specialties you currently want to put forward.
Projects	Keeps one row for each project you want to profile.
Members	Keeps one row for each principal engineer whose biographical information you want to show.
Clients	Keeps one row for each client you want to put forward as a reference.
Hours	Keeps consultant hours for a project.

These Technologies, Projects, Members, and Clients are then cross-referenced using primary and foreign keys, and intersection tables.

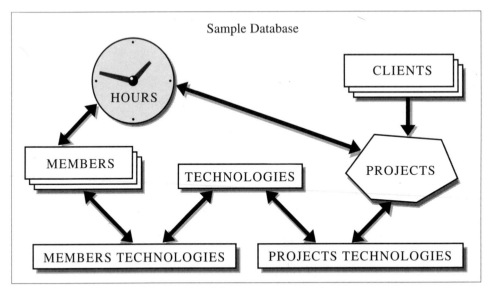

Figure 7-1. *The example database*

Install Web.sql

Although we're not going to go into great detail here, installing web.sql involves these steps:

1. Installing the http server.

2. Installing a Sybase database, or determining which remote database your web.sql code will access.

3. Loading the web.sql code onto the HTTP server machine.

4. Running the web.sql installation program, which leads you through the http server configuration file changes (for the NSAPI version) and through configuring database connections for web.sql.

Creating a Parameterized Page

In this section, we'll show you how to use web.sql to develop a parameterized Web page, as shown in Figure 7-2. Parameterizing a page allows you to change its content without changing the HTML (HTS) file. The example consulting company has to keep moving with technology and constantly develop new skills, and consequently needs to change their marketing materials frequently to reflect their most recent projects. It is easier for you, the Web page designer to put up a single template page and change the words from time to time. That way, anyone can change the information shown on the page without having to reformat the HTML pages maintained by the graphics artists.

Using the consulting company example, we will illustrate the following web.sql constructs:

- <SYB> tags

- $ws_db

- $ws_sql()

- Perl variables

- Formatting output for HTML.

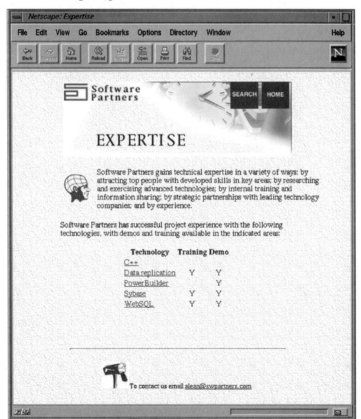

Figure 7-2. *An example parameterized Web page*

Following is the web.sql code that produced the Web page shown in Figure 7-2.

```
<HTML>
<HEAD>
<TITLE>Expertise</TITLE>
</HEAD>
<BODY background ="/images/backa.jpg">
<CENTER>
<BLOCKQUOTE><IMG SRC="/images/expertise.jpg"></BLOCKQUOTE>
</CENTER>
<P>
<BLOCKQUOTE>
<FONT SIZE = "3">
Software Partners gains technical expertise in a variety of ways: by
attracting top people with developed skills in key areas; by researching
and exercising advanced technologies; by internal training and information
sharing; by strategic partnerships with leading technology companies;
and by experience.
<P>
Software Partners has successful project experience with the following
technologies, with demos and training available in the indicated areas:
</FONT>
</BLOCKQUOTE>
<BR>
<IMG SRC=/images/brain.gif>
<CENTER>

<SYB TYPE=PERL>

$sql = "select name, name, training, demo from swp..technologies order by
name";
$format = "<TD><A HREF=atechnology.hts?t_name=%s>%s</A></TD>
<TD align=\"center\">%s</TD>
<TD align=\"center\">%s</TD><TR>";

print "<BR><TABLE BORDER = 0>";
print "<TR><TH>Technology<TH>Training<TH>Demo<TH>";
print "<TR>";
ws_sql($ws_db, $sql, $format);
print "</TABLE>";

</SYB>

</CENTER>

<BR>
<BR>
<BR>
<BR>
<HR WIDTH="450">
```

```
<CENTER>
<P ALIGN="CENTER"><IMG SRC=/images/mailbox.gif BORDER=0><FONT SIZE="2">To
contact us email
<A HREF="mailto:alean@swpartners.com">alean@swpartners.com</A></FONT>
</CENTER>
</BODY>
</HTML>
```

You may have noticed in the previous code that we did not include the clos-ing </TR> tag. We have left it out of the handwritten examples because web.sql does not generate closing </TR> tags when it automatically produces HTML code.

Now, let's discuss the constructs illustrated by this simple example.

First, note the <SYB TYPE=PERL> tag. As mentioned before, <SYB> blocks come in two flavors: SQL and Perl. If you omit the TYPE= attribute, then TYPE=PERL is assumed. You can intersperse <SYB> </SYB> blocks of either type in an HTS file, but SQL blocks can contain only SQL statements and Perl blocks can contain only Perl statements. However, you can use global Perl variables anywhere throughout the HTS file. You must define them inside a <SYB> block before you can use them outside <SYB> blocks.

Second, note how HTML is printed inside the <SYB> block. Outside the <SYB> block, you could have:

```
<TABLE>
```

but inside it, you must use a print statement like the one shown below:

```
print "<TABLE>";
```

Third, note the use of $ws_db: it is a handle to the default database connec-tion as set up on the Web.sql Administration Page. Thus, in this code segment it is assumed that a successful database connection was previously established. In the CGI version, the database connection is established when the HTS page is started up. In the NSAPI version, the database connection occurs when the first HTS page in a group is started up. The NSAPI version leaves the connec-tion open for all HTS pages in the group.

You can reassign $ws_db using the ws_connect() or ct_connect() statement. The difference between ws_connect() and ct_connect() is that ws_connect() returns a connection to one of the predefined database connections as set up on the Web.sql Administration Page, while ct_connect() returns a connection to a

server login that you supply as a parameter. The connection returned by ws_con-
nect() has the same life as the connection supplied as its parameter, while the
connection returned by ct_connect() lasts only until the end of the current HTS
file. You can use either routine to create a connection other than $ws_db.
Consider the following examples:

```
$ws_db = ws_connect("igors_conn");
$igors_db = ws_connect("igors_conn");
$ws_db = ct_connect("igor", "igor123", "SYBASE");
$igors_db = ct_connect("igor", "igor123", "SYBASE");
```

These show, respectively:

1. Resetting the default database handle to the predefined connection
    "igors_conn."

2. Setting a new database handle called "igors_db" to the same connec-
    tion.

3. Resetting the default database handle to a new connection by supply-
    ing a login, password, and server name.

4. Setting a new database handle called "igors_db" to the same connec-
    tion.

Fourth, note the use of ws_sql(). The $format parameter allows you to sup-
ply a printf-like string that is applied to every line of output. Thus, in the above
example, each line of SQL output generates an anchor in HTML. If you don't
supply the $format parameter, ws_sql() formats an HTML 3.0 table from the out-
put. In this example, you can't use a web.sql block of TYPE=SYB because you don't
want to accept the default output: rather, you want to format the output as
anchors.

The limitation of ws_sql() is that if you need to do more than just execute
the query and format the row output, you need to use ct_sql(), ws_sql()'s coun-
terpart. ct_sql() is illustrated more fully in the following examples.

Finally, note the use of t_name in the above example. Clicking on the hyperlink produced by the example ws_sql() output invokes a new HTS file called
atechnology.hts. One parameter is passed by t_name. Web.sql automatically
assigns a global Perl variable that can be used inside the HTS file. Thus, you can
use t_name inside and outside the <SYB> blocks in atechnology.hts.

A Context-sensitive Page

Suppose a visitor to your Web site goes to the Expertise page and clicks on the Sybase hyperlink. The response to the hyperlink is to call the atechnology.hts page. Using this parameter passed in as t_name—which in this case is assigned the value "Sybase"—a representative list of Project, People, and Clients is displayed to the inquirer. This is an example of dynamically building Web content that is sensitive to the previous choices made by the user. Below, we will show how to use global Perl to implement this.

The following code produces the page shown in Figure 7-3:

```
<HTML>
<HEAD>
<TITLE>Technology: $t_name</TITLE>
</HEAD>
<BODY background ="/images/backa.jpg">
<BLOCKQUOTE><IMG SRC="/images/subheadexpertise.jpg"></BLOCKQUOTE>
<H2>$t_name</H2>
<P>
If you would like to look at some <B>Projects</B> we have done with
$t_name, here is a partial list:

<BR>
<BR>
<CENTER>
<SYB TYPE=PERL>

        $sql = qq!select name, description
                    from projectstechnologies P1, projects P2
                    where technologyname = \'$t_name\'
                    and P1.projectname = P2.name
                order by description!;
        $format = qq!<A HREF=aproject.hts?p_name=%s>%s</A><BR>!;
        ws_sql($ws_db, $sql, $format);

</SYB>
</CENTER>
<BR>
<BR>

The following <B>Clients</B> can vouch for our experience with $t_name.

<BR>
<BR>
<CENTER>
<SYB TYPE=PERL>

        $sql = qq!select distinct P.clientname, P.clientname
```

```
                from projects P, projectstechnologies PT \n
               where PT.technologyname =\'$t_name\' \n
                  and PT.projectname = P.name \n
            order by P.clientname!;

      $format = qq!<A HREF=aclient.hts?c_name=%s>%s</A><BR>!;
      ws_sql($ws_db, $sql, $format);

</SYB>
</CENTER>
<BR>
<BR>

Short biographies of some of our <B>People</B> skilled
in $t_name may be viewed here:

<BR>
<BR>
<CENTER>
<SYB TYPE=PERL>

      $sql = qq!select MT.memberlname, M.fname, MT.memberlname
                from members M, memberstechnologies MT
               where MT.technologyname =  \'$t_name\'
                  and MT.memberlname = M.lname
             order by MT.memberlname!;
      $format = qq!<A HREF=amember.hts?m_name=%s>%s %s</A><BR>!;
      ws_sql($ws_db, $sql, $format);

</SYB>
</CENTER>
<BR>
<CENTER>
<HR WIDTH=100>
<IMG SRC="/images/brain.gif">
</CENTER>

</BODY>
</HTML>
```

Note how `$t_name` is used in the title, text, and SQL query that is sent to `ws_sql()`. Also note that all three queries are executed with a single database connection. If you're using the NSAPI version, these three queries can be done with the same open database connection as in the previous screen.

You now have what you want: a customized list with just a few selected profiles that illustrate your expertise in Sybase applications. Building this page from a database query prevents you from having to build a separate page for each item on the Expertise list.

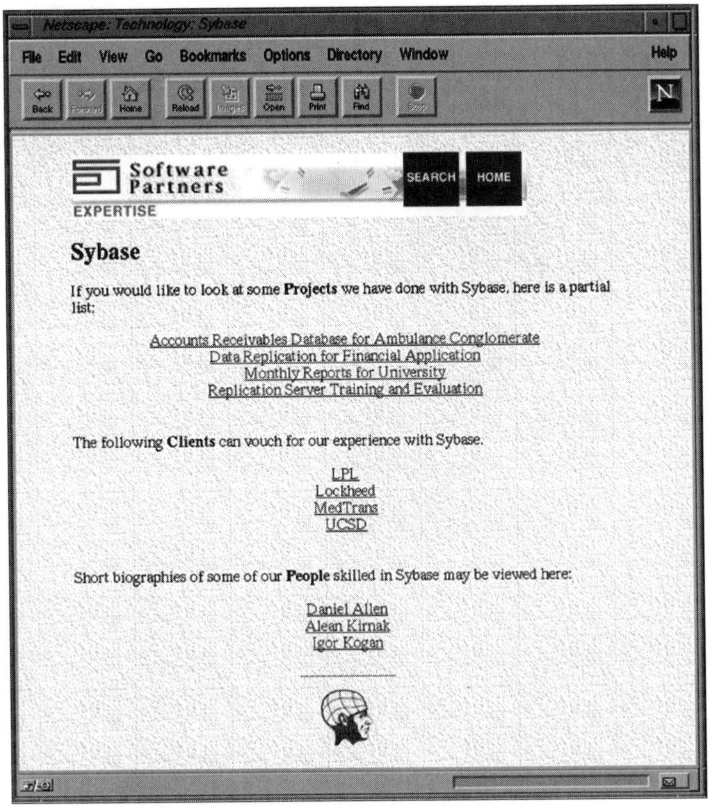

Figure 7-3. *A context-sensitive page*

A Template Page

The next example shows you how to create a single template page, then select the database rows with which to fill it. The application is a biography page for each of your consultants. Because the user can choose from a number of people, you want to create one HTML page and fill it from the database, rather than maintaining a different page for each consultant. Using this example, we will illustrate the following web.sql constructs:

- `ct_sql()`

- `ws_error()`

- `ct_results()`

- `ct_fetch()`

The consultant bio page looks like the one shown in Figure 7-4.

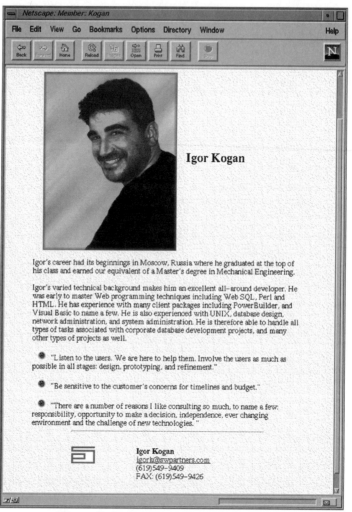

Figure 7-4. *An example template page*

The bio page in Figure 7-4 was produced by the following code:

```
<HTML>
<HEAD>
<TITLE>Member: $m_name</TITLE>
</HEAD>
<BODY background ="/images/backa.jpg">
<BLOCKQUOTE><IMG SRC="/images/subheadmembers.jpg"></BLOCKQUOTE>
```

```
<SYB TYPE=PERL>
$sql = qq!select image,
               fname,
               lname,
               email,
               phone,
               fax,
               file,
               quote1,
               quote2,
               quote3
    from members where lname = \'$m_name\'!;

if (($rc = ct_sql($ws_db, $sql)) != &CS_SUCCEED)
{
    ws_error ("<P><B> $rc ct_execute fail</B></P>");
}

while (($ret = ct_results($ws_db, $result_type)) == &CS_SUCCEED)
{
    RESULTS:
    {
        if (($result_type == &CS_CMD_SUCCEED) ||
            ($result_type == &CS_CMD_FAIL))
        {
            last RESULTS;
        }
        if ($result_type == &CS_ROW_RESULT)
        {
            while ( ($image,
                        $fname,
                        $lname,
                        $email,
                        $phone,
                        $fax,
                        $file,
                        $quote1,
                        $quote2,
                        $quote3) = ct_fetch($ws_db))
            {
                print "<H1><IMG ALIGN=middle SRC=",
                        "$image",
                        " HSPACE=20>",
                        $fname,
                        " ",
                        $lname,
                        "</H1>";

                print "<P>";
                $fullname = $pathprefix.$file;
                print `cat \"$ws_document_root$file\";
```

```
        print "<P>";
        print "<IMG SRC=/images/dot.gif HSPACE=10>", "\"",
            $quote1, "\"", "<P>";
        print "<IMG SRC=/images/dot.gif HSPACE=10>", "\"",
            $quote2, "\"", "<P>";
        print "<IMG SRC=/images/dot.gif HSPACE=10>", "\"",
            $quote3, "\"" ;

        print "<HR WIDTH=400>";
        print "<BR>";
        print "<TABLE>";
        print "<TR><TD VALIGN=TOP>";
        print "<IMG SRC=/images/swpartnerslogo.jpg HSPACE=80>";
        print "<TD>";
        print "<FONT SIZE=3>";
        print "<B>$fname $lname</B> <BR>",
            "<A HREF=mailto:", $email, ">",
                    $email,
                    "</A>",
                    "<BR>",
                    $phone,
                    "<BR>",
                    "FAX: ",
                    $fax;
        print "</FONT>";
        print "</TABLE>";
        print "<BR>";
        print "<HR WIDTH=400>";
    }
    last RESULTS;
        }
    }
}
</SYB>
</BODY>
</HTML>
```

What can you learn from this example? First, it illustrates using `ct_sql()` as opposed to using `ws_sql()`. We used `ct_sql()` because the formatting is really too complicated to do in one line of code, and because we wanted to concatenate a text file using the `cat file` command in Perl, which can't be done in the context of the `$format` parameter.

> **Note:** These examples use external files for text and images.
> Web.sql also allows you to store text and images directly in the
> database.

The `ct_sql()` command takes a database handle and a query string as parameters, as does `ws_sql()`. The `ct_sql()` command differs from `ws_sql()` in that it does not take the optional `$format` parameter, and it returns an error code. The `ws_sql()` command prints a default message if a command fails; `ct_sql()` gives you the opportunity to issue your own message using `ws_error()`, which takes one parameter, a message, prints it, and causes the current HTS file to exit. This can be extremely useful when you don't want to execute more queries if the first one fails.

After calling `ct_sql()`, you must enter a loop to retrieve the results of the call using `ct_results()`. A return of `CS_SUCCEED` from `ct_results()` signals that there are command results available for processing. Because results are returned in buffers, and because there may be more than one buffer returned, `ct_results()` must be called in a loop until `CS_END_RESULTS`, `CS_FAIL`, or `CS_CAN-CELED` is returned. The `$result_type` parameter returns the type of result set. Result set types include:

- Regular row results

- Compute row results

- Parameter results for stored procedures

- Status results for stored procedures

- A message arrival.

When the Sybase SQL Server receives any statement, including a batch with more than one statement, it processes all statements in the batch and sends the results back in buffers. It is your job to peel off those results and interpret them. The results arrive in groups of a uniform result type.

Thus, there may be a bunch of data rows followed by some stored procedure output parameters, which are in turn followed by stored procedure results and an indication that a certain number of rows were inserted. All of these results have to be processed in a `ct_results()` loop.

Some commands such as `insert`, `update`, or `delete` return no results other than status messages indicating that a certain number of rows were successfully updated. Only one type of result data is included in a single result set.

If results are available, they need to be scanned off using `ct_fetch()`, which returns an array or an associative array of data. Thus, you could have used the following command:

```
%row = ct_fetch($ws_db, 1);
```

and referred to the rows as $row{"image"}, $row{"fname"}, and so forth.

When programming with ct_sql(), you use the results loop repeatedly with
different variations depending upon the results type returned. A good skeleton
results loop is distributed with web.sql as an example. Look for results.hts.
Briefly, a good skeleton results loop might look like this:

```
while (($rval = ct_results($ws_db, $results_type)) == CS_SUCCEED)
{
        RESULT:
        {
                #insert/update/delete successful - no rows returned
                if ($results_type == CS_CMD_SUCCEED) {
                        #take appropriate action
                }
                #last SQL command failed
                elsif ($result_type == CS_CMD_FAIL) {
                        #take appropriate action
                }
                #regular data row
                elsif ($result_type == CS_ROW_RESULT) {
                        while (%row = ct_fetch($ws_db, 1)
                        .
                        .
                }
                #compute clause result
                elsif ($result_type == CS_COMPUTE_RESULT) {
                        while (%row = ct_fetch($ws_db, 1
                        .
                        .
                }
                #stored procedure status value
                elsif ($result_type == CS_STATUS_RESULT) {
                        while (@row = ct_fetch($ws_db)
                        .
                        .
                }
                #stored procedure output parameter value
                elsif ($result_type == CS_PARAM_RESULT) {
                        while (@row = ct_fetch($ws_db)
                        .
                        .
                }
                #a single command in the batch has completed
                elsif ($result_type == CS_CMD_DONE) {
                        #take appropriate action
                }
}
```

A Form for Updating Data

Up until now, everything you have done has involved a select from the database. In this section, we're going to show you some updates and HTML forms.

First, we'll show you a form for updating a bio page (shown in Figure 7-4) that allows the consultants to write and update their own bio pages using an HTML form. The example also illustrates the following web.sql constructs:

- `ct_res_info()`

- An update statement.

The first thing you're going to do is allow the consultants to log in to their own accounts. Figure 7-5 shows the login screen.

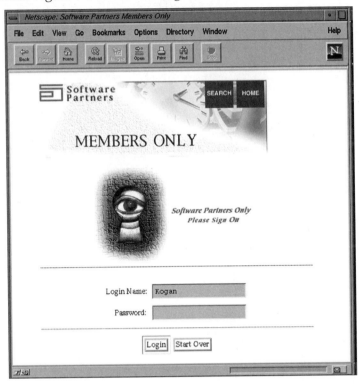

Figure 7-5. *The login screen*

Next, you have a main screen where users can choose from functions that are available only to the personnel in your company. Note that the "Message of the Day" example discussed on previous pages was used to produce the Message of the Day shown in Figure 7-6.

Figure 7-6. *The main screen*

Let's say that Igor has chosen the Your Bio Page link. He gets a screen that looks like Figure 7-7.

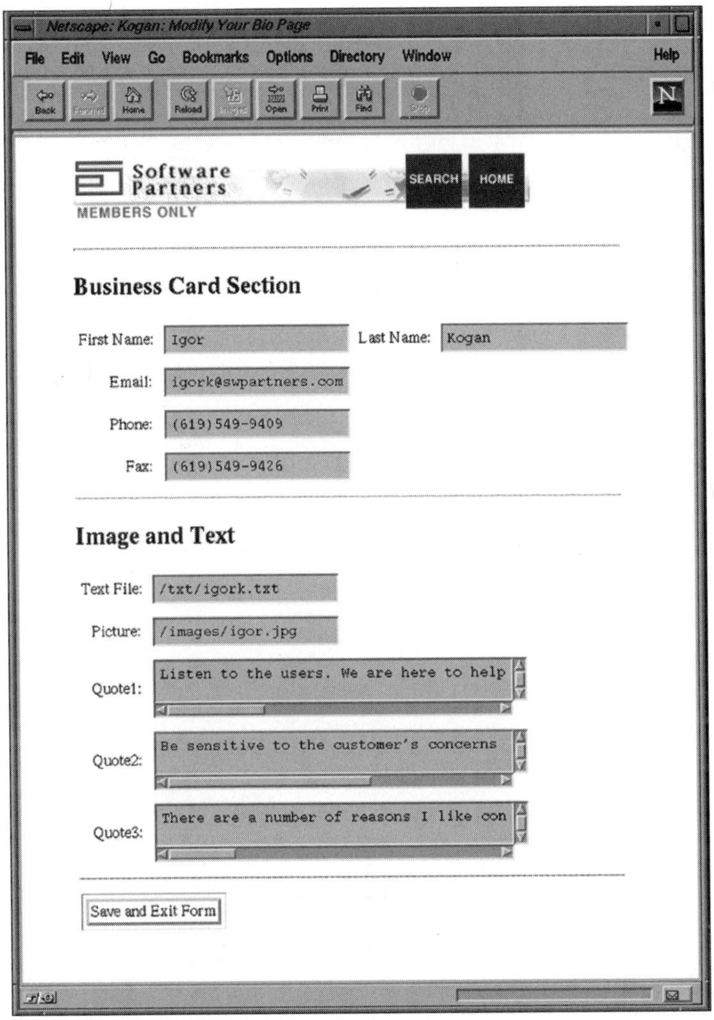

Figure 7-7. A data entry screen

The code for Figure 7-7 appears as follows:

```
<html>
<head>
<title>Modify Your Bio Page</title>
</head>
<BODY background=/images/back.gif>
<p>

<SYB>
```

```
$sql = qq!select lname,
          fname,
          email,
          phone,
          fax,
          file,
          quote1,
          quote2,
          quote3,
          image
     from members where login = \'$login\'!;

if (($rc = ct_sql($ws_db, $sql)) != CS_SUCCEED) {
    ws_error ("<P><B>Connect to database failed</B></P>");
}

while (($ret = ct_results($ws_db, $result_type)) == CS_SUCCEED) {
    RESULTS:
    {
        if ($result_type == CS_CMD_SUCCEED)
        {
            last RESULTS;
        }
        elsif ($result_type == CS_CMD_DONE)
        {
            $rowcount = ct_res_info($ws_db, CS_ROW_COUNT);
            if ($rowcount > 1)
            {
                ws_error ("<P><B>There is more than one row for
$login!</B><P>");
            }
            last RESULTS;
        }
        elsif ($result_type == CS_CMD_FAIL)
        {
            ws_error ("<P><B>SQL command failed</B></P>");
            last RESULTS;
        }
        elsif ($result_type == CS_ROW_RESULT)
        {
            ($login,
                $fname,
                $email,
                $phone,
                $fax,
                $file,
                $quote1,
                $quote2,
                $quote3,
                $image) = ct_fetch($ws_db);
            while (ct_fetch($ws_db))
```

```
            {
            }
            last RESULTS;

        }
        else
        {
            ws_error ("<P><B>What!!!</P></B>");
        }
    }
}

</SYB>

<HR>
<FORM ACTION=modmembersql.hts METHOD=POST>

<A NAME=Topform></A>
<A HREF=#Endform>Go to End</A>

<H2>Business Card Section</H2>
<TABLE>
<TR><TD ALIGN=RIGHT>First Name:     <TD><INPUT NAME=fname VALUE="$fname">
    <TD ALIGN=RIGHT>Last Name:     <TD><INPUT NAME=login VALUE="$login">
<TR><TD ALIGN=RIGHT>Email:     <TD><INPUT NAME=email VALUE="$email">
<TR><TD ALIGN=RIGHT>Phone:     <TD><INPUT NAME=phone VALUE="$phone">
<TR><TD ALIGN=RIGHT>Fax:     <TD><INPUT NAME=fax VALUE="$fax">
</TABLE>

<HR>
<H2>Image and Text</H2>
<TABLE>
<TR><TD ALIGN=RIGHT>Text File:     <TD><INPUT NAME=file VALUE="$file">
<TR><TD ALIGN=RIGHT>Picture:     <TD><INPUT NAME=image VALUE=$image>
<TR><TD ALIGN=RIGHT>Quote1:
    <TD><TEXTAREA NAME=quote1 ROWS=6 COLS=40>$quote1</TEXTAREA>
<TR><TD ALIGN=RIGHT>Quote2:
    <TD><TEXTAREA NAME=quote2 ROWS=6 COLS=40>$quote2</TEXTAREA>
<TR><TD ALIGN=RIGHT>Quote3:
    <TD><TEXTAREA NAME=quote3 ROWS=6 COLS=40>$quote3</TEXTAREA>
</TABLE>
<HR>

<INPUT TYPE=SUBMIT VALUE="Save and Exit Form">
</FORM>

<A HREF=#Topform>Go to Top</A><SP><A NAME=Endform> End of Form</A>

</BODY>
</html>
```

Note that this HTS file fills the form from the database. It performs a select, then uses the returned values as the VALUE attribute for the various form fields. The code initializes longer text fields including the database output between the <TEXTAREA> and </TEXTAREA> tags.

The ct_res_info() call is used to ensure that you retrieved only one row from the database. After all, there should be only one row per consultant in the database. The ct_res_info() call can return:

- The number of rows affected by the current command

- The number of columns in the order by clause

- The number of items in the current result set

- The number of compute clauses in the current command.

Note that another HTS file is used as the SUBMIT action. When Igor is done updating his bio information and presses the Submit button, the current page disappears and the following HTS file is loaded:

```
<HTML>
<BODY background=/images/backb.gif>
<BLOCKQUOTE><IMG SRC="/images/subheadmbronly.jpg"></BLOCKQUOTE>
<BR>
<HR>
<P>
Saving data for $login...
<SYB TYPE=SQL>
update members
        set fname = "$fname",
        lname = "$lname",
        email = "$email",
        phone = "$phone",
        fax = "$fax",
        file = "$file",
        quote1 = "$quote1",
        quote2 = "$quote2",
        quote3 = "$quote3",
        image = "$image"
        where login = "$login"
</SYB>

<SYB>

<BR>
<BR>
<CENTER>
<IMG SRC=/images/highlightsm.jpg>
```

```
</CENTER>
<BR>
...Done.
<HR>

</BODY>
</HTML>
```

The previous code updates the database and then shows the Web page shown in Figure 7-8.

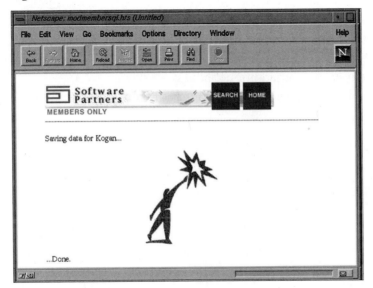

Figure 7-8. *The database is updated*

A `TYPE=SQL` call here is perfectly adequate. If an error occurs, a message is printed on the screen, which is easy to program.

Generally, to receive user input and respond with a database query of any kind, you need to go to a different HTS form. This limitation is dictated by the design of HTML. There are some possibilities for getting around it, and more are being developed all the time. Generally speaking, however, the HTML design dictates moving from page to page when using forms.

A More Complex Database Query

To further illustrate a few more concepts, we will show a page that uses slightly more complex database queries over the Web. In this example, the screen shown in Figure 7-9 allows consultants to view and enter their billable hours.

The example also illustrates a few final constructs:

- `ws_fetch_rows()`
- `ct_cancel()`
- Submitting a batch query using `ct_sql()`
- Getting stored procedure results
- Getting compute results.

The page calls a stored procedure that returns the boundaries of the current billing period. It uses these dates to recall all the hours entered to date for the billing period, computing totals by project as well as overall totals. It then allows the user to enter additional hours.

The code for implementing the form in Figure 7-9 is as follows:

```
<HTML>
<HEAD>
<TITLE>Hours for $login</TITLE>
</HEAD>
<BODY background ="/images/backa.jpg">
<BLOCKQUOTE><IMG SRC="/images/subheadmbronly.jpg"></BLOCKQUOTE>
<BR>

<CENTER>
<BR>
<BR>
<BR>
<FONT SIZE=4>
Current Billing Period
<BR>
<IMG SRC=/images/clocksrunning.gif>
<BR>
<BR>

<SYB TYPE=PERL>

print "<FORM>";
$any_results = 0;

# stored proc
$sql = qq!declare \@startdate datetime,
                  \@enddate datetime
         exec getBillPeriod \@startdate output, \@enddate output
         select convert(char(10), date, 1), project, hours
                from hoursreported
                where date >= \@startdate
```

```
                         and date <= \@enddate
                         and member = \'$login\'
                         order by project
                         compute sum(hours) by project
                         compute sum(hours)
                  !;

if (($rc = $ws_db->ct_sql($sql)) != &CS_SUCCEED)
{
    ws_error ("<P><B> $rc ct_execute fail</B></P>");
}
while (($ret = $ws_db->ct_results($result_type)) == &CS_SUCCEED)
{
    RESULTS:
    {
        if ($result_type == &CS_CMD_SUCCEED)
        {
            last RESULTS;
        }
        elsif ($result_type == &CS_CMD_DONE)
        {
            last RESULTS;
        }
        elsif ($result_type == &CS_STATUS_RESULT)
        {
            if (($status = ct_fetch($ws_db)) != 0)
            {
                print "Bad return status! $status";
            }
            last RESULTS;
        }
        elsif ($result_type == &CS_PARAM_RESULT)
        {
            ($fromdate, $todate) = ct_fetch($ws_db);

            print "<TABLE ALIGN=CENTER>";
            print
"<TR><TD ALIGN=RIGHT>From:<TD><INPUT NAME=fdate VALUE=\"",
                "$fromdate","\">";
            print
"<TR><TD ALIGN=RIGHT>To:<TD><INPUT NAME=tdate VALUE=\"",
                "$todate", "\">";
            print "</TABLE>";

            print "<P>";
            print "<TABLE BORDER = 2>";
            print "<TR><TH>Date<TH>Project<TH>Hours<TH>";
                last RESULTS;
        }
        elsif ($result_type == &CS_COMPUTE_RESULT)
        {
```

```
        while (@c_row = ct_fetch($ws_db))
        {
                if ($any_results == 0)
                {
                    print "<TR><TD>",
                "<TD><B>Grand Total</B><TD ALIGN=RIGHT><B>",
                    @c_row[0], "</B>";
            }
                else
                {
                print "<TR><TD><TD>", "Total",
                    "<TD ALIGN=RIGHT>", @c_row[0];
                }
                $any_results = 0;
        }
        last RESULTS;
    }
    elsif ($result_type == &CS_MSG_RESULT)
    {
                last RESULTS;
    }
    elsif ($result_type == &CS_CMD_FAIL)
    {
                ct_cancel($ws_db, CT_CANCEL_ALL);
                ws_error ("<P><B>Could not execute SQL !!!</B></P>");
                last RESULTS;
    }
    elsif ($result_type == &CS_ROW_RESULT)
    {
        ws_fetch_rows($ws_db,
        "<TR><TD>%s<TD>%s<TD ALIGN=RIGHT>%s");
        $any_results = 1;
            last RESULTS;
    }
          else {
        print "You shouldn't be here!!!";
          }
    }
}
# end of stored proc
print "</TABLE>";
</SYB>

<P>
<TABLE ALIGN=CENTER>
<TR><TD ALIGN=RIGHT>Date:<TD><INPUT TYPE=TEXT NAME=newdate>
<TR><TD ALIGN=RIGHT>Project:<TD><INPUT TYPE=TEXT NAME=newproj>
<TR><TD ALIGN=RIGHT>Hours:<TD><INPUT TYPE=TEXT NAME=newhours>
</TABLE>
<BR>
<BR>
<HR>
```

```
<INPUT TYPE=SUBMIT ACTION=addhours.hts VALUE="Insert">
<INPUT TYPE=RESET ACTION=hours.hts VALUE="Start Over">
</FORM>
</CENTER>
</BODY>
</HTML>
```

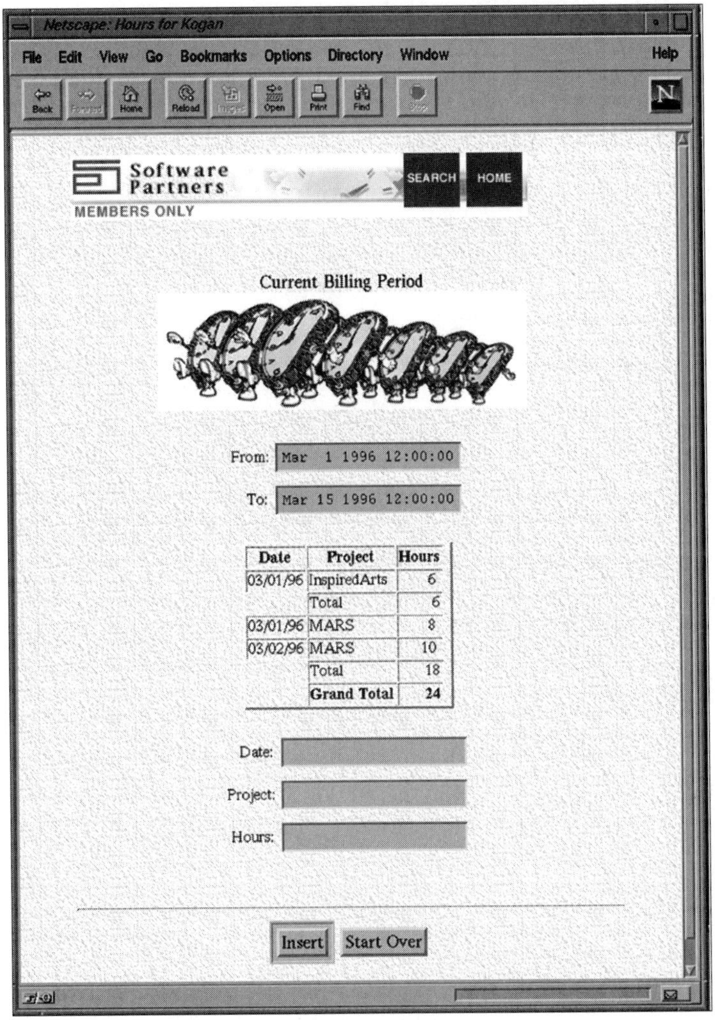

Figure 7-9. A batch database query in web.sql

Notice that the SQL statement submitted to `ct_sql()` contains two queries: a call to a stored procedure followed by a select with a compute clause. The stored procedure returns two parameters, `@startdate` and `@enddate`.

The `ct_results()` loop, then, needs to get:

- The stored procedure output
- The row output
- The compute clause output.

The following steps show how the results loop works:

1. The parameters `@startdate` and `@enddate` are returned along with the status of the stored procedure.

2. Data row output alternates with compute results.

3. The last row of compute results give the overall total, which you want to handle differently. In our example, we provided a flag to determine when you are receiving the last row.

Next, note the use of `ct_cancel()`. It discards the rest of the results, stopping more output from being returned by the server. You must use `ct_cancel()` to do this if you do not expect to use the remaining results.

Finally, note the use of `ws_fetch_rows()`, which provides an alternative to `ct_fetch()` for data rows. `ws_fetch_rows()` processes all the data rows and formats the output according to the `$format` parameter. If a `$format` parameter is not supplied, the output is formatted as an HTML 3.0 table.

Winding Up

By now, you should know enough web.sql commands to program a variety of applications in web.sql. The few commands we didn't cover in this chapter are listed here for reference and to encourage you to develop your own applications for them.

`ws_print`	Like the Perl `printf()` command, but expands variable references.
`ct_callback`	Installs a callback routine.
`ct_options`	Sets SQL Server options such as `noexec`.
`ct_col_types`	Retrieves column types for a row.
`ct_col_names`	Retrieves column names for a row.

Tips and Tricks

Web.sql provides powerful constructs for interfacing directly with a database and producing HTML for Web browsers. It carries out most actions on the server side, isolating database code from the Web and maximizing performance opportunities. Web.sql also gives the programmer a succinct environment for writing Web code by allowing a variety of constructs to appear in one file, the HTS file. Here are some tips and tricks for use in developing web.sql-enabled Web sites:

1. Use the simplest web.sql technique possible to do your database query. For example:

    *   Use `<SYB TYPE=SQL>` whenever appropriate.

    *   Usually, `ws_sql()` is the simplest of the API calls.

2. Perl global variables can appear outside the `<SYB>` blocks. Thus, if the value of `$database_company` is "Sybase," using the statement

    `$database_company`

    in the HTML part of the file produces

    Sybase

    on the user's screen. Use parameters to pass context from screen to screen and to automatically create Perl global variables.

3. Some of the most interesting Web-related opportunities have to do with connecting existing databases to the Web. To this end, Sybase provides an extremely strong set of tools to accompany web.sql. Not discussed in this document, but closely related to the topic, is the use of data replication and connectivity tools in conjunction with web.sql. These tools offer ways for not only connecting to newly-developed databases, but also to existing, heterogeneous databases. In the future, we'll have applications that replicate data into a special database for the Web, and also replicate it back. A discussion for another time.

8

Security Issues
for the Web

Although there is a universal recognition that the lack of agreement on security standards for the World Wide Web is a major stumbling block for serious commercial Web applications, there are no standards for World Wide Web (WWW) security today. This chapter describes the basic challenges of network security, some of the exposures that lurk on the Internet, and the solutions for security that appear to have the most promise and momentum today.

Modern cryptography is a branch of mathematics devoted to maintaining the secrecy of messages. The subject is difficult to explain without erring on the amount of detail to include or omit, but we'll take our chances because cryptography is a cornerstone of future Web technology. We'll review the latest security systems proposed by network strategists because it's likely that we'll soon see official standards that combine the best features of these efforts. We'll also take a look at some important security-related considerations for working with a Web server as a developer or an administrator. Throughout this chapter, we'll use the Netscape products in examples because their Navigator and Commerce Server solution has significantly influenced the direction of WWW security.

This chapter contains the following sections:

- General Principles for Securing Your Server
- Controlling Access to Your Server
- Reducing Application Programming Exposures
- Addressing Internet Security Concerns with Modern Cryptographic Methods
- Applying Cryptography to the World Wide Web
- Testing Security Systems Against Attacks
- Securing the Client
- SSL Resources.

General Principles for Securing Your Server

This section covers some of the more important principles related to reducing security risks when running a WWW server. We'll include general security principles that apply to all server operating system environments as well as security principles specific to UNIX.

Use Dedicated Computers

If you have a choice, it is best to use a dedicated computer for your server for the following reasons:

- If your server security is compromised, other applications are not affected
- There are fewer ways for people to attack your server as long as you don't run telnet or network applications like Network File System (NFS)
- It reduces coordination issues if you need to reboot your machine.

You may need to provide WWW services that address completely unrelated needs. For instance, your organization might use forms and scripts for internal purchase order processing, and a merchandise shipment tracking application for your remote Internet customers. It's certainly possible to use a single server for both purposes, but why jeopardize your internal system? What are your savings if you inadvertently leave a door open and cause your internal application to be unavailable for a few days? It's much more reasonable to use separate servers on different computers for unrelated applications.

Consider Physical Security

Your server should operate within a physically-secure location where unwanted visitors are limited. If possible, make sure that your computer's boot configuration is password-protected. You want to prevent someone from taking control of your machine by simply powering off the machine and rebooting from alternate media.

Consider Firewalls and Inter-Network Security

If your organization has a significant internal network implementation, you should consider using a network *firewall* to protect your investment. A firewall is usually a special-purpose computer that controls traffic between an organization's internal network and one or more external networks such as the Internet. The important concept is that *all* inbound and outbound traffic must go through the firewall: the control program uses your management policies to permit or deny the traffic. The firewall's narrow port of entry makes it easy to quickly change your security policy because you only need to reconfigure a single computer. A typical implementation is a computer that allows internal users to exchange electronic mail with the Internet, but denies all other access from either side of the firewall.

If you want to allow internal users to access Internet resources in a controlled manner, use a *proxy*. A proxy is a program that can communicate with both sides of a firewall. For example, an organization may set up a *proxy server* for use by the organization's WWW browsers. All browser requests to HTTP, FTP, and GOPHER resources on the external Internet are sent to the proxy server, which performs the actual contact outside the firewall and relays the results back to the browser.

Setting up a firewall or a proxy server can be complicated. There are many excellent resources that explain how to do this using free software, but we will leave those discussions for others. A good general reference on firewalls is: *Firewalls and Internet Security*, by William R. Cheswick and Steven M. Bellovin.

Use Appropriate User and User IDs

It is important to understand the difference between the user that starts the server and the user ID that is used to execute scripts or retrieve documents. If you intend to use TCP port 80 for HTTP and port 443 for HTTPS, then the root user must start the server because these ports are restricted. After the server is started, it listens for requests on its assigned port. When a connection request comes in, the server creates a separate or *child* process to service the request. The child process has an *effective* user ID that is specified in the server's configuration files. The user ID "nobody" is often used, but on some systems that user ID cannot execute programs. If "nobody" won't perform properly on your system, ask your system administrator to create a user ID for the server that doesn't belong to any UNIX groups.

Set UNIX File Permissions

We'll assume that you are the Web administrator and that you share application development duties with other people. Follow these steps to set UNIX file permissions:

1. Create a group for everyone that needs to create documents for the server. Choose a name that's meaningful to you, like "wdev" (for "WWW development").

2. Create a user ID that owns everything (such as "www"), and make it a member of the "wdev" group. You will use that user ID when you need to do server maintenance using an explicit login or the command `su - www`.

3. Add your fellow developers to the "wdev" group. Depending on your operating system, they may need to use the command `newgrp - wdev` to change their primary group before they create new documents.

4. Set up the server's document tree so that:

    •   The "www" user ID owns the document root, all subdirectories, and initially, all documents

    •   All directories, subdirectories and documents belong to the "wdev" group

- All directories and subdirectories have file permissions set to allow owner read-write-execute, group read-write-execute, and world read-execute or octal 775

- All documents have file permissions set to allow owner read-write, group read-write, and world read or octal 664.

Use the UNIX Chroot Command to Start the Server

You can use the UNIX `chroot` (change root) command to start the server so that it does not know about, and therefore cannot access any files or directories above a certain point in the UNIX file system. That point becomes the new "root" of the file system from the server's viewpoint (hence the name of the command). This gives you increased security in case someone manages to take control of your server because the host computer's operating system files are not accessible to the intruder. However, there is a price for this protection. Any commands or files that the server needs to use, such as the Perl interpreter or ISQL must also be located within this portion of the file system. To make the commands or files available to the server, you must copy them into the chroot environment you are preparing. Your operating system manuals or man pages will explain what to do in more detail.

Controlling Access to Your Server

If you have a general-purpose server, you probably need to control access to certain resources. Some of your scripts might access databases or other objects that should be restricted to internal use only. For example, let's say that the network specialist at your company wants to do a trial evaluation of a WWW training package from an outfit called "Sam's Routers-R-Us." One of the terms of the trial agreement is that you will not allow anyone outside the company to use the tutorials. You need to restrict access for the materials to your company's Internet domain or a pattern of IP addresses used in your organization. Sometimes it is necessary to deny access to everyone except a few individuals.

This section shows you how to edit configuration files in order to enforce user authentication, and how to prevent outside users from accessing your server. We show you how to edit the configuration files directly, but if you prefer a graphical interface, you can use the Netscape Administration Server shipped with Netscape servers to alter these files. Figure 8-1 shows part of an Administration Server screen.

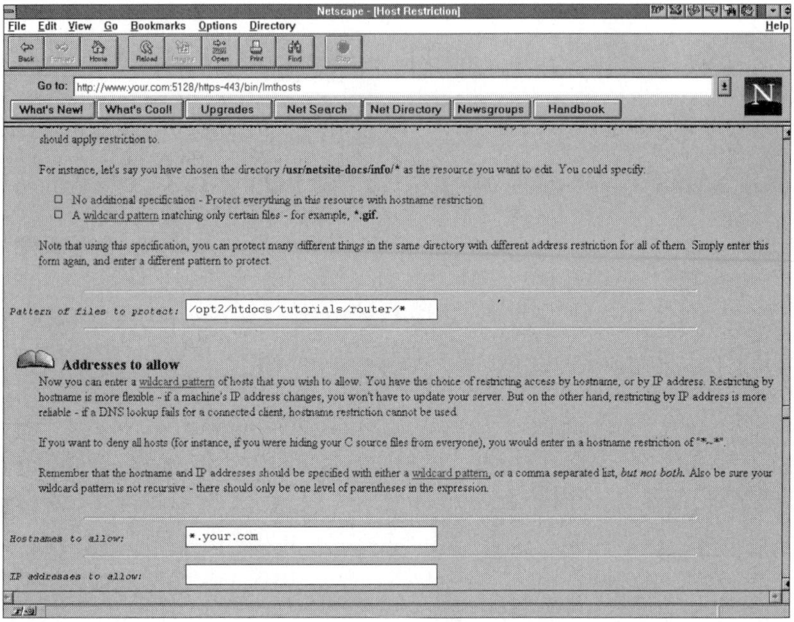

Figure 8-1. *A screen portion of Netscape's Administration Server*

Note: Do not use the Netscape Administration Server tool remotely because it does not use the SSL.

Considerations for User IDs and Passwords

Before you begin editing configuration files to enforce user authorization, you should decide how you want to manage user IDs and passwords. All servers allow you to create security databases to secure parts or all of a server's document tree. These databases usually consist of username:password pairs and are stored as plain-text files that you can edit directly, or DataBase Management (DBM) format files that you can access through special utility programs.

Managing User IDs

DBM files provide a significant performance benefit for large lists of user IDs, but they are less convenient to administer than plain-text files. The Netscape and NCSA HTTPd 1.5 servers allow you to choose either format. Netscape provides a program to convert a plain-text database to DBM, and NCSA offers the C source code, std2dbm.c and dbm2srd.c, to convert in both directions.

After you have implemented user ID and password authorization on your server, you are faced with the ongoing management responsibility of adding or removing users and changing passwords. Netscape offers a compiled program that allows you to change your password if you know the current one, which can be easily integrated into a screen for your users. You can add, remove, or change entries in your database by compiling the source dbmpasswd.c from NCSA.

The NCSA and Netscape servers also allow you to use group lists to provide additional access control. The Netscape server only supports group files in plain-text format: if you try to identify more than one group in a file, it does not work properly. Also, if you decide to use group files, Netscape's manual instructs you to use DBM format for the user ID database rather than the plain-text format. Again, NCSA HTTPd 1.5 allows you to choose plain-text or DBM format.

User IDs, CGI Scripts, and Forms

CGI scripts run under the UNIX user ID of the Web server unless something in the script explicitly changes it. Putting scripts in a password-protected directory provides some measure of protection against those scripts being run by unauthorized users.

Sybase itself requires its own user IDs and passwords, and you can build a section of the HTML form requesting this information. Providing access to a limited number of reports and requiring the user to enter their user ID and password each time they access each form is probably not a burden. However, if your entire Sybase user application is built around the Web, requiring the user to retype their user ID and password before they can access each screen will be tedious for them. Unfortunately, you cannot request the Sybase user ID and password once and then have them reliably passed from form to form because you never know exactly where a user might enter the application. One useful technique for handling this situation is configuring the Web server to require user authentication, and recording within the Sybase database who changed what and when.

A Web server configured to require user authentication makes the user ID available through the REMOTE_USER environment variable. This information can be used to log who is making changes to the database. Depending upon your security needs, this method may provide enough accountability, allowing the actual access to Sybase SQL Server itself to be accomplished through a single user ID. If you want to provide access to Sybase through a single user ID such as the Web server's user ID, you must either hard-code the Sybase user ID and password into each application, or store them someplace else and have the application access them. The method illustrated below uses Tcl as the CGI script language, and assumes that a Sybase password file exists for the Web server user ID. This file is read, write only to the owner and contains the Sybase server name, user ID, and password on a single line separated by tabs, enabling a single file to handle multiple servers.

```
set tempid [exec id]
set fchar [string first "(" $tempid]
set lchar [string first ")" $tempid]
set fchar [expr $fchar + 1]
set lchar [expr $lchar - 1]
set userid [string range $tempid $fchar $lchar]

if  { $userid == ""  } {
     append err_msg "COULD NOT GET USER ID"
     do_exit
}

if { ! [file readable $pwdir] } {
     append err_msg "PASSWORD FILE INACCESSIBLE FOR USER"
     do_exit
}
set fd [open $pwdir]

if { [gets $fd syb_passwd] <= 0 } {
     append err_msg "COULD NOT READ PASSWORD"
     do_exit
}

close $fd
```

Accessing the REMOTE_USER environment variable for updating a table that tracks who changed what is as simple as accessing the $env array in Tcl, as shown below:

```
set update_user $env(REMOTE_USER)
```

The `update_user` variable can then be put into a field in the database to track who changed the record.

Another use for the `REMOTE_USER` environment variable is to track who is accessing which scripts. Using a Tcl procedure, you can track who is running the script, the name of the script being run, and any script arguments by appending the information to a log.

Enforcing User Authorization

The NCSA and Netscape servers use different syntax in their directives enforcing user authorization. Both servers have global authorization configuration files: NCSA uses *access.conf*, and Netscape uses *obj.conf*. NCSA also allows you to specify local security directives within individual document directories using hidden files named *.htaccess*. The following sections summarize the directives and offer examples for using the NCSA and Netscape global authorization configuration files.

Using NCSA's Global Authorization Configuration File

Table 8-1 shows the directives and options that form the NCSA user authorization statements.

Table 8-1. *NCSA User Authorization Statements*

Directive	Description
`<Directory {pathname} >` `options </Directory>`	Specifies the resource to protect
`AuthType Basic`	Specifies the type of authorization
`AuthName {name}`	Conveys the reason for the restriction
`AuthUserFile {filename}`	The location of the user:password database
`AuthGroupFile {filename}`	The location of the group list file
`<Limit {GET|PUT|POST} >` `options </Limit>`	Contains a Require directive
`Require {user|group} name`	Grants access to the user or group

In the example, we'll assume that we have already created a DBM format database called user.dbm. The user.dbm database is populated with user ID:password pairs for all of your company's employees.

1. Create a new file called *group.txt* that defines a group called STUDENT. Initially, the file should contain this single line:

   ```
   STUDENT:
   ```

2. Add three user IDs to the STUDENT group: these user IDs are already part of the user.dbm database.

   At this point, group.txt consists of a single line:

   ```
   STUDENT:bwood sjones tfletcher
   ```

3. Add the following section of directives to your access.conf file:

   ```
   <Directory /opt2/htdocs/tutorials/router>

   AuthType Basic
   AuthName Routers-R-Us
   AuthUserFile /opt2/httpd/userdb/user.dbm
   AuthGroupFile /opt2/httpd/userdb/group.txt
   <Limit GET>
   Require group STUDENT
   </Limit>
   </Directory>
   ```

4. Restart your server to put the changes into effect.

Anyone accessing the .html files in the router subdirectory will be required to supply a user ID and password. If the user ID and password match an entry in the user.dbm database, the server will check to see if they are a member of the STUDENT group. If the user ID is one of the three you put into group.txt, the server allows the user to view the files.

Using Netscape's Global Authorization Configuration File

Table 8-2 shows the obj.conf directives used to enforce user authorization.

***Table 8-2.** Obj.conf Directives Used to Enforce User Authorization*

Directive	Description
`<Object ppath= name>` `options </Object>`	Specifies the resource to protect
`AuthTrans {parameters}`	Specifies the user ID database and group file using the following parameters:
`fn=basic-ncsa`	Specifies basic server authorization scheme
`auth-type= {type}`	Specifies the type of authorization
`dbm= {filename}`	Path and name of DBM user ID database
`userfile= {filename}`	Path and name of plain-text user ID database
`grpfile= {filename}`	Path and name of group file
`PathCheck {parameters}`	Specifies access restrictions using the following parameters:
`realm= {message}`	Quoted string identifying the type of resources protected
`fn=require-auth`	Only allow access if user or group is authorized
`auth-type=basic`	Only basic type is allowed
`auth-user= {list}`	Quoted string to identify users allowed access
`auth-group= {list}`	Quoted string to identify groups allowed access

Add the following section of directives to your obj.conf file in order to restrict access to the tutorial materials. A valid user ID, password, and membership in the STUDENT group is required to view the documents.

```
<Object ppath="/opt2/htdocs/tutorials/router/*">
AuthTrans fn="basic-ncsa" dbm="/opt2/httpd/userdb/user.dbm" auth-
type="basic" grpfile=/opt2/httpd/userdb/group.txt
PathCheck realm="Router Tutorial" fn="require-auth" auth-type=basic auth-
group="STUDENT"
</Object>
```

Preventing Outside Users from Accessing the Server

Now that you've created user IDs to authorize specific users to access your server, you want to prevent users outside your company from using those ID's. Assume that your Internet domain name is *your.com*. In the examples that follow, we will build upon the earlier configuration files. Again, NCSA and Netscape allow you to do many of the same things, but the syntax is different.

Using NCSA to Prevent Outside Access

Table 8-3 shows the directives and options that form the NCSA remote host authorization statements:

Table 8-3. *NCSA Remote Host Authorization Statements*

Directive/options	Description
`<Limit {GET|PUT|POST} >` `options </Limit>`	Contains all other directives
`Order {deny,allow|allow,deny}`	Specifies the order in which to apply restrictions
`Deny from {host|IP address| all}`	Specifies who should not have access
`Allow from {host|IP address|all}`	Specifies who should have access

You want to replace the directives you added earlier to your access.conf file with these:

```
<Directory /opt2/htdocs/tutorials/router>
AuthType Basic
AuthName Routers-R-Us
AuthUserFile /opt2/httpd/userdb/user.dbm
AuthGroupFile /opt2/httpd/userdb/group.txt
<Limit GET>
Order deny, allow
deny from all
allow from .your.com
Require group STUDENT
</Limit>
</Directory>
```

Using Netscape to Prevent Outside Access

Table 8-4 shows the directives and options that form the Netscape remote host authorization statements.

Table 8-4. *Netscape Remote Host Authorization Statements*

Directive/options	Description
`<Object ppath=` `{name}> {options} </Object>`	Specifies the resource to protect
`<Client {parameters}` `>{options} </Client>`	Specifies network access using these parameters:
`ip= {addresses}`	A quoted string containing the IP address
`dns= {hosts}`	A quoted string identifying hosts by registered name
`PathCheck {parameters}`	Specifies access restriction parameters
`fn="deny-existence"`	Allows you to tell a remote user that your server could not find a resource, rather than telling it that you do not want to allow access.

Replace the directives you added earlier to your object.conf file with these:

```
<Object ppath="/opt2/htdocs/tutorials/router/*">
<Client dns="*~*.your.com">
PathCheck fn="deny-existence"
</Client>
AuthTrans fn="basic-ncsa" dbm="/opt2/httpd/userdb/user.dbm" auth-
type="basic" grpfile=/opt2/httpd/userdb/group.txt
PathCheck realm="Router Tutorial" fn="require-auth" auth-type=basic auth-
group="STUDENT"
</Object>
```

Placing Multiple Servers on a Single Computer

Sometimes it is necessary to provide a different set of server resources to users outside your organization. Or you might have a requirement to provide a Web server for an additional group using the same computer.

One way to do this is to run a second WWW server that listens to a logical port other than 80 or 443, such as port 8000. The problem with this solution is that the Domain Name Service (DNS) only uses hostnames and IP addresses—not port numbers—so you cannot register the second server and hide the fact that you are sharing the same computer.

A cleaner way to solve this problem involves using different server configurations to handle requests (including access policies), depending on the IP address used to reach your computer. This is one of the more interesting features of the NCSA 1.5 server. Most computers can be configured to use additional communication adapters (for example, ethernet cards), each with a separate IP address. You can register the second IP address with a name that represents the second server and then add a VirtualHost section in the httpd.conf configuration file containing directives that override the server parameters specified before it. For example, the following directives create the appearance of a separate WWW server.

```
<VirtualHost 132.239.30.3>
ServerName www.free-ride.com
</VirtualHost>
```

For more details, consult:

```
http://hoohoo.ncsa.uiuc.edu/docs/howto/multihome.html
```

Reducing Application Programming Exposures

When you go beyond providing simple documents and begin offering interactive programs to users, you inevitably expose your server's computer to types of access you did not intend to provide. It is difficult to anticipate all the different ways renegade users can subvert your programs, primarily because your mental focus when programming is to make things work, create value, and share things—not to defend yourself.

The unfortunate reality is that if you offer services on the Internet, you must always assume that someone is going to test your doors and windows while you're sleeping. The good news is that many of the gaping security holes are well documented, so you can eliminate the majority of potential problems by following the simple guidelines suggested in this section.

Use SCCS in UNIX Environments

If your server's environment is UNIX, consider using the Source Code Control System (SCCS) for your programs. The SCCS allows you to control versions of your scripts, and makes it difficult for someone to accidentally overwrite a current program with an older copy from their private directory. It takes a bit of effort to convert existing scripts into SCCS, but it is easy to use from then on.

Make Your Scripts Exposure-resistant

Does someone try to break your scripts before you make them generally available? Obviously, you test your scripts to ensure that they're working, but it is often difficult to see past your own assumptions about how your script will be used. Someone else might see an exposure that you overlook.

Following are some general principles for reducing exposures that apply across all scripting or programming languages:

- Check all input supplied to a script or program. Decide what is valid input and extract the input by pattern matching. Reject everything else.

- Avoid all situations where user input is directly passed to a system call. In Perl, system calls include the `eval` statement and the `exec()` and `system()` functions, and invoke external programs via backticks or pipes.

- If you do decide to use a system call, make sure that you use the program's fully-qualified pathname. For example, enter `/usr2/bin/stats` instead of `stats`. By doing so, you won't risk executing a different program named `stats` that someone surreptitiously added to the current working directory or one of the directories included in your `PATH` environmental variable.

- If you use a form to provide input, understand that the form does not control what can be passed to the script *in any way at all*. Your script and its input can be called independently as a URL or from a form on another server. Don't make the assumption that the choices you offer on the form will prevent someone from supplying other input independently to your script.

- Remember that hidden form variables can be viewed by the user. Netscape Navigator users can choose the View|Source menu option to view hidden form variables. Some valid reasons for using hidden form variables are: 1) to make it easier to test a form/script combination; and 2) to communicate the identity of a form to a script that works with multiple forms. If you find other reasons to use this feature, just remember that it does not really hide anything. Most importantly, do not use hidden form variables to set passwords.

- If you decide to use server access restrictions to limit who can use your form, make sure you add the same protection to the script called by the form.

- Scripts are usually easier to break than compiled programs. On a UNIX system, you should be extremely careful about giving a script set-user-on-execution (setuid) permission. If you need to do this, never allow root to serve as the temporary user ID for the script.

- Compiled programs should never make assumptions about the size of input supplied by the remote user. If the program's input buffer length is exceeded, it may be possible for the user to execute a command. Use dynamic allocation for these areas and provide error handling in case the program exhausts the amount of memory available.

- Perl has a built-in mechanism called *tainting* that can help you protect yourself. When taint checking is active, any environmental variables, command-line input, or standard input cannot be used by your script in any command that starts a subshell or modifies directories or files. You must use pattern matching to extract the data from these sources before using it.

- To turn on tainting for Perl version 4, use

```
#!/usr/local/bin/taintperl
```

instead of

```
#!/usr/local/bin/perl
```

- For Perl5, tainting is specified using the following command line flag:

```
#!/usr/local/bin/perl -T
```

If you use Perl to write your CGI scripts, review *Safe CGI Programming* by Paul Phillips. You can find it at this location:

```
http://www.cerf.net/~paulp/cgi-security/safe-cgi.txt
```

Considerations for Sybase

If your WWW scripts use ISQL as the CGI-to-Sybase SQL Server link, you must consider the possibility that your Sybase user ID and password may be exposed to sniffers. This section shows you how to reduce security exposures by using ISQL in batch mode, how to maintain user passwords, and how to encrypt passwords.

Using ISQL in Batch Mode

Typically, you invoke ISQL with a command similar to the following:

```
$ISQL -U user_name
```

After you respond to the password prompt, you are inside the program and ready to enter Transact-SQL (Sybase's SQL language) commands. This is the *interactive* method for using ISQL, which is impractical when using ISQL with Web servers because of the security risks implicit with the ability to invoke any Transact-SQL command directly against the database. For example, using ISQL interactively would allow a user to enter the `delete table` command, wreaking havoc on the database.

You want to use ISQL in *batch* mode so you can manually script the entire interaction between ISQL, the CGI program, and Sybase SQL server to avoid these security risks. Using ISQL in batch mode means that you need to bypass the ISQL command prompt and find another method for supplying a password.

One option is to use the `-P` command-line argument to ISQL, as follows:

```
$ISQL -U user_name -P password
```

Unfortunately, this is not a secure way of supplying a password. For example, when you type the system command in UNIX:

```
ps -ef
```

you see the entire command line that invoked ISQL as part of the output of the ps command. This is not secure because the ISQL user's password is displayed on the command line each time someone invokes the program in this fashion.

A better approach is to place this command into a script and make the script executable. Consider the following C-Shell (csh) script. It contains the same command in the preceding example.

```
#!/bin/csh
$ISQL -U user_name -P password
```

You could set the permissions so that only the appropriate users can see the contents of the preceding script, but it does not completely solve the security problem. Even if you set the permissions correctly and use a CGI program to invoke the preceding csh script, the command line for ISQL can still be read using the ps command, as we described before. The following changes to the csh script solve this problem.

```
#!/bin/csh
$ISQL -U user_name  << EOF
password

quit
EOF
```

Note that the preceding script looks different than the previous one. Let's look at what it is doing. The append input operator << tells UNIX to invoke the ISQL program and pass whatever appears up to the label EOF to the ISQL program. If you think of how the interactive program works, when you type:

```
$ISQL -U user_name
```

you would next be prompted for a password. This prompting occurs here as well. Because the code that appears before the label EOF is passed to ISQL, if you make sure you have the password as the first value followed by a carriage return, then the password is supplied just the same. If you type the ps command after the preceding csh script is invoked, you will only see the code up to the <<

appear as the output of `ps`, which hides the password. Assuming that the correct file permissions are set for the csh script, the password is fairly safe.

There is a caveat, though. The actual prompt appears as part of the output. The result set that the CGI script sees includes the following prompt as the very first value in the result set:

```
Password:
```

You need to filter this out of your output with the CGI script before displaying it as a Web page. We discuss how to do this filtering in Chapter 4, "Creating CGI Scripts Using Perl."

Maintaining Passwords

Using the preceding method to handle passwords requires you to go into each csh script containing ISQL code and change the password value each time you need to change a user's ISQL password. This could become a maintenance nightmare after you create many scripts. By taking advantage of the UNIX operating system, you can reduce the maintenance overhead.

To begin, you need to create two user IDs: a UNIX user ID with ownership access to the Web server software, and a Web ISQL Server ID for making Sybase SQL Server accessible from within a Web session. Only the Web master should have access to these two accounts.

When you create a UNIX user ID for the Web server, give all the permissions for running CGI scripts to the Web user ID (for example, WWW_User) from within the Web server. (See the configuration instructions for your particular Web server to set the permissions for CGI execution.) Create a hidden file that contains the ISQL password for the WWW_User ID. Hidden files in UNIX have names beginning with a period. For example, you could name your hidden password file as follows:

```
.WWW_Userid_Pwd
```

Simply naming the file with a leading period does not automatically make the file secure. Change the UNIX file permissions so that only the WWW_User ID can read or write to the file, as follows:

```
chmod 600 .WWW_Userid_Pwd
```

In this password file, type the password value for the Web ISQL user, not the UNIX password, for the WWW_User ID. After these are in place, you can use a csh script like the following to access Sybase SQL Server from the Web server.

```
#!/bin/csh
$ISQL -U user_name << EOF
`cat /export/home/WWW_User/.WWW_Userid_Pwd`

quit
EOF
```

Notice that the line where we previously supplied the password value begins and ends with a backquote (`): this is not the same as a single quote character. (The backquote usually shares the same keyboard key as the tilde (~), but it may be in a different place on your keyboard.) The backquote has special meaning in UNIX. It tells UNIX to run the command between the backquotes and place the result of the command in the file as if it had been entered there. In our example, we're running the cat command, which concatenates or reads the file that follows it on the command line. In the preceding script, the cat command reads the hidden password file for the WWW_User ID, which contains the password to the ISQL Web user ID. You achieve the same result as with the previous csh script, but in this case, if you need to change a user's password, you only have to do it in one place instead of changing it in each script.

Encrypting the Password

Sybase warns that if you supply a password to ISQL in interactive or batch mode and the server crashes, the password value is readable in the core file left by the crashed server. Sybase supplies the -X command-line option that encrypts the password between the client and server, making it unreadable in the core file if the server crashes. This option changes the preceding csh script slightly:

```
#!/bin/csh
$ISQL -U WWW_User -X -i /export/home/WWW_User/sp_help.sql << EOF
`cat /export/home/WWW_User/.WWW_Userid_Pwd`

quit
EOF
```

Note: In our examples in this section, we showed you scripts pointing to a single hidden password file in the WWW_User's home directory. It is more likely, and highly recommended, that you have different passwords for each server. As a result, you may have one password file in the WWW_User's home directory for each server.

Addressing Internet Security Concerns with Modern Cryptographic Methods

If you're planning to use the Internet for commercial applications, you face an interesting challenge. The things that make the Net successful—high speed communications and ease of access—also introduce serious security exposures for anyone hoping to utilize the Net as a reliable path for business transactions. Today, the primary network security concerns are *authentication*, *message integrity*, and *privacy*. We'll define each of these terms by the questions they raise:

- *Authentication*—Is your transaction partner (server, client) really who it says it is?

- *Message integrity*—Is there a guarantee that your messages will not be modified by any outsiders? How will you know?

- *Privacy*—Can someone other than your transaction partners intercept and read your messages?

An additional issue that has not yet received a lot of attention—yet—is the situation where a Web transaction involving money is later repudiated by one of the parties. For example, if your organization uses the Web for electronic commerce and a customer orders something from you and pays with her MasterCard account, do you have a way to prove later that she agreed to those payment terms? If challenged, will your proof hold up in a court of law? You should think about these issues when making decisions about which security system to employ. Digital signatures will solve part of the repudiation problem by allowing us to replace paper documents with ones propagated and stored by computers.

All WWW servers provide ways to selectively restrict access to some or all documents on the basis of a browser's Internet address or domain. Authorization by user name and password, discussed earlier, is also a standard feature. These basic controls, while useful, don't guarantee the safety of network transactions between the browser and the server. The Internet relies on many intermediate computers to provide routing services, but unfriendly people can break into any of these machines and use them to eavesdrop or to modify network traffic. Cryptography is the only way to protect transactions that must traverse the outside world. This section discusses the concepts and nomenclature of some of the more popular encryption methods used today. Applying these methods to the World Wide Web is illustrated in the section, "Applying Cryptography to the World Wide Web."

Overview of Cryptographic Tools

This section discusses some of the more popular encryption methods employed by modern network security systems. Most cryptographic methods use *keys* to encrypt messages. A key is a unit of data, similar in concept to a password, that is used by encryption methods to make a message or transaction temporarily unreadable. The cryptographic methods are summarized below:

- *Symmetric*, or "secret key" cryptographic techniques, in which the key used by the message sender to encrypt the transaction is also used by the message receiver to decrypt the transaction

- *Asymmetric*, or "public key" techniques that allow the message sender and receiver to use different keys to encrypt and decrypt the same message

- Special keyless functions called *message digests* that are used to check the integrity of the data transmitted

- *Digital certificates*, used to validate your partner's identity.

The latest packaged WWW security solutions, which we will examine in "Applying Cryptography to the World Wide Web" use a combination of these methods. The following sections describe each method more fully.

Symmetric Cryptography (Secret Key) Methods

There are many secret key encryption methods available today. The more popular secret key methods are the DES, RC2 and RC4 ciphers, which are described in this section. The most important differences between them are key size, length of time in common service, patent rights, and U.S. export restrictions. Regardless of their strengths, they all share the same problem: how to distribute secret keys to a remote recipient without risking interception. Public key encryption systems, described in the next section, are ideally suited for exchanging secret keys.

The Data Encryption Standard (DES) was developed in the early 1970s by IBM and the National Security Agency (NSA). Its 56-bit key size doesn't provide much security from today's powerful computers. A stronger method called Triple-DES has an effective key size of 90 bits and is much more secure. DES is a *block cipher*—it encrypts and decrypts messages in chunks.

RSA Data Security, Inc. offers two proprietary encryption algorithms for license in the United States. The Rivest's Code 2 and 4 (RC2 , RC4) functions can be used with any key size from 1 to 1024 bits. These routines were developed by Ron Rivest, an MIT professor who co-founded RSA with fellow mathematicians Adi Shamir and Len Adleman. RC2 is a block cipher like DES, but RSA claims that it is approximately twice as fast. RC4 is a *stream cipher*—it encrypts a message by using a number string of the same length. Hardware or software using RC2 or RC4 can be legally exported from the United States if the implementation uses a key size of 40 bits or less. The reasoning behind this is that the small key size produces encrypted code that is relatively easy to break, and does not pose a threat to national security.

Asymmetric Cryptography (Public Key) Methods

Asymmetric cryptography techniques rely on the mathematical presumption (but not proof) that certain numerical operations can be performed easily in one direction (encryption), but not in the reverse direction (decryption) unless you know the value of one of the original inputs. Under this scheme, each trading partner has a public key that can be advertised to the world, and a private key that must be kept secret.

To send an encrypted message to a trading partner, it is only necessary to know the partner's public key, encrypt the message using that key, and transmit the message. Upon receipt, the trading partner uses their private key to decrypt the message. An outsider intercepting the encrypted message and the public key would only be able to decrypt the message by repetitive computations taking many months or years of computer time, or by finding a new discovery in mathematics. The RSA public key method, developed in the mid-1970s, is the best known of these technologies.

Because public key cryptography requires a lot of computational overhead, it is mainly used to authenticate the session partners and hide the symmetric cryptographic keys negotiated at the beginning of a transaction. For example, when a Netscape Navigator browser first interacts with a Netscape Commerce Server in secure mode, the Navigator randomly generates a symmetric key, then uses the Commerce Server's public key to asymmetrically encrypt a message containing the symmetric key. If the Commerce Server is not an impostor, it has the correct private key to decrypt the message, and can then use the symmetric key to proceed with the secure session.

Message Digest Functions

Message digest functions use an entire message of any size as input, and produce a fixed-size number (the message *digest*) as output. The message digest can be used later by the recipient to tell if the message has been altered in any way. Message digest functions are one-way: you cannot use the number to reconstruct the original message. It is practically impossible for someone to construct another message that will produce the same message digest, so these functions are particularly useful in producing digital signatures. The most widely used algorithms for creating message digest functions are MD2, MD4, MD5 and SHA.

The *MD* family of functions was written by Ron Rivest. MD2 is the slowest of the three, while MD4 is the fastest. MD5 is used most often because it is more secure than MD4, but its execution rate is about a third slower than MD4's. The message digests are 128 bits long. These algorithms are publicly available as Internet RFCs.

The Secure Hash Algorithm (SHA) is a U.S. Government standard developed by the National Institute of Standards and Technology (NIST). It was modeled after the MD4 algorithm, but produces a 160-bit message digest.

Digital Certificates

Digital certificates are used to prevent impostors from using public key systems. They are only issued by well-known, trusted organizations called Certificate Authorities (CA). WWW browsers use a server's certificate to verify the name of the server's organization. The certificate contains several pieces of information including a serial number, the name of the server, the server's public key, the public key's expiration date, and the name of issuer. It also contains the CA's digital signature, which cannot be forged. The signature is created by using a message digest function to digitally summarize the other certificate information, then encrypting the message digest using the CA's private key.

The widely-distributed Netscape Navigator browser is currently programmed to work with only a small list of Certificate Authorities. One of these is Verisign, Inc., a spin-off company of RSA. If you build your own SSL server instead of using the Netscape Commerce Server, you still need to have your public key signed by one of Netscape's preferred CA's. The CA requires you to submit legal proof of your right to use your organization's name, and pay a fee. The certificate eventually expires, so you must arrange for a renewal in advance or lose your ability to use the SSL.

U.S. Export Restrictions and Cryptography

If you intend to implement a secure WWW server and anticipate an international clientele, you need to know some legal ramifications related to cryptography. Cryptographic machinery, which includes computer programs as well as hardware devices, is considered to be a munition under U.S. law, and is not legally exportable to most foreign countries without a license from the State Department.

The reasons for the law come from the experiences of World War II, and are understandable. However, the enforcement of the law is inconsistent. For example, descriptions of cryptographic algorithms in the form of flowcharts or mathematical formulae *are not* subject to export restrictions, while implementations of the same algorithms as executable computer programs or hardware devices *are* restricted.

Why is this relevant to your secure WWW server? If you have customers outside the United States, you should ensure that the ciphers used in your security solution are available in the browsers. At this time, browsers using RSA's

RC2 and RC4 ciphers are legally exportable to foreign customers if the key size is no greater than 40 bits.

Applying Cryptography to the World Wide Web

Several schemes are available to provide complete, browser-to-server ("end-to-end") Internet transaction security for the WWW. These approaches all use the component cryptographic methods presented earlier, but differ in how they combine those methods, as well as in their use of network layers and key management. For example, the Secure Socket Layer uses a combination of public key and secret key cryptographic methods to provide a packaged security solution superior to using either method by itself. This section discusses the most widely-publicized systems, which are:

- Secure Socket Layer (SSL)

- Secure HyperText Transport Protocol (S-HTTP)

- Kerberos

- Pretty Good Privacy (PGP).

The Secure Socket Layer (SSL)

Netscape advocates the SSL protocol for providing privacy over the Internet. A formal proposal of the protocol exists as an *Internet-Draft*: see the following sidebar, "Getting More Information About WWW Security" for more details. Netscape's Web products provide the ability for browsers (clients) to authenticate the servers they contact. HTTP is the first protocol to be extended to use the SSL. This implementation is the HTTP+SSL or HTTPS, and port 443 is reserved as the well-known port for the protocol. Although Netscape has integrated SSL in its Navigator browser and Commerce Server products, they consider it to be an open, nonproprietary protocol. The SSL is employed below the application layer, but above the transport protocol layer, providing a secure channel for applications. Figure 8-2 shows the architecture.

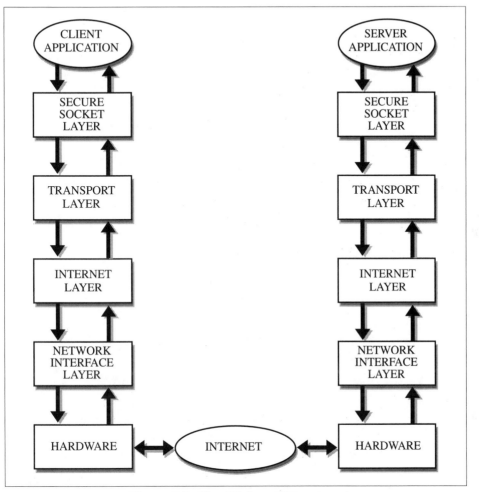

***Figure 8-2.** The SSL in a TCP network*

Getting More Information About WWW Security

There are many sources of information to help you keep up with what's new in efforts to secure the Internet and the WWW in particular. *Internet-Drafts* are draft documents used by the Internet Engineering Task Force (IETF) and other groups to put forth new proposals for review and discussion. These documents may change at any time and are valid for no more than six months. The SSL and S-HTTP proposals are currently Internet-

Drafts. The status of these documents is available in the file *id-abstracts.txt* in the *internet-drafts* directories at these FTP sites:

> ftp.is.co.za (Africa)
> nic.nordu.net (Europe)
> munnari.oz.au (Pacific Rim)
> ds.internic.net (US East Coast)
> ftp.isi.edu (US West Coast)

Security Alerts

The Computer Emergency Response Team (CERT) distributes advisory notices to subscribers of its e-mail list. A portion of a notice is included in Figure 8-3. The mailings may point out a newly-discovered operating system vulnerability, explain the seriousness of the problem, tell you where to get a patch, and what to do in the mean time. To join the CERT list, send mail to:

cert@cert.sei.cmu.edu

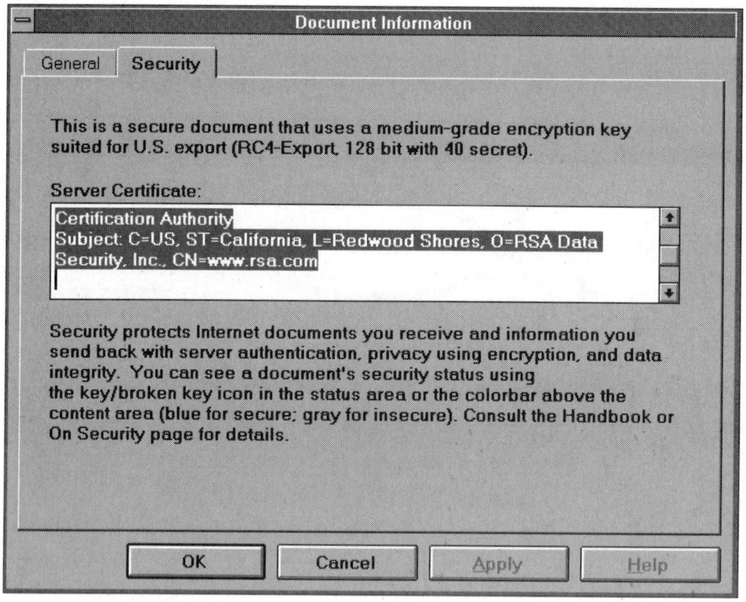

Figure 8-3. *Part of a security alert from CERT*

Newsgroups

These groups may have the answers to your security questions:

> snews://secnews.netscape.com/netscape.security
> news:comp.security.firewalls
> news:comp.security.misc
> news:comp.security.unix
> news:comp.unix.admin

WWW Security Web Pointers

Most of these security-oriented Web Pages have pointers to other places that you should find interesting:

"WWW Security References:"
`http://www-ns.rutgers.edu/www-security/reference.html#lists`

"Security Issues in WWW:"
`http://www.cs.unc.edu/wwwc/public/hanes/security.html`

"The World Wide Web Security FAQ:"
`http://www-genome.wi.mit.edu/WWW/faqs/www-security-faq.html`

"Cryptography And Security:"
`http://theory.lcs.mit.edu/~rivest/crypto-security.html`

"Netscape Data Security:"
`http://www.netscape.com/newsref/ref/netscape-security.html#com`

"RSA's Frequently Asked Questions About Today's Cryptography:"
`http://www.rsa.com/rsalabs/faq/faq_gnrl.html`

How Netscape Implements SSL

Following is a summary of how the Netscape Navigator (which we'll call the client) and the Netscape Commerce Server (server) conduct a new secure transaction using the SSL. The uppercase words correspond to the description used in the formal SSL specification:

1. The server listens for https requests.

2. The client contacts the server and sends a plain-text CLIENT-HELLO message that lists the client's encryption capabilities (RC4 with 40-bit key, for example), as well as some CHALLENGE-DATA that will be used later to authenticate the server.

3. The server returns a plain-text SERVER-HELLO message containing the server's encryption capabilities, a copy of the server's certificate, and a random CONNECTION-ID. The certificate contains the server's public key.

4. The client selects the encryption cipher to use and randomly generates a *master key* that will later be used with the CONNECTION-ID to form the *session key*. The session key does the majority of the encryption.

    The client uses the server's public key to encrypt some or all of the master key. If the client is limited to 40-bit encryption for U.S. export law reasons, then only that length of the master key is encrypted. The rest is sent unencrypted (or "in the clear"), but the result is a key with a length of 128 bits. The client includes this in a CLIENT-MASTER-KEY message that is sent to the server.

5. The server uses its *private key* to decrypt the master key chosen by the client. It uses the CONNECTION-ID and the master key to derive the session key, then encrypts the CHALLENGE-DATA using the session key. The server sends this data to the client in a SERVER-VERIFY message.

6. The client uses the session key to decrypt the CHALLENGE-DATA returned by the server. If it matches the original CHALLENGE-DATA sent in the CLIENT-HELLO message, the server is authenticated. The server has proven that it possesses the private key that works with the public key contained in the certificate.

7. The client encrypts the CONNECTION-ID with the agreed-upon session key and sends the server a CLIENT-FINISHED message.

8. The server decrypts the CLIENT-FINISHED message and compares the CONNECTION-ID with the value the server originally sent. If it matches, the handshake phase of the conversation is complete.

9. The client and server exchange application data.

Maintaining Security of the Private Key

If you are using public key cryptography, it's imperative to securely store your private key. As with all files related to the server configuration, the private key should not be kept within the directory tree that the server uses for documents. Obviously, it should not be world-readable.

What are the exposures if someone manages to copy your private key? They could decrypt any messages sent to you if they are able to intercept your communications, at least until your certificate expires. What would prevent the thief from using the key to impersonate you on a server somewhere else? Because your server sends your certificate in the clear all the time, it would be easy for someone to obtain the certificate using Netscape Navigator from anywhere in the world. To use your keys in another Netscape Commerce Server, however, the thief would need to know the password that you used to generate the private key because the Commerce Server requires it at start-up time.

If you have gone to the trouble of implementing a server that uses modern cryptographic methods, it makes sense to be consistent in the other ways you or others access the machine. For example, the Netscape Commerce Server provides an HTML-based accessory called the Administration Server to help you perform configuration tasks. This facility prompts you for a user ID and password before you can change the Commerce Server's configuration. Unfortunately, it uses HTTP rather than HTTPS. If you use Netscape Navigator from a remote workstation to access the Administration Server, you are broadcasting this powerful user ID and password as clear text.

Secure HTTP (S-HTTP)

This protocol is proposed in an Internet-Draft by Enterprise Integration Technologies (EIT) as a backwards-compatible extension to HTTP. It provides end-to-end security over the Internet at the application level, rather than as part of the underlying transport layer. S-HTTP provides a great deal of flexibility in how the browser and server interact to form a secure conversation. You can prearrange secret keys outside the S-HTTP session, or you can negotiate them when the session is initiated. You can also handle a request in a transaction mode other than a reply. The browser and server can agree to use or not use authentication, encryption and digital signatures, in any combinations.

Kerberos

MIT's Kerberos authentication system uses trusted security servers to perform encryption key management for a network. Kerberos provides clients with a *ticket* used to prove their identity to application servers, such as rlogind. Organizations with Kerberos in place might consider using it for their internal WWW needs. The NCSA 1.5 server supports Kerberos V4 and V5 for network security. Kerberos can also be used to provide security for implementations of S-HTTP. You can learn more about using Kerberos with the NCSA HTTP server at:

```
http://hohoo.ncsa.uiuc.edu/docs/howto/kerberos.html
```

PGP (Pretty Good Privacy)

Phil Zimmerman used RSA's patented public key algorithm in his controversial encryption program first released in 1991. The program found its way to the Internet, quickly spread across the world, and became the de facto standard for electronic mail encryption. The 2.6 version of the program uses software licensed by RSA Data Security, Inc. Versions 2.3a and earlier should not be used in the United States because they may be in violation of RSA's patent. The program is available for non-commercial use in the United States from MIT. Use the distribution instructions available via:

```
ftp://net-dist.mit.edu/pub/PGP/README
```

PGP can be compiled into the NCSA's HTTPd server, but there is no browser support readily available today. To view a PGP-protected document, you must download the encrypted file to the browser's host and manually decrypt it using a local PGP program. For additional information, a proposal for a browser interface that works with PGP-capable servers is presented in the document *CCI-Based Web Security: A Design Using PGP*, available at:

```
http://sdg.ncsa.uiuc.edu/~jweeks/www4/paper/current_rev.html
```

Testing Security Systems Against Attacks

After you have chosen and implemented a security system, you need to make sure that it can withstand unwanted invasions. Peer review is the classic method for testing a new cryptographic technique. The length of time that you subject an encryption algorithm or security system to public testing by anyone— including the people who earn their livelihood that way—will determine how much confidence you should place in its strength. There are a number of scenarios that cryptographers and network programmers use to predict the strengths and vulnerabilities of a new system. The more commonly discussed scenarios are:

- Man-in-the-middle
- Replay
- Plain-text.

We will look at the mechanics of each scenario, and discuss how a modern security system, the SSL, defends against them.

Before we describe each scenario, assume that there are three computers in your building: your workstation, a router that connects to your workstation, and a larger computer that also connects to the router. Your workstation uses the Netscape Navigator, and the larger computer runs the Netscape Commerce Server in secure mode. The router connects to your company's high-speed network. Unfortunately for you, the router is occasionally controlled by Sam, a university student in a nearby city who broke into the machine last month. Sam uses a network *sniffer* program on the router to examine network traffic and save any information that might help him attack other computers later.

The Man-in-the-middle Scenario

Sam is testing a new program on the router that allows him to intercept and automatically respond to data that your Navigator attempts to send to the Commerce Server. He has a copy of your server's signed certificate and knows the server's public key because he can see these digital streams in the clear when you start a new session with the server.

Today, when you try to use your Navigator, his program intercepts your CLIENT-HELLO message containing CHALLENGE-DATA. Sam's program immediately sends back a SERVER-HELLO message that looks like it is from the server. Your Navigator returns a CLIENT-MASTER-KEY message that is encrypted with the server's public key. Sam's program is now stalled because the next thing that he needs to return to your Navigator is a SERVER-VERIFY message. His program cannot decrypt your CLIENT-MASTER-KEY message because Sam does not know the server's private key. His program cannot derive the session key that the Navigator chose and therefore cannot send back the CHALLENGE-DATA properly encrypted to satisfy the Navigator. Sam's man-in-the-middle attack fails.

Replay

Sam has another program ready to test. He has a digital recording of every data packet that was exchanged last week between your Navigator and the server. Sam's program re-sends the data that your Navigator sent to the server earlier, thus recreating the transactions.

His program begins executing and sends the original CLIENT-HELLO message to the server. The server responds with a fresh SERVER-HELLO message. Sam's program sends back the original CLIENT-MASTER-KEY message. The server now has the original CHALLENGE-DATA, an original master key, and a fresh CONNECTION-ID. The server randomly assigns the CONNECTION-ID, derives the session key from the re-sent master key and the fresh CONNECTION-ID, encrypts the CHALLENGE-DATA, and sends the SERVER-VERIFY message to Sam's program.

Sam's program cannot read the server's message because the new session key does not match the recorded one, but remember: the purpose of this message is to *authenticate the server to the client*. Sam's program does not care about authentication and it proceeds to send the server the next recorded message, CLIENT-FINISHED. Since this message is encrypted with the old session key, the server can't decrypt it to compare the CONNECTION-ID data. The handshake fails and Sam's replay attack is thwarted.

Plain-Text

Sam knows that every time your Navigator sends a request to the server, there's a very good chance that he can predict the content of a portion of the request because he knows a few things about the HTTPS protocol. He correctly decides that the encrypted value of the plain-text character string GET is the most common component in the exchange after the Navigator/server handshake phase is complete. He reasons that he should construct a *dictionary database* in which every possible session key your Navigator might select is indexed by the corresponding encrypted value of GET.

After doing this, it is relatively simple for Sam to intercept your encrypted exchanges, detect portions of the encrypted data that occur with the greatest frequency, and use that data in a simple look-up operation against the database. These actions determine the value of your session key and Sam uses it to decode your entire transmission.

Sam is excited about this project, but he realizes that he has to do some capacity planning to carry out this attack. How much disk storage is needed to construct the dictionary database? Sam knows the Navigator uses a 128-bit session key, even though only 40 bits is encrypted. The size of the key determines the number of keys possible. Sam determines that the amount of disk space in bytes required to solve GET is $((128 \times (2 ** 128) \times 24) / 8)$. This figure is greater than the number of atoms in the known universe. Sam reflects on the size of this number for a moment and abandons his plain-text attack for practical reasons.

Securing the Client

Most of the material in this chapter discusses the various things you should consider to protect the integrity of your server's data as well as the host computer itself. Now it is time to look at the other side of the picture. As the WWW grows, it becomes increasingly likely that unscrupulous people or even criminals will operate servers or have access to a server's host computer, which might be a small workstation. Why is this possibility relevant to you? Consider these points:

- If you propose to use the WWW to offer commercial transactions to the public, you must understand all the security implications well enough to present a business case, either formally as a legal offer or indirectly as persuasive and reassuring advertising. Why should someone that does not know you, cannot see you, and cannot talk to you give you their credit card number on a form displayed on their computer? You must be able to explain why the mechanism can be trusted.

- Your server collects information from users that is potentially harmful to them if divulged to third parties. You have an ethical responsibility to take reasonable precautions with the records or logs that your server creates. You might be legally liable, as well.

Identifying the Server

The Netscape Navigator displays a doorkey icon in the lower left corner of the window border when you are viewing a document securely using the SSL. A broken doorkey in the same location indicates that the SSL is not being used to access the document. If the Navigator is using the SSL to view a page containing a combination of secure and non-secure documents, the unbroken doorkey displays, but the non-secure references do not display. These visual cues give you a quick assessment of end-to-end security conditions.

An unbroken doorkey by itself does not mean that you can trust the server to conduct a sensitive transaction. It only proves that the server possesses:

- A valid digital certificate with the signature of a Navigator-trusted Certificate Authority

- The correct private key matching the public key contained in the certificate.

The organization legitimately authorized to use the certificate and private key might be deceptively using another organization's name in the content of the document you are browsing. There is nothing in Netscape's current implementation of the SSL that automatically protects you in this case. Before you start typing your credit card number on a WWW form to place an order, examine the certificate to protect yourself. To do this, select the Navigator's File|Document Info|Security menu and examine all of the certificate information. Figure 8-4 shows the Document Information Window.

```
CERT Summary CS-95:03
November 28, 1995

The CERT Coordination Center periodically issues the CERT Summary to draw
attention to the types of attacks currently being reported to our incident
response staff. The summary includes pointers to sources of information for
dealing with the problems. We also list new or updated files that are
available for anonymous FTP from ftp://info.cert.org

Past CERT Summaries are available from
     ftp://info.cert.org/pub/cert_summaries
-------------------------------------------------------------------------

Recent Activity
---------------

Since the September CERT Summary, we have seen these continuing trends in
incidents reported to us. The majority of reported incidents fit into four
categories:

1. Packet Sniffers

We continue to see daily incident reports about intruders who have installed
sniffers on compromised systems. These sniffers, used to collect account names
and passwords, are frequently installed with a kit that includes Trojan horse
binaries. The Trojan horse binaries hide the sniffer activity on the systems
on which they are installed.
```

***Figure 8-4.** Examining a server's certificate with Navigator*

Browsers and Privacy

Servers record the details of every access attempt in log files, including the IP address or hostname of the browser, the date and time of the transaction, the URL access method (GET, POST, and so on), the requested URL, and the version of the browser. If the access is authenticated, the server also records the user's name. The log also includes the name/value variable pairs set by any form using the GET method: this is true even for encrypted transactions on the Netscape Commerce Server. The Commerce Server also uses a special log file named "secure" to record the IP address, date, time, and the size of the bulk cipher key used in the transaction.

Proxy servers provide controlled access to the WWW and other Internet resources by running on firewall computers. These servers maintain logs of all outbound WWW requests from organizations, which presents a very sensitive privacy issue. Because most browsers are found on personal workstations, the log of a proxy server provides a concise summary of how users are spending the organization's time. However, a proxy server is not able to know the URL of a request between a browser and a server that use the SSL due to encryption. In this case, the proxy server's log only contains information identifying the browser's host (workstation) and the destination server's hostname and port.

SSL Resources

Following is a list of other SSL products available:

- SSLeay and SSLapps—Two Australian programmers, Eric A. Young and Tim J. Hudson offer an impressive independent implementation of the SSL, which they offer freely on the Internet under the reasonable condition that if you use their code, you must explicitly recognize their work. The software packages, SSLeay and SSLapps are available via FTP. The packages incorporate independent implementations of the DES, RC4, IDEA and RSA algorithms. If you import their work into the United States (remember, an FTP is an import!), you should be sure that you are not in violation of RSA's U.S. patent rights. For more information, see:

  `http://psych.psy.uq.oz.au/%7Eftp/Crypto/`

Alex Tang has documented his successful WWW implementation of SSLeay in the United States. He explains the financial and paperwork requirements for obtaining a signed digital certificate from a Certificate Authority. His experiences are available at:

```
http://petrified.cic.net/~altitude/ssl/ssl.saga.html
```

- Netscape's SSL Toolkit—If you're a C programmer, you can add SSL support to any TCP client/server application pair, including WWW browsers and servers. Netscape provides SSLRef as a reference implementation and development aid: it is free for non-commercial use. For details, see:

```
http://home.netscape.com/newsref/std/sslref.html
```

- SSL for Winsock—If you're a Microsoft Windows programmer, Netscape offers information that you can use to implement SSL in your applications at:

```
http://home.netscape.com/newsref/std/ssl_integration.html
```

- Netscape's Electronic Commerce Payment Protocol—If you're interested in the future of Internet credit card transactions, you will want to learn more about this three-way protocol. It proposes a secure system between a customer, a merchant, and a payment gateway that represents a bank. The protocol consists of a secure transport layer (the SSL) and an electronic payment protocol layer. This system provides the customer special protection because the merchant never knows the credit card number. You can read the details at:

```
http://home.netscape.com/newsref/std/credit.html
```

Summary

We've covered a lot of ground in this chapter. Some lengthy discussions were necessary to provide a foundation for proper explanation of important but sometimes complicated security topics. Now, it's time to review the key points that you should keep in mind for your World Wide Web project:

- When possible, use a dedicated, physically-secure computer for your Web server.

- Make sure that application developers are aware of the many security exposures that can be introduced to your server through the CGI. There are free references that explain these exposures in depth—read them.

- If you are using the Web for commerce, you should employ a packaged security solution that uses modern cryptographic methods.

- Understand the concerns of the Web client—your customer.

HTML 2.0 DTD

Following is a Quick Reference guide for the HTML 2.0 DTD. Because we are assuming that you will be normalizing your code, we excluded the minimization indicators, but included the occurrence and sequence indicators. Deprecated and obsoleted content models have also been excluded from the following list, and because of the lack of browser support for MATH elements, we have also excluded all sibling MATH elements except the MATH element. We also excluded attribute declarations except for those that are required: required attributes are placed within curly brackets next to the element.

HTML Elements

HTML

```
(HEAD,BODY,PLAINTEXT?)
```

HEAD

```
(TITLE & ISINDEX? & BASE? & NEXTID? & META* & LINK*)
```

The elements contained within the HEAD content model are as follows, and are listed in alphabetical order:

BASE

```
EMPTY
```

ISINDEX

```
EMPTY
```

LINK

```
EMPTY
```

META

```
EMPTY
```

NEXTID

```
EMPTY
```

TITLE

```
#PCDATA
```

BODY

```
((H1|H2|H3|H4|H5|H6)|(#PCDATA|A|IMG|BR|(EM|STRONG|CODE|SAMP|KBD|VAR|CITE)|(
TT|B|I)|(P|(UL|OL|DIR|MENU)|DL|PRE|BLOCKQUOTE)|HR|ADDRESS)*
```

PLAINTEXT

```
CDATA
```

The elements contained within the BODY content model are as follows, and are listed in alphabetical order:

A
```
((H1|H2|H3|H4|H5|H6)|(#PCDATA|A|IMG|BR|(EM|STRONG|CODE|SAMP|KBD|VAR|CITE)|(
TT|B|I)))*  -(A)
```

ADDRESS
```
((#PCDATA|A|IMG|BR|(EM|STRONG|CODE|SAMP|KBD|VAR|CITE)|(TT|B|I)))|P)*
```

B
```
(#PCDATA|A|IMG|BR|(EM|STRONG|CODE|SAMP|KBD|VAR|CITE)|(TT|B|I)))*
```

BLOCKQUOTE
```
((H1|H2|H3|H4|H5|H6)|(#PCDATA|A|IMG|BR|(EM|STRONG|CODE|SAMP|KBD|VAR|CITE)|(
TT|B|I)|(P|(UL|OL|DIR|MENU)|DL|PRE|BLOCKQUOTE)|HR|ADDRESS)*
```

BR
```
EMPTY
```

CITE
```
(#PCDATA|A|IMG|BR|(EM|STRONG|CODE|SAMP|KBD|VAR|CITE)|(TT|B|I)))*
```

CODE
```
(#PCDATA|A|IMG|BR|(EM|STRONG|CODE|SAMP|KBD|VAR|CITE)|(TT|B|I)))*
```

DD
```
((#PCDATA|A|IMG|BR|(EM|STRONG|CODE|SAMP|KBD|VAR|CITE)|(TT|B|I)))|(P|(UL|OL|
DIR|MENU)|DL|PRE|BLOCKQUOTE))*
```

DIR
```
(LI)+  -(P|(UL|OL|DIR|MENU)|DL|PRE|BLOCKQUOTE)
```

DL
```
(DT|DD)+
```

DT
```
(#PCDATA|A|IMG|BR|(EM|STRONG|CODE|SAMP|KBD|VAR|CITE)|(TT|B|I)))*
```

EM
```
(#PCDATA|A|IMG|BR|(EM|STRONG|CODE|SAMP|KBD|VAR|CITE)|(TT|B|I)))*
```

FORM   {ACTION, METHOD}

```
((H1|H2|H3|H4|H5|H6)|(#PCDATA|A|IMG|BR|(EM|STRONG|CODE|SAMP|KBD|VAR|CITE)|(
TT|B|I)|(P|(UL|OL|DIR|MENU)|DL|PRE|BLOCKQUOTE)|HR|ADDRESS)*  -(FORM)
+(INPUT|SELECT|TEXTAREA)
```

H1 - H6

```
(#PCDATA|A|IMG|BR|(EM|STRONG|CODE|SAMP|KBD|VAR|CITE)|(TT|B|I)))*
```

HR

```
EMPTY
```

I

```
(#PCDATA|A|IMG|BR|(EM|STRONG|CODE|SAMP|KBD|VAR|CITE)|(TT|B|I)))*
```

IMG

```
EMPTY
```

INPUT

```
EMPTY
```

ISINDEX

```
EMPTY
```

KBD

```
(#PCDATA|A|IMG|BR|(EM|STRONG|CODE|SAMP|KBD|VAR|CITE)|(TT|B|I)))*
```

LI

```
((#PCDATA|A|IMG|BR|(EM|STRONG|CODE|SAMP|KBD|VAR|CITE)|(TT|B|I)))|(P|(UL|OL|
DIR|MENU)|DL|PRE|BLOCKQUOTE))*
```

LISTING

```
CDATA
```

MENU

```
(LI)+-(P|(UL|OL|DIR|MENU)|DL|PRE|BLOCKQUOTE)
```

OL

```
(LI)+
```

OPTION

```
(#PCDATA)*
```

P

```
(#PCDATA|A|IMG|BR|(EM|STRONG|CODE|SAMP|KBD|VAR|CITE)|(TT|B|I)))*
```

PRE
(#PCDATA|A|HR|BR)*

SAMP
(#PCDATA|A|IMG|BR|(EM|STRONG|CODE|SAMP|KBD|VAR|CITE)|(TT|B|I)))*

SELECT
(OPTION+) -(INPUT|SELECT|TEXTAREA)

STRONG
(#PCDATA|A|IMG|BR|(EM|STRONG|CODE|SAMP|KBD|VAR|CITE)|(TT|B|I)))*

TEXTAREA
(#PCDATA)* -(INPUT|SELECT|TEXTAREA)

TT
(#PCDATA|A|IMG|BR|(EM|STRONG|CODE|SAMP|KBD|VAR|CITE)|(TT|B|I)))*

UL
(LI)+

VAR
(#PCDATA|A|IMG|BR|(EM|STRONG|CODE|SAMP|KBD|VAR|CITE)|(TT|B|I)))*

Element Abbreviation Definitions

Following is a definition for each element.

A	anchor
ADDRESS	address block
B	bold
BODY	document body
BLOCKQUOTE	quoted passage
BR	line break
CITE	name or title of cited work
CODE	used to display source code
DD	definition of term within a definition list

DIR	directory listing
DL	definition list
DT	definition term within a definition list
EM	emphasis
FORM	fill-out form
H1	heading, level 1
H2	heading, level 2
H3	heading, level 3
H4	heading, level 4
H5	heading, level 5
H6	heading, level 6
HEAD	document head
HR	horizontal rule
HTML	hypertext markup language document
I	italic
IMG	image
INPUT	data input type within a form
ISINDEX	document is a searchable index
KBD	data that represents user input, depicting keyboard text type
LI	list item
LISTING	computer listing
MENU	menu listing
OL	ordered list
OPTION	an option within a select list
P	paragraph

PLAINTEXT	plain text passages
PRE	preformatted text
SAMP	sample text
SELECT	selection of option(s) within a drop-down list
STRONG	strong emphasis
TEXTAREA	text input area
TT	typewriter text
UL	unordered list
VAR	variable phrase or substitutable phrase

HTML 3.0 DTD

Following is a Quick Reference guide for the HTML 3.0 DTD. Because we are assuming that you will be normalizing your code, we excluded the minimization indicators, but included the occurrence and sequence indicators. Deprecated and obsoleted content models have also been excluded from the following list, and, because of the lack of browser support for MATH elements, we have also excluded all MATH elements except the MATH element. We also excluded attribute declarations except for those that are required: required attributes are placed within curly brackets next to the element.

HTML Elements

HTML
```
(HEAD, BODY)
```

HEAD
```
(TITLE & ISINDEX? & BASE? & STYLE? & META* & LINK* & RANGE*)
```

The elements contained within the HEAD content model are as follows, and are listed in alphabetical order:

BASE   {HREF}
EMPTY

ISINDEX
EMPTY

LINK   {HREF}
EMPTY

META   {CONTENT}
EMPTY

RANGE   {FROM, UNTIL}
EMPTY

STYLE   {NOTATION}
(#PCDATA)

TITLE
(#PCDATA)

The elements contained within the BODY content model follow the BODY element shown below, and are listed in alphabetical order:

BODY
(BANNER?,BODYTEXT)   +(SPOT)

BANNER
(DIV|(H1|H2|H3|H4|H5|H6)|(#PCDATA|SUB|SUP|B|((U|S|TT|I|BIG|SMALL)|(EM|STRON
G|CODE|SAMP|KBD|VAR|CITE)|(TAB|MATH|A|IMG|BR)|(Q|LANG|AU|DFN|PERSON|ACRONYM
|ABBREV|INS|DEL)))|(P|(UL|OL)|DL|PRE|BQ|FORM|ISINDEX|FN|TABLE|FIG|NOTE)|HR|
ADDRESS)*

BODYTEXT
(DIV|(H1|H2|H3|H4|H5|H6)|(#PCDATA|SUB|SUP|B|((U|S|TT|I|BIG|SMALL)|(EM|STRON
G|CODE|SAMP|KBD|VAR|CITE)|(TAB|MATH|A|IMG|BR)|(Q|LANG|AU|DFN|PERSON|ACRONYM
|ABBREV|INS|DEL)))|(P|(UL|OL)|DL|PRE|BQ|FORM|ISINDEX|FN|TABLE|FIG|NOTE)|HR|
ADDRESS)*

SPOT   {ID}
EMPTY

The elements that are contained within the BANNER and BODYTEXT content models are as follows, and are listed in alphabetical order:

A
```
(#PCDATA|SUB|SUP|B|((U|S|TT|I|BIG|SMALL)|(EM|STRONG|CODE|SAMP|KBD|VAR|CITE)
|(TAB|MATH|A|IMG|BR)|(Q|LANG|AU|DFN|PERSON|ACRONYM|ABBREV|INS|DEL)))+ -(A)
```

ABBREV
```
(#PCDATA|SUB|SUP|B|((U|S|TT|I|BIG|SMALL)|(EM|STRONG|CODE|SAMP|KBD|VAR|CITE)
|(TAB|MATH|A|IMG|BR)|(Q|LANG|AU|DFN|PERSON|ACRONYM|ABBREV|INS|DEL)))+
```

ACRONYM
```
(#PCDATA|SUB|SUP|B|((U|S|TT|I|BIG|SMALL)|(EM|STRONG|CODE|SAMP|KBD|VAR|CITE)
|(TAB|MATH|A|IMG|BR)|(Q|LANG|AU|DFN|PERSON|ACRONYM|ABBREV|INS|DEL)))+
```

ADDRESS
```
((#PCDATA|SUB|SUP|B|((U|S|TT|I|BIG|SMALL)|(EM|STRONG|CODE|SAMP|KBD|VAR|CITE)|
(TAB|MATH|A|IMG|BR)|(Q|LANG|AU|DFN|PERSON|ACRONYM|ABBREV|INS|DEL)))*|P*)
```

AU
```
(#PCDATA|SUB|SUP|B|((U|S|TT|I|BIG|SMALL)|(EM|STRONG|CODE|SAMP|KBD|VAR|CITE)
|(TAB|MATH|A|IMG|BR)|(Q|LANG|AU|DFN|PERSON|ACRONYM|ABBREV|INS|DEL)))+
```

B
```
(#PCDATA|SUB|SUP|B|((U|S|TT|I|BIG|SMALL)|(EM|STRONG|CODE|SAMP|KBD|VAR|CITE)
|(TAB|MATH|A|IMG|BR)|(Q|LANG|AU|DFN|PERSON|ACRONYM|ABBREV|INS|DEL)))+
```

BIG
```
(#PCDATA|SUB|SUP|B|((U|S|TT|I|BIG|SMALL)|(EM|STRONG|CODE|SAMP|KBD|VAR|CITE)
|(TAB|MATH|A|IMG|BR)|(Q|LANG|AU|DFN|PERSON|ACRONYM|ABBREV|INS|DEL)))+
```

BQ
```
(BODYTEXT,CREDIT?)
```

BR
```
EMPTY
```

CAPTION
```
(#PCDATA|SUB|SUP|B|((U|S|TT|I|BIG|SMALL)|(EM|STRONG|CODE|SAMP|KBD|VAR|CITE)
|(TAB|MATH|A|IMG|BR)|(Q|LANG|AU|DFN|PERSON|ACRONYM|ABBREV|INS|DEL)))+
```

CITE
```
(#PCDATA|SUB|SUP|B|((U|S|TT|I|BIG|SMALL)|(EM|STRONG|CODE|SAMP|KBD|VAR|CITE)
|(TAB|MATH|A|IMG|BR)|(Q|LANG|AU|DFN|PERSON|ACRONYM|ABBREV|INS|DEL)))+
```

CODE
```
(#PCDATA|SUB|SUP|B|((U|S|TT|I|BIG|SMALL)|(EM|STRONG|CODE|SAMP|KBD|VAR|CITE)
|(TAB|MATH|A|IMG|BR)|(Q|LANG|AU|DFN|PERSON|ACRONYM|ABBREV|INS|DEL)))+
```

CREDIT
```
(#PCDATA|SUB|SUP|B|((U|S|TT|I|BIG|SMALL)|(EM|STRONG|CODE|SAMP|KBD|VAR|CITE)
|(TAB|MATH|A|IMG|BR)|(Q|LANG|AU|DFN|PERSON|ACRONYM|ABBREV|INS|DEL)))+
```

DD
```
((#PCDATA|SUB|SUP|B|((U|S|TT|I|BIG|SMALL)|(EM|STRONG|CODE|SAMP|KBD|VAR|CITE)
|(TAB|MATH|A|IMG|BR)|(Q|LANG|AU|DFN|PERSON|ACRONYM|ABBREV|INS|DEL)))|(P|(UL|
OL)|DL|PRE|BQ|FORM|ISINDEX|FN|TABLE|FIG|NOTE))
```

DEL
```
(#PCDATA|SUB|SUP|B|((U|S|TT|I|BIG|SMALL)|(EM|STRONG|CODE|SAMP|KBD|VAR|CITE)
|(TAB|MATH|A|IMG|BR)|(Q|LANG|AU|DFN|PERSON|ACRONYM|ABBREV|INS|DEL)))+
```

DFN
```
(#PCDATA|SUB|SUP|B|((U|S|TT|I|BIG|SMALL)|(EM|STRONG|CODE|SAMP|KBD|VAR|CITE)
|(TAB|MATH|A|IMG|BR)|(Q|LANG|AU|DFN|PERSON|ACRONYM|ABBREV|INS|DEL)))+
```

DIV
```
(DIV|(H1|H2|H3|H4|H5|H6)|(#PCDATA|SUB|SUP|B|((U|S|TT|I|BIG|SMALL)|(EM|STRONG
|CODE|SAMP|KBD|VAR|CITE)|(TAB|MATH|A|IMG|BR)|(Q|LANG|AU|DFN|PERSON|ACRONYM|
ABBREV|INS|DEL)))|(P|(UL|OL)|DL|PRE|BQ|FORM|ISINDEX|FN|TABLE|FIG|NOTE)|HR|
ADDRESS)*
```

DL
```
(LH?,(DT|DD))
```

DT
```
(#PCDATA|SUB|SUP|B|((U|S|TT|I|BIG|SMALL)|(EM|STRONG|CODE|SAMP|KBD|VAR|CITE)
|(TAB|MATH|A|IMG|BR)|(Q|LANG|AU|DFN|PERSON|ACRONYM|ABBREV|INS|DEL)))+
```

EM
```
(#PCDATA|SUB|SUP|B|((U|S|TT|I|BIG|SMALL)|(EM|STRONG|CODE|SAMP|KBD|VAR|CITE)
|(TAB|MATH|A|IMG|BR)|(Q|LANG|AU|DFN|PERSON|ACRONYM|ABBREV|INS|DEL)))+
```

FIG   {SRC}
```
(OVERLAY*,CAPTION?,FIGTEXT,CREDIT?)   -(FIG | IMG)
```

FIGTEXT
```
(DIV|(H1|H2|H3|H4|H5|H6)|(#PCDATA|SUB|SUP|B|((U|S|TT|I|BIG|SMALL)|(EM|STRONG
|CODE|SAMP|KBD|VAR|CITE)|(TAB|MATH|A|IMG|BR)|(Q|LANG|AU|DFN|PERSON|ACRONYM|A
BBREV|INS|DEL)))|(P|(UL|OL)|DL|PRE|BQ|FORM|ISINDEX|FN|TABLE|FIG|NOTE)|HR|ADD
RESS)*
```

FN
```
(DIV|(H1|H2|H3|H4|H5|H6)|(#PCDATA|SUB|SUP|B|((U|S|TT|I|BIG|SMALL)|(EM|STRONG
|CODE|SAMP|KBD|VAR|CITE)|(TAB|MATH|A|IMG|BR)|(Q|LANG|AU|DFN|PERSON|ACRONYM|
ABBREV|INS|DEL)))|(P|(UL|OL)|DL|PRE|BQ|FORM|ISINDEX|FN|TABLE|FIG|NOTE)|HR|
ADDRESS)*
```

FORM   {ACTION}
```
(DIV|(H1|H2|H3|H4|H5|H6)|(#PCDATA|SUB|SUP|B|((U|S|TT|I|BIG|SMALL)|(EM|STRONG
|CODE|SAMP|KBD|VAR|CITE)|(TAB|MATH|A|IMG|BR)|(Q|LANG|AU|DFN|PERSON|ACRONYM|
ABBREV|INS|DEL)))|(P|(UL|OL)|DL|PRE|BQ|FORM|ISINDEX|FN|TABLE|FIG|NOTE)|HR|
ADDRESS)*  +(INPUT | SELECT | TEXTAREA)  -(FORM)
```

H1 - H6
```
(#PCDATA|SUB|SUP|B|((U|S|TT|I|BIG|SMALL)|(EM|STRONG|CODE|SAMP|KBD|VAR|CITE)
|(TAB|MATH|A|IMG|BR)|(Q|LANG|AU|DFN|PERSON|ACRONYM|ABBREV|INS|DEL)))+
```

HR
```
EMPTY
```

I
```
(#PCDATA|SUB|SUP|B|((U|S|TT|I|BIG|SMALL)|(EM|STRONG|CODE|SAMP|KBD|VAR|CITE)
|(TAB|MATH|A|IMG|BR)|(Q|LANG|AU|DFN|PERSON|ACRONYM|ABBREV|INS|DEL)))+
```

IMG   {SRC}
```
EMPTY
```

INPUT   {NAME (except for submit and reset), VALUE (for radio and checkbox)}
```
EMPTY
```

INS
```
(#PCDATA|SUB|SUP|B|((U|S|TT|I|BIG|SMALL)|(EM|STRONG|CODE|SAMP|KBD|VAR|CITE)
|(TAB|MATH|A|IMG|BR)|(Q|LANG|AU|DFN|PERSON|ACRONYM|ABBREV|INS|DEL)))+
```

KBD
```
(#PCDATA|SUB|SUP|B|((U|S|TT|I|BIG|SMALL)|(EM|STRONG|CODE|SAMP|KBD|VAR|CITE)
|(TAB|MATH|A|IMG|BR)|(Q|LANG|AU|DFN|PERSON|ACRONYM|ABBREV|INS|DEL)))+
```

LANG
```
(#PCDATA|SUB|SUP|B|((U|S|TT|I|BIG|SMALL)|(EM|STRONG|CODE|SAMP|KBD|VAR|CITE)
|(TAB|MATH|A|IMG|BR)|(Q|LANG|AU|DFN|PERSON|ACRONYM|ABBREV|INS|DEL)))+
```

LH
```
(#PCDATA|SUB|SUP|B|((U|S|TT|I|BIG|SMALL)|(EM|STRONG|CODE|SAMP|KBD|VAR|CITE)
|(TAB|MATH|A|IMG|BR)|(Q|LANG|AU|DFN|PERSON|ACRONYM|ABBREV|INS|DEL)))+
```

LI

```
((#PCDATA|SUB|SUP|B|((U|S|TT|I|BIG|SMALL)|(EM|STRONG|CODE|SAMP|KBD|VAR|CITE
)|(TAB|MATH|A|IMG|BR)|(Q|LANG|AU|DFN|PERSON|ACRONYM|ABBREV|INS|DEL)))|(P|
(UL|OL)|DL|PRE|BQ|FORM|ISINDEX|FN|TABLE|FIG|NOTE))
```

MATH

```
(#PCDATA)*   -(%notmath)  +(%math)
```

NOTE

```
(DIV|(H1|H2|H3|H4|H5|H6)|(#PCDATA|SUB|SUP|B|((U|S|TT|I|BIG|SMALL)|(EM|STRONG
|CODE|SAMP|KBD|VAR|CITE)|(TAB|MATH|A|IMG|BR)|(Q|LANG|AU|DFN|PERSON|ACRONYM|
ABBREV|INS|DEL)))|(P|(UL|OL)|DL|PRE|BQ|FORM|ISINDEX|FN|TABLE|FIG|NOTE)|HR|
ADDRESS)*
```

OL

```
(LH?,LI+)
```

OPTION

```
(#PCDATA)
```

OVERLAY   {SRC}

```
EMPTY
```

P

```
(#PCDATA|SUB|SUP|B|((U|S|TT|I|BIG|SMALL)|(EM|STRONG|CODE|SAMP|KBD|VAR|CITE)
|(TAB|MATH|A|IMG|BR)|(Q|LANG|AU|DFN|PERSON|ACRONYM|ABBREV|INS|DEL)))+
```

PERSON

```
(#PCDATA|SUB|SUP|B|((U|S|TT|I|BIG|SMALL)|(EM|STRONG|CODE|SAMP|KBD|VAR|CITE)
|(TAB|MATH|A|IMG|BR)|(Q|LANG|AU|DFN|PERSON|ACRONYM|ABBREV|INS|DEL)))+
```

PRE

```
(#PCDATA|SUB|SUP|B|((U|S|TT|I|BIG|SMALL)|(EM|STRONG|CODE|SAMP|KBD|VAR|CITE)
|(TAB|MATH|A|IMG|BR)|(Q|LANG|AU|DFN|PERSON|ACRONYM|ABBREV|INS|DEL)))+   -
(TAB | MATH | IMG |BIG | SMALL | SUB | SUP)
```

Q

```
(#PCDATA|SUB|SUP|B|((U|S|TT|I|BIG|SMALL)|(EM|STRONG|CODE|SAMP|KBD|VAR|CITE)
|(TAB|MATH|A|IMG|BR)|(Q|LANG|AU|DFN|PERSON|ACRONYM|ABBREV|INS|DEL)))+
```

S

```
(#PCDATA|SUB|SUP|B|((U|S|TT|I|BIG|SMALL)|(EM|STRONG|CODE|SAMP|KBD|VAR|CITE)
|(TAB|MATH|A|IMG|BR)|(Q|LANG|AU|DFN|PERSON|ACRONYM|ABBREV|INS|DEL)))+
```

SAMP
```
(#PCDATA|SUB|SUP|B|((U|S|TT|I|BIG|SMALL)|(EM|STRONG|CODE|SAMP|KBD|VAR|CITE)
|(TAB|MATH|A|IMG|BR)|(Q|LANG|AU|DFN|PERSON|ACRONYM|ABBREV|INS|DEL)))+
```

SELECT   {NAME}
```
(OPTION+)  -(INPUT | TEXTAREA | SELECT)
```

SMALL
```
(#PCDATA|SUB|SUP|B|((U|S|TT|I|BIG|SMALL)|(EM|STRONG|CODE|SAMP|KBD|VAR|CITE)
|(TAB|MATH|A|IMG|BR)|(Q|LANG|AU|DFN|PERSON|ACRONYM|ABBREV|INS|DEL)))+
```

STRONG
```
(#PCDATA|SUB|SUP|B|((U|S|TT|I|BIG|SMALL)|(EM|STRONG|CODE|SAMP|KBD|VAR|CITE)
|(TAB|MATH|A|IMG|BR)|(Q|LANG|AU|DFN|PERSON|ACRONYM|ABBREV|INS|DEL)))+
```

SUB
```
(#PCDATA|SUB|SUP|B|((U|S|TT|I|BIG|SMALL)|(EM|STRONG|CODE|SAMP|KBD|VAR|CITE)
|(TAB|MATH|A|IMG|BR)|(Q|LANG|AU|DFN|PERSON|ACRONYM|ABBREV|INS|DEL)))+
```

SUP
```
(#PCDATA|SUB|SUP|B|((U|S|TT|I|BIG|SMALL)|(EM|STRONG|CODE|SAMP|KBD|VAR|CITE)
|(TAB|MATH|A|IMG|BR)|(Q|LANG|AU|DFN|PERSON|ACRONYM|ABBREV|INS|DEL)))+
```

TAB
```
EMPTY
```

TABLE
```
(CAPTION?,TR*)
```

TD
```
(DIV|(H1|H2|H3|H4|H5|H6)|(#PCDATA|SUB|SUP|B|((U|S|TT|I|BIG|SMALL)|(EM|STRONG
|CODE|SAMP|KBD|VAR|CITE)|(TAB|MATH|A|IMG|BR)|(Q|LANG|AU|DFN|PERSON|ACRONYM|
ABBREV|INS|DEL)))|(P|(UL|OL)|DL|PRE|BQ|FORM|ISINDEX|FN|TABLE|FIG|NOTE)|HR|
ADDRESS)*
```

TEXTAREA   {NAME, ROWS, COLS}
```
(#PCDATA)  -(INPUT | SELECT | TEXTAREA)
```

TH
```
(DIV|(H1|H2|H3|H4|H5|H6)|(#PCDATA|SUB|SUP|B|((U|S|TT|I|BIG|SMALL)|(EM|STRONG
|CODE|SAMP|KBD|VAR|CITE)|(TAB|MATH|A|IMG|BR)|(Q|LANG|AU|DFN|PERSON|ACRONYM|
ABBREV|INS|DEL)))|(P|(UL|OL)|DL|PRE|BQ|FORM|ISINDEX|FN|TABLE|FIG|NOTE)|HR|
ADDRESS)*
```

TR
```
(TH|TD)*
```

TT
```
(#PCDATA|SUB|SUP|B|((U|S|TT|I|BIG|SMALL)|(EM|STRONG|CODE|SAMP|KBD|VAR|CITE)
|(TAB|MATH|A|IMG|BR)|(Q|LANG|AU|DFN|PERSON|ACRONYM|ABBREV|INS|DEL)))+
```

U
```
(#PCDATA|SUB|SUP|B|((U|S|TT|I|BIG|SMALL)|(EM|STRONG|CODE|SAMP|KBD|VAR|CITE)
|(TAB|MATH|A|IMG|BR)|(Q|LANG|AU|DFN|PERSON|ACRONYM|ABBREV|INS|DEL)))+
```

UL
```
(LH?,LI+)
```

VAR
```
(#PCDATA|SUB|SUP|B|((U|S|TT|I|BIG|SMALL)|(EM|STRONG|CODE|SAMP|KBD|VAR|CITE)
|(TAB|MATH|A|IMG|BR)|(Q|LANG|AU|DFN|PERSON|ACRONYM|ABBREV|INS|DEL)))+
```

Element Abbreviation Definitions

Following is a definition for each element.

A	anchor
ABBREV	abbreviation
ACRONYM	acronym
ADDRESS	address block
AU	author
B	bold
BANNER	document banner
BASE	document base pathname
BIG	offset text to a bigger font size
BODY	document body
BODYTEXT	container element for body text
BQ	quoted passage
BR	line break

CAPTION	table or figure caption
CITE	name or title of cited work
CODE	used to display source code
CREDIT	person who receives credit for quoted passage
DD	definition of term within a definition list
DEL	used to mark deleted text
DFN	definition within the body text
DIV	document division
DL	definition list
DT	definition term within a definition list
EM	emphasis
FIG	figure
FIGTEXT	figure text
FN	footnote
FORM	fill-out form
H1	heading, level 1
H2	heading, level 2
H3	heading, level 3
H4	heading, level 4
H5	heading, level 5
H6	heading, level 6
HEAD	document head
HR	horizontal rule
HTML	hypertext markup language document
I	italic
IMG	image

INPUT	data input type within a form
ISINDEX	document is a searchable index
KBD	data that represents user input, depicting keyboard text type
LANG	language
LH	list heading
LI	list item
LINK	a link from the document
MATH	math
META	meta-information
NOTE	used to mark a note, caution or warning
OL	ordered list
OPTION	an option within a select list
OVERLAY	image overlay within a figure
P	paragraph
PERSON	used to mark a person's name
PRE	preformatted text
Q	quoted text
RANGE	range values
S	strikeout text
SAMP	sample text
SELECT	selection of option(s) within a drop-down list
SMALL	offset text to a smaller font size
SPOT	used to insert IDs at arbitrary places
STRONG	strong emphasis
STYLE	pointer to link style sheet

SUB	subscripted text
SUP	superscripted text
TAB	used to set document tabs
TABLE	table
TD	table data cell
TEXTAREA	text input area
TH	table column or row heading
TITLE	title of document
TR	table row container
TT	typewriter text
U	underline
UL	unordered list
VAR	variable phrase or substitutable phrase

CGI Environment Variables and Return Codes

The Web server program communicates with CGI gateway programs by setting values in environment variables. CGI is the standard for the environment variables being used for passing data between the CGI gateway programs and the Web server. The environment variables are then manipulated by the CGI gateway scripts or programs and processed further.

CGI Environment Variables

This section divides the CGI environment variables into Universal and Gateway categories.

Universal Environment Variables

The following environment variables are passed regardless of the client type.

GATEWAY_INTERFACE

This variable contains a value indicating the CGI specification level that the server supports. The value is in the form:

```
specification/whole-number digit.incremental-number digit
```

For example, for the CGI 1.1 specification, the value in the variable would be CGI/1.1.

SERVER_NAME

Contains the server's hostname, DNS alias, or IP address.

SERVER_SOFTWARE

Provides the name and version number of the current Web server. The value is in the format "server name/version number." For example, this variable could contain:

```
Netsite/1.0, NCSA/1.0, etc.
```

Gateway Environment Variables

The following variables are set when the gateway program is executed.

AUTH_TYPE

If the server program supports authentication, this variable contains the value for the authorization scheme. If the server does not support authentication, or if no value is supplied by the client program, this value is null.

CONTENT_LENGTH

The value in this variable is an integer describing the number of bytes being sent by the client program. Early Web servers did not provide an end-of-file (EOF) marker, so the bytes had to be counted when read. For example, if your CGI gateway program is querying a database and the result set is 120 bytes in length, the value in this variable would be 120.

CONTENT_TYPE

If data is sent to the CGI gateway program from a form that used the POST method, then the value in this variable describes the type of data being sent to the CGI program. The format of this variable follows the Content-type HTML header. That is, the values indicate the Multipurpose Internet Mail Extension (MIME) type of the data being sent. If the GET method is used, or if the data type is undetermined, the value in this variable is null.

HTTP_?

The HTTP_? variables are determined by the client program used to send the Web page originally. The client program can send its own variables as headers. The Web server program makes a few changes to the headers and turns them into environment variables. If the protocol from the client program was HTTP, then server prepends HTTP_ to the beginning of the header variable name and converts its name to all upper case. Additionally, if there are any hyphens (-) in the name of the header variable, they are converted to underscores (_).

Some examples of these variables are HTTP_ACCEPT, HTTP_FROM, and HTTP_USER_AGENT. HTTP_ACCEPT is used to indicate the types of data the client program can accept or handle. For example, image/tif, image/gif, and so on.

HTTP_FROM contains the value of the E-Mail address of the sender, assuming the client browser program supports headers such as this. For example:

```
fred@bedrock.slate.com.
```

HTTP_USER_AGENT indicates the client browser used to send the request.

PATH_INFO

This variable contains a value that is appended after the URL path for the CGI program. For example, assume that in the following URL, the CGI script name is cgi_script.cgi:

```
http://fred.wilma.com/cgi-bin/cgi_script.cgi/val1/val2
```

The PATH_INFO variable would contain:

```
/val1/val2
```

The PATH_INFO variable is often used to pass arguments to a CGI script.

PATH_TRANSLATED

If the value in the PATH_INFO variable (supplied with the URL) is a relative path, this variable contains the actual value. Consider the following example URL PATH_INFO value:

```
../../../../../../foobar
```

The PATH_TRANSLATED value would be the actual path value, such as:

```
/one/two/three/four/five/six/seven/foobar
```

QUERY_STRING

When an HTML form uses the GET or ISINDEX methods, the values supplied by the user are contained in this variable. QUERY_STRING is one of two main ways to retrieve values the user supplied in an HTML form. The other is with the POST method, where the CGI gateway script reads a stream for CONTENT_LENGTH bytes.

REMOTE_ADDR

This variable contains the IP address of the host server making the request.

REMOTE_HOST

This variable contains the domain name value for the host server making the request. For example, the value might be java.sun.com. We suggest that you use this variable with REMOTE_ADDR.

REMOTE_IDENT

This variable is set only when the HTTP server supports RFC 931 identification. If it does, then the value in this field is the remote user name retrieved from the server.

REQUEST_METHOD

This variable contains the value GET, POST or HEAD as set in the METHOD attribute of the FORM tag in an HTML form. HEAD is usually not called directly by CGI programs. If it is, it behaves as a GET request method. For example, the following FORM tag sets the method to GET. As a result, the value GET is in the REQUEST_METHOD variable.

```
<FORM METHOD="GET" ACTION="http://fred.wilma.com/cgi-bin/cgi_script.cgi">
```

REMOTE_USER

If the client program supports authentication, the value of the user name is retrieved into this variable.

SCRIPT_NAME

For CGI gateway scripts that reference themselves, this variable contains the relative path to the script being executed. In other words, it contains the value pointing to itself. This can be used, for example, to call the same CGI gateway script but with different command-line options that are dependent upon some event or value supplied by the user.

SERVER_PORT

Contains the value of the port set for the Web server. The default value for Web servers is port 80, but the system administrator can set it to any value from 1 to 65,535.

SERVER_PROTOCOL

Provides the name and version of the server's supported protocol level. For example, it could be:

```
HTTP/1.0, HTTP/3.0, etc.
```

CGI Return Codes

Each HTTP request returns some value indicating the result of the requested action. The returned code can give you clues about errors in your CGI or HTTP code, or some other error condition, but the problem is not always obvious.

Additionally, the HTTP return codes and their values may not all be supported by a given server. Some servers also add a few of their own return codes that are not widely supported. Below are the more common return codes and their respective meanings. The numbering scheme for return codes generally follows these guidelines: the 200 series of codes indicate some degree of success; the 300 series of codes indicate some form of redirection (such as the client program automatically handling the request with another address); and the 400 and 500 series of codes indicate some form of error condition.

As you develop CGI programs, you will most likely see codes 404 and 500. A return code of 500 is usually caused by a badly-formed CGI header. Code 404 appears whenever there is a mis-coded (or mis-named) URL. The return codes are as follows:

Code	Value	Meaning
200	OK	The request was successfully handled.
201	CREATED	Indicates that a POST method command succeeded.
202	ACCEPTED	Indicates that the request was received, but may or may not be successful when it actually performs.
203	PARTIAL INFORMATION	This follows a GET method command and indicates that the command did not come completely from the server. For example, you could manually code the `?attribute=value&attribute=value...` line following a URL.
204	NO RESPONSE	Indicates successful request fulfillment, but that there is no HTML page to be returned as a response.
301	MOVED	The previously requested data has been relocated. Note that some browsers can automatically re-link to the forwarded location, whereas others will receive this return value.
302	FOUND	If the client program supports Location headers, it will be redirected to a new URL. This is used with the GET method.
303	METHOD	Similar to 302, it tells the client program to try another address. This code supports the POST method.
304	NOT MODIFIED / USE LOCAL COPY	Indicates that the header sent with the request was an "if-modified-since" header and that the data in the request has not been modified. These types of requests are used to manage a local cache with a single request.

Code	Value	Meaning (cont.)
400	BAD REQUEST	The request had bad HTTP syntax.
401	UNAUTHORIZED	A parameter is sent with the request for those servers that support authentication. This code indicates either a poorly formed parameter or an unauthorized request.
402	PAYMENT REQUIRED	This code is fairly obscure and not yet used frequently. The request can supply a "chargeto" header for payment. This code indicates an unacceptable "chargeto" header.
403	FORBIDDEN	The client request is not allowed to be performed.
404	NOT FOUND	The server could not find all or part of the request.
500	INTERNAL ERROR	The server could not process the request due to an unexpected condition. This return code is generated for a number of error conditions.
501	NOT IMPLEMENTED	Indicates that a request was received for a service this server does not support.
502	SERVICE OVERLOADED	When the request was received, the server was already processing the maximum number of requests. Note that the maximum number of requests is usually a configurable option for servers.
503	GATEWAY TIME-OUT	This return code occurs when a request causes a server to contact another service and the other service does not respond in a timely fashion.

ASCII Conversion Chart

Note: all of the following vxalues begin with a % sign.

HEX	ASCII	HEX	ASCII
00	null	0D	carriage return
01	start of heading	0E	shift out
02	start text	0F	shift in
03	end text		
04	end of trans	10	data link escape
05	enquiry	11	DC1 - X-ON
06	acknowledge	12	DC2
07	bell	13	DC3 - X-OFF
08	backspace	14	DC4
09	horizontal tab	15	neg acknowledge
0A	linefeed	16	synchronous idle
0B	vertical tab	17	end of trans blck
0C	formfeed	18	cancel

HEX	ASCII	HEX	ASCII
19	end of medium	33	3
1A	substitute	34	4
1B	escape	35	5
1C	file separator	36	6
1D	group separator	37	7
1E	record separator	38	8
1F	unit separator	39	9
		3A	:
20	space	3B	;
21	!	3C	<
22	"	3D	=
23	#	3E	>
24	$	3F	?
25	%		
26	&	40	©
27	'	41	A
28	(	42	B
29	)	43	C
2A	*	44	D
2B	+	45	E
2C	,	46	F
2D	-	47	G
2E	.	48	H
2F	/	49	I
		4A	J
30	0	4B	K
31	1	4C	L
32	2	4D	M

HEX	ASCII		HEX	ASCII
4E	N		67	g
4F	O		68	h
			69	i
50	P		6A	j
51	Q		6B	k
52	R		6C	l
53	S		6D	m
54	T		6E	n
55	U		6F	o
56	V			
57	W		70	p
58	X		71	q
59	Y		72	r
5A	Z		73	s
5B	[		74	t
5C	\		75	u
5D	]		76	v
5E	^		77	w
5F	_		78	x
			79	y
60	`		7A	z
61	a		7B	{
62	b		7C	l
63	c		7D	}
64	d		7E	~
65	e		7F	del
66	f			

The CT-Lib API

The following API calls are for a subset of the Sybase::CTlib API, and should satisfy most of your application needs. For each API call, we'll show you associated arguments and provide a brief description.

General API calls

The status return value for all CT-Lib calls is CS_SUCCEED, CS_FAIL, or CS_CANCELED, depending on the return state of the command.

ct_callback

```
ct_callback($type, $cb_func)
```

Installs a callback routine for messages from the server or CT-Lib. Set $type to CS_CLIENTMSG_CB for a CT-Lib callback, and to CS_SERVERMSG_CB for a server callback.

ct_cancel

```
$dbh ->ct_cancel($type)
```

Used to cancel commands. If `$type` is `CS_CANCEL_ALL`, then the current command terminates immediately. If `$type` is `CS_CANCEL_ATTN`, then the result sets are discarded the next time the application reads from the server.

ct_col_names

```
@names = $dbh ->ct_col_names()
```

Returns the names of the columns in the current query. If the current query doesn't contain columns, an empty array is returned.

ct_connect

```
$dbh = Sybase::CTlib->ct_connect([$user [, $passwd [, $server [,$app-
name]]]])
```

Initiates a connection to a Sybase server, and is a constructor that returns a Perl object used to call the API's methods. If supplied, it uses the specified username, password, server, and application name for the connection.

ct_col_types

```
@types = $dbh ->ct_col_types([$doAssoc])
```

Returns the column types or an associative array of column name column type. If `$doAssoc` is non-zero, it returns an associative array. If `$doAssoc` is zero, it returns only the types.

The possible column types can be found in the `cstypes.h` include file. Following is a list of types and their associated value from Sybase 10.0.2 on Solaris 2.4.

```
CS_ILLEGAL_TYPE        -1
CS_CHAR_TYPE            0
CS_BINARY_TYPE         1
CS_LONGCHAR_TYPE       2
CS_LONGBINARY_TYPE     3
CS_TEXT_TYPE           4
CS_IMAGE_TYPE          5
CS_TINYINT_TYPE        6
CS_SMALLINT_TYPE       7
CS_INT_TYPE            8
```

CS_REAL_TYPE	9
CS_FLOAT_TYPE	10
CS_BIT_TYPE	11
CS_DATETIME_TYPE	12
CS_DATETIME4_TYPE	13
CS_MONEY_TYPE	14
CS_MONEY4_TYPE	15
CS_NUMERIC_TYPE	16
CS_DECIMAL_TYPE	17
CS_VARCHAR_TYPE	18
CS_VARBINARY_TYPE	19
CS_LONG_TYPE	20
CS_SENSITIVITY_TYPE	21
CS_BOUNDARY_TYPE	22

ct_execute

```
$status = $dbh ->ct_execute($sql)
```

Sends `$sql` to the server for execution. Multiple commands are allowed. You need to read in all results using `ct_results` or issue a `ct_cancel` before submitting a new request or ending the Perl program.

ct_fetch

```
@data = $dbh ->ct_fetch([$doAssoc])
```

Returns a row of data. If `$doAssoc` is non-zero, it returns an associative array of the column name and the value. If `$doAssoc` is zero, it returns only the values.

ct_fetchable

```
$ret = $dbh ->ct_fetchable($restype)
```

Returns true if the current result set has returnable rows.

newdate

```
$date = $dbh->newdate($initialValue);
```

CT-Lib allows you to create Sybase date types to avoid loss of precision due to rounding errors and incompatible types. When manipulating date objects, be sure to use the date methods, especially for assignment. If you don't use the set method, you will lose the special properties associated with date objects.

ct_results

```
$status = $dbh ->ct_results($res_type)
```

Returns the status for the previous command in $res_type. Some possible values for $res_type are: CS_ROW_RESULT, CS_CMD_DONE, CS_CMD_SUCCEED, CS_COMPUTE_RESULT, and CS_CMD_FAIL.

CS_CMD_DONE is returned when all result sets are processed. CS_ROW_RESULT is returned if rows are returned. CS_CMD_SUCCEED is returned if a command that returns no data was successful. CS_COMPUTE_RESULT is returned when data is generated due to a compute command.

ct_res_info

```
$res_info = $dbh ->ct_res_info($info_type)
```

Returns information about the current result set. $info_type is used to determine the subject of the information returned. Possible values include: CS_NUM_COMPUTES, CS_NUMDATA, CS_NUMORDERCOLS, and CS_ROW_COUNT.

ct_sql

```
$ret |@ret = $dbh ->ct_sql($cmd [, \&rowcallback])
```

Executes the SQL command $cmd. In the scalar context, it returns a reference to an array of references, which returns an array of row values. In the array context, ct_sql simply returns an array of references to rows. If you supply the rowcallback argument, the function is called on each row returned.

This loads the whole result set into memory, so it may be resource-intensive.

Date API calls

Date objects have special manipulation methods in native format. Use these only if you need to avoid any rounding errors or loss of precision. It appears that using data in native format runs slower than using the same data in Perl format. CT-Lib is being expanded to offer both native and Perl format approaches so you can use native format where exact precision is absolutely necessary, and use the Perl version when speed is an issue.

For Web-based reports, speed is often an issue, and you will want to seriously weigh the benefits of using values in native formats. In our example in the "Using CGI Scripting and SybPerl to Build an Internet Application" section in Chapter 4, "Creating CGI Scripts Using Perl," we use dates in native format to show how it should be done, but keep in mind that this approach may not be the best for your application. Following is a subset of the date methods. Look at the CT-Lib man page for a comprehensive listing.

crack

`@arr = $date->crack`

Breaks the date out into an array containing the following components: (`$year`, `$month`, `$month_day`, `$year_day`, `$week_day`, `$hour`, `$minute`, `$second`, `$millisecond`, `$time_zone`).

str

`$date->str`

Converts the date to a string. This is automatically called when you print a date object.

Money/Numeric API calls

Money and numeric objects have their own set of methods. These objects come with the same caveats as the date object. Make sure you use the same method, or you will replace the money object with the scalar to which you set its variable.

calc

`$mny->calc($mny2, $op)`

Performs a precise calculation on a money or numeric object. The possible calculations are addition, subtraction, multiplication, and division. `$op` can be one of the following: +, -, *, or /.

newmoney

```
$mny = $dbh->newmoney([$initialValue]);
```

Allows you to create a new money object.

newnumeric

```
$num = $dbh->newnumeric([$initialValue]);
```

Allows you to create a new numeric object.

num

```
$mny->num
```

Converts a money or numeric object to a floating point number.

set

```
$mny->set($number)
```

Sets the value of `$mny` to `$number`. Make sure you use this instead of =, or your object will lose its special type.

str

```
$mny->str
```

Converts the money or numeric object to a string. This is automatically called when you print a money or numeric object.

Index

A

C

C language
   compared to Java, 182, 183, 190,
      193
   Netscape's SSL Toolkit, 306
   passing data to Open Client/Open
      Server script, 75
C++ language
   compared to Java, 182, 183, 184,
      190, 193
   passing data to ISQL script or Open
      Client/Open Server script, 75
Cancel() method, Java, 218
capitalization, for Perl variables, 99
case sensitivity, Java, 184
catch command, Tcl, 155
centralized data lookups, 5, 7
Certificate Authorities (CA), 293, 304,
      306
CGI (Common Gateway Interface)
      scripts
   See also Perl (Practical Extraction
      and Report Language); Tcl
      (Tool
      Command Language)
   argument processing code, 117
   building an Internet application,
      128–142
   calling ISQL script, 76
   checking for typos in, 123
   creating forms, 4–5, 24–25
   data integrity, 165–166, 176
   data-values passed to, 37–38
   environment variables
      gateway, 330–333
      universal, 329–330
   exit procedure to deliver error mes-
      sages, 166
   filtering user-supplied information,
      25
   headers, 112–113
   interpreting ISQL result lines, 88

linking data to columns, 36
parsing form results, 114–121
in password-protected directories,
   275
querying Sybase SQL Server, 5, 6
retrieving unordered lists from database, 92
return codes, 333–335
for server-side processing, 16
subroutines for sending information
   to client machine, 121–125
with web.sql, 8
char data type, Java, 186
CHECKBOX option, for TYPE
      attribute of <INPUT> element,
      33–38
CHECKED attribute of <INPUT> ele-
      ment, 36, 47
checksum, 54
ciphers, 291, 293
CLASS (Classification) attribute
   of <INPUT> element, 47
   of <SELECT> and <OPTION> ele-
      ments, 53
   of <TEXTAREA> element, 58
classes, Java, 187–190
CLASSPATH environment variable,
      Java, 191
Client Library
   application, 77
   routines, in web.sql, 239–240
Client/Server database systems
   See also Web applications
   application
      accessing with the Web, 2
      design considerations, 2–3
      implementing, 11–18
   hardware issues, 11
   query *vs.* transactional, 3
   server-side processing, 4, 5
   workload distribution, 4–11
client-side processing
   for forms, 12